Tiger in the
Barbed Wire

Also by Howard R. Simpson

A Very Large Consulate (1988)
A Gathering of Gunmen (1987)
Junior Year Abroad (1986)
The Jumpmaster (1984)
The Obelisk Conspiracy (1975)
Rendezvous Off Newport (1973)
The Three-Day Alliance (1971)
Assignment for a Mercenary (1965)
To a Silent Valley (1961)

Tiger in the Barbed Wire

An American in Vietnam 1952–1991

HOWARD R. SIMPSON

Foreword by
PIERRE SALINGER

BRASSEY'S (US), Inc.
A Division of Maxwell Macmillan, Inc.

WASHINGTON · NEW YORK · LONDON · OXFORD
BEIJING · FRANKFURT · SÃO PAULO · SYDNEY · TOKYO · TORONTO

Brassey's (US), Inc.

Editorial Offices	*Order Department*
Brassey's (US), Inc.	Brassey's Book Orders
8000 Westpark Drive	c/o Macmillan Publishing Co.
First Floor	100 Front Street, Box 500
McLean, Virginia 22102	Riverside, New Jersey 08075

Library of Congress Cataloging-in-Publication Data

Simpson, Howard R., 1925–
   Tiger in the barbed wire : an American in Vietnam, 1952–1991 / Howard R. Simpson ; foreword by Pierre Salinger.
      p. cm.
   Includes index.
   ISBN 0–02–881008–2 :
   1. Indochinese War, 1946–1954—Personal narratives, American.
   2. Vietnamese Conflict, 1961–1975—Personal narratives, American.
   3. Vietnam—Description and travel—1975– 4. Simpson, Howard R., 1945– . I. Title.
   DS553.5.S56   1992
   959.704'38—dc20   91–34016
                                                                      CIP

Brassey's (US), Inc., books are available at special discounts for bulk purchases for sales promotions, premiums, fund-raising, or educational use through the Special Sales Director, Macmillan Publishing Company, 866 Third Avenue, New York, New York 10022.

10 9 8 7 6 5 4 3 2 1

Printed in the United States of America

In 1952 a captain in charge of a sector in the mountains of central Vietnam was awakened at 0300 hrs. by the jangling of his field telephone. It was a call from a young lieutenant in an outlying post.

"Mon *capitaine*," the lieutenant spluttered, "there's a tiger in the barbed wire!"

"Well, kill it!" the captain ordered.

"I can't," the lieutenant replied, "I don't have my shoes on."

An anecdote of the French
Expeditionary Corps
reflecting the incongruous
quality of the Indochina War

To my wife and daughters

Contents

Foreword

When the Gulf War came to an end, it was generally felt that the Vietnam War had been shoved into the past. But Howard Simpson's excellent book, *Tiger in the Barbed Wire*, adds a great deal of historic information that many Americans have not been aware of.

Few Americans were involved for as long and as deeply in the Vietnam conflict as Howard Simpson. He first went there in 1952 as a press officer in the U.S. Embassy at a time when the war was seen strictly as a French conflict. But the fact was that American involvement in the crisis was rising at that time, along with the conflict between the French and the Americans. The French saw the war as a need to maintain colonial power. The Americans were already pushing the French toward accepting a more independent Vietnam.

Two years after Simpson arrived there, the French participation in the war was dramatically brought to an end by the French loss at Dien Bien Phu. We learn through this book how the French military leaders made disastrous mistakes that led to the Dien Bien Phu defeat. Soon afterward the Geneva accord of 1954 was signed, dividing Vietnam at the seventeenth parallel. A year later the French pulled out of the country, and the Vietnam crisis became an American problem.

Before the Geneva accord, the Americans had decided that their solution was to place in power Ngo Dinh Diem as prime minister of Vietnam. When Simpson arrived in Saigon, he was assigned as Diem's press adviser. At the same time, the CIA had sent Ed Lansdale to Vietnam to put together an operation trying to stabilize the Vietnamese military forces. When the Geneva accord took place and the communists came to power in Hanoi, North Vietnam, the Americans ran an important campaign to encourage as many people as possible to leave North Vietnam, to "vote with their feet" against the communist regime. The operation was a general success, but it soon became clear that the Diem government faced increasing threats from internal sects trying to take it over.

Simpson left Vietnam in late 1955 and had assignments in Nigeria, and Marseille and Paris, France. From a distance he watched the evolution of the Vietnamese situation. During the Kennedy administration the number of U.S. military advisers in Vietnam had risen from 500 to 16,000, and Diem had been overthrown as prime minister and killed. A month later John Kennedy was assassinated. It was not long after Lyndon Johnson took power that Simpson was again sent to Vietnam. He would only stay a year this time, but later he became the deputy director of the State Department's East Asia/Pacific Bureau of Public Affairs, returning to Vietnam as the American presence broke down and was finally eliminated.

This massive experience in Vietnam provides Simpson with a special and in-depth view of the long crisis. It was not an easy time. But his book gives us a rare view of this history, something which few books on this subject have done before. Before finishing the book, Simpson, now retired from the Foreign Service, went back to Vietnam to evaluate what has happened since the American defeat. There he had a spectacular meeting with Gen. Vo Nguyen Giap, the vice president of the Vietnamese Council of Ministers but better known as the man who defeated the French at Dien Bien Phu. He said, comparing the American soldier to the French, "The American soldier . . . was better armed. When he was in the field there were helicopters that brought provisions, even water. He knew the terrain less well, the Vietnamese people even less. As to the American commanders, . . . they knew less than the soldiers they were commanding." A 1991 appraisal of the Vietnam War from the Vietnamese point of view, but probably very accurate, and perhaps explains why the Americans lost.

PIERRE SALINGER

Preface

This book is a personal account of what it was like to serve in Indochina as a Foreign Service officer during both the French and American periods of conflict. It is also a description of my on-the-job training in such varied fields as diplomacy, political intrigue, war reporting, information gathering, psychological warfare, press relations, and the frustrating task of "advising" Vietnamese prime ministers.

I arrived in Saigon in early 1952 on my first assignment as the Franco-Vietminh war of attrition was approaching its crucial phase. Nothing, including my World War II Army service, my studies, my brief newspaper career, or a quick course at the Foreign Service Institute, had prepared me for what I was to find in Indochina. On the surface the Indochina War was a "white hat, black hat" situation, but a few months of on-the-ground experience was to put events and those involved in them under a gray filter.

In the ensuing years I witnessed the drama of colonial decline and the slow but certain progression toward direct U.S. involvement in Vietnam. I was introduced to the realities of guerrilla warfare, subversion, and political terrorism. Fate, and a series of assignments from 1952 to 1971, allowed me to live the struggle for Indochina at first hand, both in the field and in Saigon.

More recently, in the spring of 1991, I returned to Vietnam for a three-week stay as a journalist. My prime purpose was to gather material, but I also wanted to close the circle of my Vietnam experience. Vietnam has been a part of my life since I first stepped out into the blazing heat at Saigon's Tan Son Nhut Airport. I met my American wife in Saigon and the eldest and youngest of our four daughters were born there. The old French Indochina hands, *les anciens d'Indo*, used to refer to *le mal jaune*, an indefinable, nostalgic attraction to that deceptively calm, often brutal land. A number of Americans, including myself, still suffer from its effects.

Many of the situations and characters I describe are as clear in my mind today as they were then. But memory can be fickle. I have double-checked my notes, scanned a number of publications, and availed myself of the Freedom of Information Act to cut slippage to a minimum. I can only say that these were my experiences.

Acknowledgments

A number of books on Vietnam have served to jog my memory, fill information gaps and pinpoint events, dates and participants. These include: *Pour une parcelle de gloire* by Gen. Marcel Bigeard, Plon, 1975; Dennis Bloodworth's *An Eye for the Dragon*, Farrar Straus & Giroux, 1970; *L'Aventure* by Lucien Bodard, Gallimard, 1967; *Edward Lansdale: The Unquiet American* by Cecil B. Curry, Houghton Mifflin, 1988; *De Lattre au Vietnam* by Pierre Darcourt, *La Table Ronde*, 1965; *Dien Bien Phu* by Gen. Vo Nguyen Giap, *Éditions en langues Étrangères*, 1964; David Halberstam's *The Best and the Brightest*, Random House, 1969; Stanley Karnow's *Vietnam: A History*, Viking, 1983; *La Bataille de Dien Bien Phu* by Jules Roy, Julliard, 1963; *The Word War* by Thomas Sorensen, Harper & Row, 1968; and *The Pentagon Papers* as published by *The New York Times*, Bantam Books, 1971.

I would like to thank James L. Binder, the editor in chief of *Army*, for allowing me to use excerpts from some of my articles previously published in that magazine. My thanks also to the Information and Privacy Staff of the Department of State for digging deep into the recent past to supply me with declassified telegrams and memorandums under the provisions of the Freedom of Information Act.

Finally, I would like to thank my wife, who lived through the events described in this book with courage and abiding good humor and whose memory and editorial judgment contributed to the final product.

Prologue

In January of 1952 the French war in Indochina, the British counterguerrilla campaign in Malaya, and the UN Police Action in Korea were all seen by the United States as essential, interlocking efforts in the Western strategy of preventing the Communist domination of Asia and containing Chinese expansionism. In Vietnam, Ho Chi Minh, the revolutionary Communist who had fought the Japanese with assistance from the American OSS during World War II, had become the wartime Vietminh leader "Uncle Ho," supported by the Soviet Union and the Chinese Communists. The collapse of Franco-Vietminh negotiations at Fontainebleau in 1946 and the beginning of hostilities later the same year had plunged the Indochinese Peninsula into the long chain of violence and suffering that continues to this day.

The Vietminh military commander, Gen. Vo Nguyen Giap, had built a formidable "people's army" of over 100,000 regulars supported by Regional forces and local militia. Giap's battle-hardened divisions, equipped and trained by the Chinese, had already dealt humiliating defeats to the French at Dongkhe, Cao Bang, and Lang Son in 1950.

Later the same year the arrival of the charismatic, innovative Gen. Jean-Marie de Lattre de Tassigny, the new French commander in Indochina, had momentarily changed the course of the war. Blunting three of Giap's offensives in early 1951 and inflicting heavy losses on the Vietminh, de Lattre restored the morale of the French Expeditionary Corps, lobbied the Truman administration for increased American aid, pushed for more active Vietnamese participation in the war with the Communist Vietminh, and threatened to take active measures against corruption and large-scale trafficking in the Vietnamese piaster.

This had all changed by early 1952. General de Lattre had died in France of cancer and been replaced by his deputy, Gen. Raoul Salan; General Giap was waiting for the end of the rains to launch a new offensive into the T'ai tribal region of northwestern Vietnam. The tempo of U.S. military and economic aid shipments in support of the Franco-Vietnamese war effort had increased. American policymakers, operating in a glacial Cold War environment, had decided that France was "fighting the good fight" in Indochina but had insisted that the French accelerate movement toward a true independence for Vietnam and, eventually, Cambodia and Laos. Washington considered the establishment of a viable Vietnamese national army as the key to an independent, noncommunist Vietnam.

The French, who had grudgingly granted Vietnam the status of an Associated State within the French Union in 1949, still controlled the country's finances, its defense, its police, and the puppet, playboy emperor of Vietnam, Bao Dai. Franco-American agreements and French government policies formulated in Paris traveled badly. Many French officials in Saigon and Hanoi clearly intended to keep Indochina under the tricolor. Frequent government changes in Paris facilitated their efforts to maintain a thinly disguised colonial regime and keep political reform on a back burner.

The war that had begun in 1946 was to intensify and proliferate, culminating in the French defeat at Dien Bien Phu and the signing of the Geneva Accords in 1954 that divided Vietnam at the seventeenth parallel. U.S. involvement in Vietnam escalated with the French pullout in 1955 and the installation of the Diem government. The incapability of Diem to deal with Communist infiltration and domestic unrest, and the U.S.-condoned military coup against the Diem government in 1963, facilitated the North Vietnamese–supported Vietcong insurrection that had been growing in strength throughout South Vietnam in the early 1960s. With the arrival of U.S. combat troops in 1965, Washington experienced the frustrations of fighting a modern revolutionary war in Western terms with inappropriate conventional tactics. American soldiers in Vietnam soon learned why the French had labeled their Indochina conflict *la sale guerre*, the "dirty war." Generations of Vietnamese, Cambodians, and Laotians were destined—if they survived—to know little else but war, suffering, and personal loss.

The need to seek lessons from the traumatic record of our Vietnam experience is of particular importance. Revolutionary warfare, limited-intensity conflict, and terrorism have replaced the specter of counterproductive nuclear conflict. As the French Indochina War contained the seeds of eventual U.S. involvement, small-scale American participation, political or military, in today's secondary international conflicts can hold the same dangers. One of these is the myth that conventional military force can still be used in political-military problem-solving in Third World nations where guerrilla warfare is a common tradition. The second is exemplified by the term "nation-building," still in use in Washington. It is a presumptuous phrase that can dangerously mislead its practitioners. We were "nation-building" in Vietnam without recognizing that nations, good or bad, strong or weak, are built from within—not from without.

As we approach what has been labeled the "Pacific Century" and attempt to define our coming role in Asia, an understanding of what went wrong in Vietnam, and why, can serve as a caution and guide to the future. I hope the events, happenings, and observations in the following pages will contribute in some way to that understanding.

Tiger in the Barbed Wire

CHAPTER 1

The Tarnished Pearl

The Air France Constellation swung wide over the green rice paddies and palm-shaded villages on its landing approach to Saigon's Tan Son Nhut Airport. It had been a long trip from Paris, with stops in Rome, Beirut, Karachi, and Bangkok. The two French officers across the aisle finished their champagne and tightened their neckties. I noted a change in engine noise as the aircraft slowed and the pilot pointed its nose downward. We'd been forewarned by the stewardess. Our abrupt descent was designed to foil any Vietminh snipers that might be concealed near the runway.

It was a perfect landing. We taxied past French Air Force C-47s and a Moraine observation plane. Grass-tufted mounds of earth at the edge of the runway were crowned with concrete pillboxes. Protective barbed wire, hung with drying laundry, glinted in the bright sunlight. Ten minutes later I stepped out onto the landing ramp and into the heavy, furnacelike heat. It was January 1952 and I had arrived in the "Pearl of the Orient."

The busy airport was noisy and crowded. French businessmen and personnel from the rubber plantations wearing white shirts, shorts, and knee socks; Vietnamese merchants in sharkskin suits; French officers with swagger sticks; graceful Vietnamese women in flowing *ao dais* of pastel silks; and cadaverous, perspiring porters carrying three times their weight in baggage vied for space in the gritty terminal. Squeaking ceiling fans stirred the torpid air. The enclosed customs area reverberated to the sound of Bearcat fighter planes taking off on a mission, gray napalm canisters under their stubby wings.

It was the beginning of my Foreign Service career and my first visit to Asia.

Behind me were World War II Army service in Europe, art studies in Paris on the GI Bill, a brief stint as a newspaper artist, appointment to the State Department, a quick course at the Foreign Service Institute in Washington, and a hurried consultation in Paris. None of this had prepared me for what I was to find in Indochina.

The tall, taciturn U.S. Information Service officer who'd come to meet me eased us through the immigration and police controls. Waiting outside, while he went to get his Jeep station wagon, I had my first real taste of the sun's heat. Slow-moving cotton-ball clouds provided only fleeting relief. My escort drove into the chaotic traffic with calm restraint. Small blue Renault taxis darted like uncertain beetles from side roads, horns blaring; racketing cyclomotors filled with passengers swerved through the flow of military vehicles, leaving a trail of acrid smoke; cyclo-pousse drivers with muscle-knotted legs shouted, jangled their bells, and waved their arms, warning of imminent cross-traffic turns.

The signs of war were obvious. Watchtowers and pillboxes guarded crossroads and bridges. Senegalese sentries with fixed bayonets stood in the shade of their guard posts, concertina wire festooned the approaches to a police station, and a sandbagged machine gun position dominated a nearby rail siding. Street vendors squatted on the curbs, fanning their small braziers, grilling pork or beef on bamboo skewers. Soup carts, decorated with garish designs of colored glass, offered steaming bowls of *soupe chinoise* or *pho*, redolent of rich broth and coriander.

The setting changed as we reached the outskirts of Saigon, the crowds faded, the traffic lessened. The broad residential streets were almost empty. High whitewashed walls crested with jagged shards of broken glass surrounded opulent colonial villas shaded by dark-green foliage. Flame trees spread their scarlet crowns over sun-dappled alleys, and Vietnamese policemen in white uniforms directed traffic through the quiet intersections. We drove past the tall, red brick cathedral and the imposing bulk of the post office. Apart from the lush gardens, the bright tropical flowers, and the heat, we could have been in a somnolent French provincial town.

My guide insisted on showing me the Rue Catinat, Saigon's main street, before dropping me off at my temporary quarters. If I'd been intrigued by what I'd seen so far, I was fascinated by Rue Catinat. Sidewalk cafés and restaurants, complete with antigrenade netting over their terraces, were serving French, Vietnamese, and Chinese customers. Tall, leafy plane trees shaded the wide, pedestrian-filled sidewalks. There were attractive Vietnamese women with waist-length black hair secured by a single silver clip; khaki-clad Foreign Legionnaires with luxuriant mustaches; fat Chinese shopowners; elderly French colonials with panama hats; chic Frenchwomen with deep tans; and small bands of Vietnamese street urchins with shoeshine boxes, bare feet, and salvaged cigarette butts stuck behind their ears.

A rich, unfamiliar aura hung over the city. It was a mix of fragrance from balcony flowers and plants; the pungent miasma of the distant mangrove swamps only slightly diluted by the breeze from the Saigon River; a whiff of copra from the docks; the smell of sun-softened macadam; and the aromas of grilled food, *nuoc mam*, garlic, strong coffee, and black tobacco.

By the time we pulled to a stop near a government-leased apartment building my travel fatigue and the hangover I'd brought with me from Paris had been forgotten. Saigon was rated a 25 percent hardship post in Washington, but I couldn't believe my good fortune. I had the feeling I'd stepped into a *Terry and the Pirates* scenario, the perfect environment for a young bachelor. It was far from my art department desk at the San Francisco *Call Bulletin*, but I was convinced I'd made the right move. There might be a war going on in Indochina, but it didn't seem omnipresent. My guide shattered that illusion.

"You got any cotton?" he asked as we unloaded my bags.

"Cotton?" I replied, puzzled.

"That's a military hospital across the street," he told me, indicating a walled complex topped by a French tricolor. "Most of their casualties come from night attacks and they operate into the early-morning hours. The screams can keep you awake if you don't plug your ears."

Someone had been thoughtful enough to stock the apartment's refrigerator. I opened a beer and began to unpack, taking note of my new surroundings. The ceiling fan started with a shower of sparks and an ominous grating sound. Small green gecko lizards clung motionless to the wall, and two large cockroaches had obviously made the bathtub their home. I didn't have to report to work until the next day, after I'd recovered from the trip, but I'd already decided to explore Rue Catinat on my own. I lay down for a short nap and awakened at 10:00 A.M. the next morning. Neither the racketing cyclomotors, the shrill gossiping of resident Chinese servants, nor screams from the hospital had disturbed my sleep.

I reported to Lee Brady, the chief of USIS Saigon, that afternoon. His office was above the Galerie Eden, just off the Rue Catinat. Brady was a quiet intellectual with a wry sense of humor who had served with the Office of War Information during World War II. He spoke impeccable French and had close contacts with a number of influential French and Vietnamese officials. It wasn't the first time we'd met. He'd been in San Francisco on a recruiting tour for the State Department and I'd been one of the candidates he'd interviewed. I was now a member of his staff. He lost no time in welcoming me and pointing me in the right direction. I was to report to John Pickering, Brady's deputy, who was in overall charge of information and press matters.

John "Black Jack" Pickering, the deputy director of USIS Saigon, shouted for me to come in. Despite the small rotating fan on his desk, the small office was stifling. He looked up at me from under his bushy eyebrows as if I were a newly hired cub reporter, shook his jowls, and suggested I take off my coat and tie. I was wearing the Foggy Bottom uniform according to State: a seersucker tropical suit and a subdued, striped necktie.

"You can wear that getup when you call on the ambassador," Pickering growled, "not when you're working." Black Jack, despite his official position, was straight out of *The Front Page*. A former Chicago newsman who'd worked for the old Paris edition of the *Herald-Tribune* and covered Lindbergh's arrival in France, he hadn't lost the requisite gruffness of a tough city editor. I soon learned that he believed in straight talk.

He briefed me on who to see at the embassy; hinted that protocol was best ignored; suggested I start work by editing a daily news bulletin published in English, French, and Vietnamese; and asked me what I knew about Indochina. I scraped together what I could: an amalgam of what I'd read, news headlines I remembered, the few lectures I'd attended in Washington, and the crumbs of background provided by a disinterested officer during my consultation in Paris. Black Jack was clearly unimpressed. I then made the mistake of adding an after-thought.

"I understand the French are doing well in the field," I ventured, repeating what I'd been fed in Paris. Black Jack frowned as if he'd been accosted by the village idiot.

"That," he said in his gravelly voice, "is pure bullshit!"

I soon found myself in a new world where the clichés and consigns I'd learned in Washington didn't apply. The U.S. Information Service in Saigon was in full transition. As part of the State Department's international Information and Educational Exchange Program and offspring of the wartime Office of War Information, USIS had been trying to chart a peacetime course between infor-mation and cultural programs. The Cold War, the Korean conflict, and the Indochina War were changing all that. The trend was now toward a more active participation in information programs supporting U.S. policies and the "Campaign of Truth," a euphemism for counterpunching Soviet and Chinese propaganda with our own. USIS Saigon was soon to be in the front line of this effort in Indochina.

The late President Roosevelt's anticolonial view of France's role in Asia had been scrapped. Washington policymakers now saw Indochina as another dom-ino threatened by Communist China's expansionism in the Far East. We were countering this threat in Korea, and the French were "fighting the good fight" in Indochina. In return for massive U.S. military and economic aid in their struggle to defeat Ho Chi Minh's Vietminh, the French were going to build a free and independent Associated States of Indochina within the French Union. The United States was also determined to keep France an active, contributing partner in the NATO Alliance. This was a high-priority matter. Franco-U.S. cooperation in Indochina was therefore essential. Boat rocking of any kind was not to be tolerated.

Ambassador Donald Heath received me on my second day in Saigon. He was a professional diplomat, a short, thoughtful man with a disconcerting re-semblance to Stan Laurel. The United States had established an embassy in Saigon after recognizing the French-controlled government of Emperor Bao Dai in early 1950. Heath's mandate was to keep the French happy—and fight-ing. The ambassador questioned me on my experience, asked me about the quality of my French, and spoke with a certain nostalgia of his short career as a working journalist. It was not too long before he turned to policy and used the phrase "fighting the good fight." He explained that, as I would be working with the French and Vietnamese Information Services and both resident and visiting foreign correspondents, it was particularly important I understood policy and didn't stray from the official line. I left my first meeting with a working ambassador impressed by Heath's relaxed manner and the time he'd taken to speak with such a junior member of his staff. Little did I know then that in a year's time he'd be seriously considering having me recalled to Washington for flouting the policy he'd so carefully outlined.

The Continental Hotel was directly across from the entrance to the Galerie Eden. It was a white colonial pile of a building with a wide café terrace on the Rue Catinat, an open restaurant decorated with potted palms, and a tile-floored bar looking out on the Opera House square. The Continental was the rendezvous point for the old French *colons*, traveling entrepreneurs, Army officers on leave, intelligence agents, and adventurers drawn by a durable Asian war. It was also the unofficial headquarters of both Saigon-based and visiting foreign correspondents.

Black Jack Pickering suggested I make contact with the press corps before seeking out my official Vietnamese and French counterparts. "You'll learn more from them," he'd explained, "than you have from any Washington briefing." I soon made the Continental a second office. I began my real education on Indochina sitting with journalists in the bar of the Continental at the *apéro* hour. Til and Peg Durdin of *The New York Times*, Max Clos of AP, Lucien Bodard of *France-Soir*, Jacques Mootasami of Reuters, Dennis Bloodworth of the London *Observer*, Dennis Warner of the *Melbourne Herald*, Robert Shaplen of *The New Yorker* and François Sully of *Newsweek* were all regulars or visitors at the Continental. Most of them had long experience in the Far East, and all of them had a good idea what was happening beyond the confines of Saigon.

I soon learned that being a government official imposed certain limitations. I was not only a new boy on the block, I was no longer a journalist. There was a definite line that I couldn't cross, an area I couldn't enter. It wasn't a matter of distrust. It was more a reticence, a two-way manifestation of the classic antagonistic roles of media and officialdom. We could drink together and laugh together, but at a certain point the veil would fall, the inner circle would close. Considering that some of these veteran newsmen shared more information with me than I possibly could from my side of the divide showed a commendable desire to "educate" the newcomer.

The Continental Hotel was a microcosm of the *old* Indochina. Split bamboo blinds kept the sun and the monsoon rains out of the wide rooms. Whispering groups of Vietnamese room boys huddled in the corridors, gambling or gossiping, responding in slow motion to the sound of a room bell and requests for ice, mineral water, sandwiches, or the services of discreet, management-approved prostitutes. Stout Corsicans with legitimate businesses and links to both the smuggling trade and the Customs Service met to sip pastis together under the fans before moving to the dining room for a lunch of boiled fish napped with garlic-heavy aioli sauce.

Tanned French officers in fatigues, their MAS submachine guns beside them, ordered a last drink in the bar before returning to their outposts well before the roads out of Saigon were closed for the night. The traffic on Rue Catinat flowed by the Continental like a rattling, fuming metallic river. Low-slung Citroën sedans, mud-spattered military jeeps with long whip aerials, weaving Vespa scooters, and cyclomotors all contributed to the blue haze of exhaust hanging under the plane trees. Bicycles and cyclo-pousses flanked the motorized vehicles, and child vendors darted through the traffic to sell cigarettes and chewing gum to customers on the Continental's terrace.

If the Continental Hotel was a landmark of colonial Vietnam, its owner, Monsieur Mathieu Franchini, was a larger-than-life Saigon character. A Corsican who had come to Indochina as a young man after World War I, Franchini had married into a respectable provincial Vietnamese family and worked his way slowly into the business and official circles of the capital.

He had bought the moribund Continental and, over the years, turned it into a going concern. By the 1950s he also owned the luxurious Majestic Hotel fronting on the Saigon River and was an "adviser" on financial matters to the spendthrift Emperor Bao Dai and the Bank of Indochina. He also maintained a business relationship with Gen. Bay Vien, the former river pirate and corrupt commander of the Binh Xuyen Shock Police of Saigon. Some said Franchini was the *capo di capi* of Vietnam's Corsican underworld. Others swore that he was only an exalted "fixer" in the Corsican tradition. Whatever the truth, Franchini was someone to be reckoned with in Saigon. Official public receptions sponsored by the High Command of the French Expeditionary Corps, the French high commissioner, or the Vietnamese Ministry of Information were always held in Franchini's Continental. It was the place to be seen, to observe, to exchange confidences.

Five days after my arrival I moved out of the temporary apartment across from the hospital. The administrative officer had found a villa for me in a residential area. I was pleased and flattered to have a whole villa to myself. I changed my mind when I saw it. It had been a fine home to someone a long time ago, but neglect and the tropics had done their work. The garden looked like a jungle. Thick vines had grown up the stucco walls and snaked under the roof to dislodge the tiles. Fruit bat droppings were thick on the terrace. The furniture consisted of two wooden chairs; a kitchen table; a wide bed with a mosquito net; and a boxed hospitality kit of cooking utensils, cutlery, soap, towels, and bedding. The enormous living room, a study, and the two large unused bedrooms were completely empty except for a colony of furry-legged spiders and grouped deposits of rat droppings. My gratitude for the administrative officer's largesse evaporated. The American Mission had taken over a number of villas on long-term leases to accommodate incoming personnel. Until they could be put in order, it was prudent to have them occupied. The administrative officer was obviously supplying me with accommodation and ensuring the services of a house-sitter at the same time.

My "staff" arrived at dusk—a Muslim guard in a khaki uniform armed with a long, hardwood club; and two elderly Chinese women accompanied by two young girls carrying cooking pots, utensils, and bedding. The guard was supplied by the embassy. The Chinese contingent had been sent by solicitous Foreign Service wives. It included a cook, a wash *amah*, and the two girls as general backup. They were all dressed in black trousers and white cotton blouses. The cook's teeth appeared to be solid gold. Two of them had a playing card spade and club cut into the precious metal, the design accentuated by the black-painted tooth underneath. Within minutes the empty villa echoed to loud, high-pitched Cantonese and the racket of wooden clogs.

I succeeded in explaining to the cook that she and her crew could stay for a trial period, took a quick shower, and left the villa to catch a cyclo to the Continental. Before I could step out the gate, the guard stopped me to ask if I'd like a woman for the night. I declined and he went back to arranging his sleeping mat on the terrace under my window. When I returned much later, the guard was fast asleep. Strange sounds and a flickering glow came from the interior of the villa.

The Chinese servants were kneeling before a semicircle of lighted candles. The cook held fuming joss sticks in her hand; the living room was permeated with incense. Their chanting bordered on a collective moan. From time to time they'd touch their foreheads to the floor. Loath to interrupt what I took to be a religious ceremony, I retired to my room, tightened the mosquito netting, and went to sleep. The next morning, using pidgin French and dramatic gestures worthy of Chinese opera, the cook informed me the villa was inhabited by an evil spirit. She predicted that a few more nights of prayer would solve the problem. As I left for work, the watchman warned me to guard my valuables carefully as the servants were untrustworthy. The yawing, bumpy cyclo ride gave me the time to admit a definite drop in enthusiasm for villa living. On arrival at the office I'd decided to seek a small apartment near the city center.

The following week was devoted to making contact with French and Vietnamese officials. There were two lists: one a ridiculously long one of diplomatic calls demanded by the outdated rules of protocol, the other a collection of working contacts. Black Jack Pickering, red pencil in hand, shortened the diplomatic list appreciably. He explained that at my modest level I'd be received by some uninteresting underling and the prime advantage of the calls was to spot friendly officials who might be cooperative and useful. I also decided to use the visits to form a mental picture of the location of government buildings for future reference.

The diplomatic circuit was a kaleidoscope of polished floors; impressive chandeliers; oriental carpets; wide stairways; and airy, high-ceilinged halls decorated with hanging scrolls, shiny lacquer paintings, and *bleu de Hué* porcelains. From the Palais Norodom to the prime minister's palace, the governor general's residence and the General Staff Headquarters, I was met by obsequious doormen, guided through long corridors, and received by French and Vietnamese officials and military officers. They offered me iced orange soda or green tea, welcomed me to Saigon, and asked a number of questions on my professional background and experience in the Far East. The calls inevitably ended with the promise of future assistance or cooperation as needed. It was only later that I realized the French were finding such innocuous social charades useful in filling the first pages of their dossiers on the increasingly numerous and potentially trouble-some official Americans arriving in Saigon.

The first working contacts were more interesting. Jean-Pierre Dannaud, the director of the French Information Service, and his staff were friendly enough but there was a coolness and a touch of condescension in their manner. It was my first encounter with the deep and underlying French resentment of Ameri-can interference in Indochina, but I brushed it off as a bad first impression stemming from my obvious lack of previous experience in the Far East. I was wrong to do so. In the early 1950s continued Franco-American rivalry in Indo-china was to work against any positive solution of the Vietnamese problem. The two so-called allies saw the future of the Indochinese Peninsula from en-tirely different optics. The French, working from the vantage point of their own colonial history, relied on past experience and what they saw as an overrid-ing need to reestablish their hegemony in Indochina. The Americans, who tended to regard history itself as a closed book—and colonial history as tain-ted—saw their role as that of enlightened liberators. We had helped liberate Europe from Nazi tyranny and defeated the Japanese. We would now save Indo-china from Communist aggression. In order to do this the region had to be purged of any lingering vestiges of prewar colonialism. The French and Ameri-can theories were basically incompatible and provided a doubtful, shaky foun-dation for Franco-U.S. collaboration in the war against the Vietminh.

The French were wary of American objectives in Indochina. They had been struggling to pick up the pieces of their prewar colonial empire despite the obstacles put in their way. U.S. refusal to help a French military task force return to Vietnam and OSS contacts with Ho Chi Minh in 1945 had only confirmed the French suspicion that the American superpower intended to include the former French colony in its own zone of economic and political influence. The French were in a difficult, frustrating situation. To regain Indo-china they had to defeat Ho Chi Minh. To defeat Ho Chi Minh they had to depend on U.S. military and economic aid. To receive the aid they had to agree to certain American stipulations, including a pledge of eventual independence for Vietnam, Laos, and Cambodia. At the same time, to reconsolidate French supremacy, they had to rebuild a shattered infrastructure strong enough to guarantee control and keep out interlopers. All of these requirements created a dichotomy of effort and an environment of deception and suspicion that would poison Franco-American relations throughout the Indochina War.

This rivalry, masked by diplomatic language and soothing official declara-tions, was to have a direct, negative effect on the eventual American inter-vention in Vietnam. French reverses in the field and their final defeat produced a dangerous mind-set among many senior American military officers and diplo-matic officials. "The French did it wrong, so there is nothing to learn from them" was the first message. The second fateful commandment was, "We have the power, it's simply a question of applying the right dosage." The theory was that overwhelming U.S. political, economic, and military power would bring about the defeat of a Communist-led insurgency and provide the time and environment in which a noncommunist government could thrive and prosper. It looked good in State Department position papers, it scanned well in Pentagon contingency plans, but it was to fall apart in application.

Both the French and the Americans underestimated the strength and appeal of Vietnamese nationalism, a precious commodity the Vietnamese Communists drew around themselves like a magic cloak and exploited with skill and tenacity. We both worked with "our" Vietnamese nationalists, many of whom were dedicated and sincere, but we failed to recognize or admit that their very presence at our side often diminished their claim to true nationalism in the eyes of their compatriots.

The French, due in part to their long colonial rule in Indochina, rarely considered total independence a realistic option. They worked with—and through—revolving strata of Vietnamese, Laotian, and Cambodian officials and contacts who acted as front men in successive local governments while French officials continued to pull the strings.

If my meeting with Dannaud had planted certain doubts in my mind, my encounter with Captain Gardes of the French Army Information Service was more successful. The intense and direct Gardes (who later joined the revolt of the generals in Algiers against the de Gaulle government) was a whirlwind of energy and ideas. He had read Sun Tsu, the ancient Chinese master of guerilla warfare, and Mao; he was studying revolutionary warfare; and he was an advocate of increased psychological-warfare capabilities for the Franco-Vietnamese war effort.

His office was a noisy, busy operational center with officers and sergeants coming and going, telephones ringing, and combat cameramen and photographers on their way to operations in the battle zone stopping by for last-minute instructions. Through it all he managed to pour me a chilled bottle of Tiger beer and carry on a conversation. He urged me to "get out of Saigon" at the earliest opportunity to see the "reality of Indochina." He emphasized that the war would be won or lost in the villages and hamlets, not in the staff conferences and official receptions of the capital. When the time came to leave, he walked me to the door, continuing his harangue on the need to get out in the field.

"Would you like to go on an operation?" he asked. I hesitated. I was still feeling my professional way and not sure military operations fitted my job description.

"Think about it," Gardes suggested, "and call me. There's something coming up close to Saigon. You'd be away a few hours." I promised to call him back and hurried to my next appointment.

The Vietnamese Ministry of Information was gearing up for an increased role in psychological warfare and anti-Vietminh propaganda. The minister was unavailable, but I soon learned that this was no great loss as ministers of information were particularly expendable. It was a difficult job. Caught between their French "advisers" who called the shots, the newly arrived Americans brimming with untested ideas, and pressure from various Vietnamese political groups, any minister of information had to perform a hazardous balancing act. The fact that a show of efficiency or positive results might put them on the Vietminh assassination list didn't make the job any easier.

More green tea, more polite words, and the minister's staff showed me some of their output. There were three-color posters and brochures meant for use in the countryside; booklets on farming, health, and hygiene; and books extolling the lives of Vietnamese patriots, such as the Trung sisters, who had fought and defeated Chinese invaders in A.D. 40. The propaganda material for the field branded the Vietminh as puppets of the Chinese, underlined Vietminh atrocities, and made liberal use of the red-striped, yellow flag of the government. It all looked productive and meaningful. I learned later that the material I'd seen rarely reached its rural targets. The Ministry teams hung their posters and distributed their brochures under heavy guard during hurried daytime visits. At nightfall local Vietminh commanders would instruct the villagers to destroy the government output or use the paper bonanza for personal hygiene after political officers had derided the government's message in compulsory public sessions. With province chiefs and police officers having to barricade themselves into their fortified offices for the night, there were few Ministry teams willing to risk nocturnal operations. Those who did often returned to Saigon feetfirst.

My last stop was at the offices of Agence Vietnam Presse, the government-controlled news agency responsible for the distribution of French- and Vietnamese-language news and feature articles throughout the country. Here I met Monsieur L, the AVP director, a Vietnamese official and survivor with whom I would work over a number of years. A short, bespectacled man with a ready laugh, a taste for scotch, and a gift for maneuvering, Monsieur L bore facial scars from an abortive Vietminh assassination attempt. He had close links with the French Intelligence Services and was finely tuned to changes in the political wind. All this was still unknown to me as I sat, tea-logged, in Monsieur L's office and listened to his enthusiastic description of the best nightclubs in Saigon and Cholon, Saigon's Chinese twin city.

My first day of official calls made one thing painfully clear. Both the French and the Vietnamese expected me to have an official title of some kind. They operated in a well-established government hierarchy where titles were important. It was all very well to introduce myself as a member of the U.S. diplomatic mission or a USIS officer, but it was much too vague for the people I'd be dealing with. I mentioned this to Black Jack Pickering when I returned to the office. He seemed surprised that I wasn't sure of my position and told me I was to be the assistant press officer working under Gene Gregory, a human dynamo who seemed determined to save Vietnam despite itself.

I also mentioned Captain Gardes's invitation to accompany French military units on operation near the capital. Black Jack cogitated, rubbed his forehead vigorously, and cleared his throat a number of times. He finally decided it was a good idea and gave me his blessing but recommended I not mention the project to anyone at the embassy. "What they don't know won't hurt them," he mumbled as I left his office.

The USIS offices above the Galerie Eden were located in a vast warren of unairconditioned, tile-floored space divided by corridors and stairways. Vietnamese, French, Chinese, Cambodian, and Laotian translators worked side by side preparing official policy statements and press releases. Perspiring American officers edited a daily news bulletin, received by wireless from Washington for distribution to the media, government offices, and foreign embassies throughout Indochina, and brainstormed new propaganda initiatives for proposal to the French and Vietnamese. A separate room overhead housed the officers and staff of the FBIS (Foreign Broadcast Information Service—a CIA affiliate) busy monitoring the airwaves of Indochina for radio traffic, including Vietminh broadcasts and emanations from neighboring countries.

The same building complex also housed the Information Section of the U.S. Aid Mission dedicated to publicizing the use and benefits of U.S. aid to Vietnam and assisting the Vietnamese government in setting up their own publicity machinery through technical and financial assistance. The American staff, headed by Leo Hochstetter and John Donovan, was a collection of freewheeling, talented nonconformists with little regard for the niceties of diplomacy. Hochstetter and Donovan had been together as foreign correspondents in the Middle East until they'd managed to insult King Farouk during a formal dinner. Unrepentant, they now had official status in Saigon and a well-deserved reputation for hell-raising that made Ambassador Heath decidedly uneasy.

I spent the working day familiarizing myself with the office routine, meeting the Vietnamese and Chinese senior staff, and filling in for Gregory as he went off on mysterious errands carrying a bulging briefcase. It was a sad commentary on our effectiveness that, although all the USIS officers spoke French, only one spoke Vietnamese and he was stationed in Hanoi. This meant that all our printed output in Vietnamese, Cambodian, or Laotian went unchecked by an American officer. For all we knew, our daily news bulletin could have contained pro-communist material or even calls to action for Vietminh cells based in Saigon. Fortunately, our local staff was dependable and generally loyal.

If I concentrated on the nuts and bolts of our Information Program during the day, I spent the evenings and nights trying to understand the military and political picture. The "dirty little war" that had begun in 1946 as a thinly disguised colonial reconquest had escalated. The Indochina conflict was now being played for international stakes; and France, the United States, China, and the USSR were the high rollers. I had arrived in Vietnam immediately following the departure of General de Lattre de Tassigny, *"le Roi Jean,"* the commanding general who had breathed new life in the Expeditionary Corps and defeated general Giap in a series of battles in North Vietnam. Since his explosive arrival in Indochina in 1950 (he'd sent twenty colonels back to France within forty-eight hours for sins ranging from lack of offensive spirit to looking unsoldierly), de Lattre had used his broad military and civilian powers to change the tactics of the Indochina War. His coordinated use of air power, airborne troops, artillery, and naval forces had caught the Vietminh in the open during set-piece battles. In the twenty-six-day battle of the Day River in 1951 alone, General Giap had lost over 11,000 men, thanks in part to the arms, aircraft, and equipment supplied to the French by the Truman administration.

General de Lattre, crushed by the death in action of his son and suffering from cancer, had returned to France, where he died on June 11, 1952. Although he left his "marshals," a hand-picked band of colonels, in Indochina to carry on the war, de Lattre's legacy was fading fast. Without his iron hand of command the marshals had become rivals. His successor as commander in chief, Gen. Raoul Salan, known as *le Chinois* for his extensive service in the Far East, was an intelligence expert and not a tactician. But de Lattre had taught General Giap a lesson he was not to forget. A captured order of the day signed by Giap following his costly reverses stated, "Our troops, who have shown their superiority as guerrillas, should, from now on, not seek massive battle. The general counteroffensive is called off. Regional elements will enter by small groups into the towns and reinforce the urban networks. The prize of revolutionary warfare remains the population."

I picked up bits and pieces of information like small tiles in a mosaic. Much of it came from correspondents just in from the press camp in Hanoi or operations in the Tonkin Delta. Other reflections were made by our local staff, who were beginning to relax in my presence. Some food for thought was available in the daily communiqués issued by the French High Command. As a French journalist suggested, "Reverse the meaning of the communiqué until it becomes negative and work slowly back toward the possible truth."

It would be wrong to give the impression that life in Saigon was grim, serious, and depressing. The Pearl of the Orient, though tarnished, still glowed in the night. I had seen the Rue Catinat after dark and sipped cognac and soda at the bar of the Croix du Sud while an all-female French orchestra mesmerized a polyglot male audience. I'd sat over a Tuborg in the roof bar of the Majestic Hotel, where the pianist played the latest hits from Paris and bright tracers from a harassed French post across the river arced through the sky. I'd dined on grilled filet steak and asparagus at l'Amiral Restaurant, a rendezvous of French parachutists and special operations types.

Nevertheless, my newfound friends among the correspondents at the Continental decided that my education was incomplete. I was invited to join a sortie on Cholon, the Chinese city ten minutes from downtown Saigon. We commandeered two cabs and set off down the broad Boulevard Galliéni to dine at one of Cholon's famous restaurants. The Arc-en-Ciel was a huge, two-story Chinese restaurant combined with an upstairs nightclub complete with a Filipino band and floor shows including such headliners as Josephine Baker and Charles Trenet. It had the requisite anti-grenade screening on its long terrace, and the barman's gin fizz was famous throughout the Far East.

But the regular customers could do without the floor shows or the barman's special. They came for the food. The cavernous eating hall was a bedlam of noise and movement. Businesslike Chinese waiters in white coats rushed between the round tables, their arms loaded with steaming platters; young Chinese girls in tight jackets proffered steaming towels to new arrivals; and private parties of French officials or Chinese businessmen isolated behind thin screens raised their glasses of straight scotch or *kaoliang* in raucous toasts. Steam and tempting odors wafted from the kitchen as the waiters swung through the doors. The menu was a many-paged marvel of variety. There were dishes from Peking, Shanghai, Canton, and Szechuan served in generous portions on broad tables studded with iced bottles of Tiger beer or rosé de Provence.

More discreet tables were available upstairs, including one reserved for members of the Sûreté and other branches of the French security services. Well-groomed Chinese prostitutes, in skin-tight *cheong-sams* split to the thigh, spooned down bowls of rich hot-and-sour soup before drifting to their business stations in the nightclub. Directly across the street a slightly downmarket restaurant specialized in lotus bud soup, a sweetish broth touted as an effective aphrodisiac. Cyclo-pousse drivers in rags, tattered felt hats hiding their thin faces, clustered around the entrance to the Arc-en-Ciel. They rang their handlebar bells and shouted in pidgin French at people leaving the restaurant, vying for customers.

Our next stop was Le Grand Monde, the gigantic gambling emporium operated by Gen. Bay Vien, leader of the Binh Xuyen, a band of former river pirates now doubling as the "shock police" of Saigon-Cholon, more an assault group than a law-enforcement entity. I learned that Bay Vien, who'd received his general's rank from Emperor Bao Dai, also shared the rich take of Le Grand Monde with the emperor and his Imperial Cabinet. In return, Bay Vien owned the rackets of Cholon, including the opium monopoly. The Binh Xuyen were not only profiting from the benevolence of the emperor, they also sheltered under the protective wing of the French Army's 2ème Bureau, or intelligence branch, whose operatives found the ruthless Bay Vien and his swampwise gunmen useful against the Vietminh. To complicate matters further and shore up Bay Vien's position, the U.S. Aid Mission would soon equip the Binh Xuyen shock police with new jeeps, radio equipment, and arms.

Le Grand Monde's expanse was hidden by a high stucco wall at the entrance to Cholon. Heavily armed Binh Xuyen troopers patrolled the grounds and searched customers for weapons at the gates. Inside there was bedlam. Crowds of gamblers clustered around brightly painted symbols and charts displayed at tables or on oilcloth laid on the packed dirt ground. Vietnamese taxi drivers, aged Chinese servants, off-duty prostitutes, sidewalk vendors, dark-skinned Cambodians from rice sampans docked in the *Arroyo Chinois*, all pushed, shoved, and shouted, placing their bets in traditional games of chance.

We worked our way through the crush to the casino, where we were searched for the second time before entering Bay Vien's pride and joy. The casino was high ceilinged, airy, and lit by chandeliers. The low, professional voices of the croupiers were counterpointed by the click of chips and the tinkle of iced drinks being served at the tables. The whole crowded room spelled money. High-ranking French officials sporting the red *tomate* of the Legion of Honor on their lapels rubbed shoulders with well-dressed *métis* pimps. Stout Chinese bankers bet huge amounts, their impassive features hiding any reaction to losing or winning. French planters with arms like matchsticks and skin the color of yellow parchment placed their bets with shaking hands, hoping to win enough to support their opium habit. Middle-aged Vietnamese women with heavy makeup and expensive jewelry chain-smoked as they watched the roulette wheel spin and slow.

I left Le Grand Monde the equivalent of fifteen dollars ahead. As we hailed cabs and drove off to our next stop I learned more about the Binh Xuyen. Peter Lennox, a devil-may-care British cameraman working for the U.S. Aid Mission, explained that Bay Vien lived in a fortified villa across the Y-shaped concrete bridge on the other side of the *Arroyo Chinois*. Not only was it the warlord's home and command post, it also boasted a zoo containing Bay Vien's favorite pets: a magnificent tiger and a fully grown boa constrictor. Rumor had it that the tiger's diet varied depending on the unexplained, permanent disappearances of the general's enemies.

Le Parc aux Buffles, on the Boulevard Galliéni, was one of the world's largest bordellos. It was another of Bay Vien's holdings, established for the use of the French Expeditionary Corps. Its separate sections for officers and enlisted men were contained in a walled complex taking up a whole city block. We talked our way in past a doubtful Foreign Legion sentry standing under a sign specifying that all arms and grenades must be checked at the gate. The cubicles for the enlisted men formed a square around a wide earthen field where crowds of soldiers prowled on the lookout for the prostitute of their choice. It was a noisy, steamy flesh market, kept orderly by patrolling military police and the grim-faced Chinese matrons in charge of the girls.

The women came from as far away as the *djebels* of Algeria and as close as the slums of Saigon. There were short, stocky Laotians, Cambodians with long black hair and silver ear studs, Vietnamese wearing cheap copies of French dresses, tattooed professionals from the Ouled Nail tribe of Algeria, Negro women from West Africa, and a few hard-bitten, down-on-their-luck white women who would never see the red light districts of Marseille and Toulon again. Unshaded bulbs threw a garish light over this sexual corrida, soldiers' boots kicked up the dust, and popular prostitutes had two or three men waiting in line outside their cubicles.

We pushed through the sweaty crowd, a true Tower of Babel where German and Hungarian Legionnaires argued over precedence, Vietnamese prostitutes demanded fresh towels, and Chinese supervisors saw to the unloading of a military truck full of beer. Entering a narrow passageway, we left the din behind us, knocked on a locked door, and entered the officers' section of the "bullpen." We were in a long, low-ceilinged room equipped with tables and benches that faced out onto a side street. Colored lights were strung over the tables, and palm fronds were woven through the antigrenade netting to provide some privacy. Doors on each side of the passageway we'd just used led to individual cubicles.

This was the domain of "Momma," the queen bee of the officers' section. She was a Vietnamese version of James Michener's "Bloody Mary." She was short, squat, and her teeth were stained with betel juice. We were introduced, and when Momma learned I was an American official, she hastened to explain that "many diplomats" were her customers. The many diplomats were in reality one: a British vice consul who arrived once a week on his motorbike for his "Friday boom." The girls here were carefully selected for their looks and figures, although Momma wasn't above infiltrating some from the enlisted men's section when business was heavy.

There was a note waiting for me when I returned to my villa. It was from Captain Gardes. If I wanted to see an operation near Tay Ninh I was to rendezvous with a departing jeep at 0630 the next morning.

CHAPTER 2

The Plantation

I made the rendezvous at the post office with fifteen minutes to spare. I'd had a few hours' sleep, a hurried breakfast, and a cup of reheated coffee. I'd dressed in what I thought appropriate: khaki trousers, a light, short-sleeved shirt, and desert boots. I was carrying a small rucksack containing a change of clothing, toilet articles, two oranges, and a bottle of scotch. The last item was suggested by one of the correspondents. He'd called it "the ice breaker," explaining it was the best antidote to the icy reception one usually received from officers in the field. I also had an item of contraband in my sack that Ambassador Heath wouldn't approve of—an unofficial .38 caliber Colt Police Special that I'd brought with me from Washington. An old Indochina hand had suggested a handgun would not be a luxury in Vietnam and I'd taken his advice. World War II had dimmed any enthusiasm I might have had for weapons, but I considered the revolver a form of insurance policy.

The jeep that rolled into the cobblestoned courtyard of the post office was driven by a thin Moroccan noncom with a needle-sharp nose and a neatly trimmed beard. He wore a tight gray turban and his uniform was carefully pressed. He threw me a quick salute, eyed me with curiosity, and handed me an envelope. It contained my *ordre de mission*, duly signed by Captain Gardes. I was authorized to proceed in a military vehicle to join a Spahi unit of armored cavalry near Tay Ninh. I would be their guest and responsibility during my stay. The driver pointed to the rear seat of the jeep.

"For you," he said in French. Gardes had thoughtfully provided me with an army bush hat and a canteen. I nodded my recognition and climbed in beside the driver, shifting his submachine gun out of the way.

Saigon was pleasant at that time of the morning. The air was cool, a thin mist hung in the topmost branches of the high trees, and small, bicycle-powered carts were serving soup and noodles to early risers. Women and children were gathering at a public pump filling kerosene tins and jerri-cans with water. The driver explained that the daily road-opening patrol would now be busy scouring the highway for mines and possible ambushes. By the time we left Saigon behind, the road ahead should be clear.

By 1952 the war of the roads had settled into a set routine. The road complexes of Vietnam, Cambodia, and Laos were the arteries and veins of the Franco-Vietnamese war effort. There were few helicopters available. Those that were handled medical evacuation and other high-priority tasks. Supply and troop movements depended on truck transport. To protect the roads the French had built a number of mutually supporting strongpoints and posts. The more elaborate were of thick reinforced concrete along the model of a Maginot Line pillbox, complete with armored firing ports, periscopes, electric generators, and dismantled, revolvable tank turrets protruding from the roof. Some of the more elaborate posts boasted the ultimate in tidiness—a flexible tube through which spent machine gun cartridges would tumble to be deposited outside the pillbox. Unfortunately, the ground-level exit holes provided easy entry for pole-like bangalore torpedoes placed by enemy assault teams.

Simpler constructions were more common. They were often built like a crude fort using logs, mud, sandbags, and corrugated metal. The center of the complex usually featured a roofed watchtower housing an automatic weapon. These posts were protected by one or two trenches filled with sharpened bamboo stakes and rimmed with concertina rolls of barbed wire. Some positions had defensive mines at their disposal, but the mines often remained in storage. The ease with which Vietminh agents could record their placement and the danger they posed to the local populace sometimes outweighed their usefulness.

Theoretically these posts were supported by artillery units. In the event of attack they were to deliver fire according to precise map coordinates. But the Vietminh were far from stupid. The main attack would always involve feints against neighboring posts, with the French commanders all clamoring for fire support the hard-pressed artillery was unable to deliver. The roads would be closed at nightfall, the posts would button up until daylight, and the Vietminh would have the run of the countryside, mining the roads, digging them up, attacking isolated villages, and carrying out agitprop sessions among the peasants.

The posts were usually manned by Vietnamese irregulars, locally recruited militia, under the command of French junior officers or noncoms. As the Vietnamese were allowed to keep their families close by, some posts looked more like fortified farms than military installations. Children played near the pillboxes, ducks swam in the flooded ditches where the women washed clothes, and drying shirts and shorts fluttered like battle flags above the position. Posts of particular tactical importance were often manned by regulars, under the command of veterans from *la Coloniale* or the *Gendarmerie*. These posts had a more lean, military look about them, with cleared fields of fire and more disciplined, alert personnel.

We entered a zone of silence just beyond the suburbs. The traffic noises faded, the streets became almost empty, and lush tropical growth crowded the edge of the road. We bounced up a sharp rise past a stand of thin palms and pulled to a stop near the permanent roadblock marking the Saigon exit. A *Gendarmerie* sergeant checked our papers and waved us on. The driver was obviously not a talker. I reexamined my *ordre de mission*. It didn't tell me much. I'd read *Beau Geste* and knew that the Spahis were an elite Algerian cavalry unit of France's Colonial Army. I'd seen some Spahi officers wearing their powder-blue caps in Marseille in 1945. The Spahis, like all cavalry units, had now lost their horses. I wondered how they coped with the Vietminh.

I'd left a note with the washwoman and given her strict instructions to deliver it to the office. It would tell Black Jack Pickering where I'd gone and when I expected to return. I didn't quite believe that I'd be back in Saigon that evening, but there wasn't much I could do about it. The driver tapped me on the arm and pointed to the blackened carcass of a burnt-out bus lying on its side in a rice paddy next to the road.

"Landmine," he explained gravely. I almost asked when it had happened, but decided not to distract him. We were now well into the countryside. The fields and paddies were varied shades of green bisected by dun-colored earthen dikes. The isolated villages, marked by screening growths of palm and banana trees, seemed peaceful and quiet. Water buffalo herded by young boys were moving along a dike in single file. A solitary old man dressed in a black robe and holding a black umbrella waved to us for a ride as we sped past.

We had to pull over near the approach to a concrete bridge and wait for a signal to join the outgoing one-way traffic. It was a long wait. The incoming convoy of overloaded buses, market wagons, two-and-a-half-ton Dodge trucks, jeeps, and motor scooters had to move slowly over the bridge, skirting a gaping hole in the roadway. An exploding mine had blasted the concrete, sending a large chunk of the bridge down into the sluggish yellow stream. The bus passengers were buying sugarcane and coconut from roadside vendors as the buses moved slowly ahead. There was a din of quacking and clucking from the trussed ducks and chickens being taken to market. A skinny young Legionnaire with cornsilk hair was shouting at some Vietnamese workmen below near the water's edge. They were smiling up at him in apparent incomprehension.

It took us two hours to reach our destination. We had entered the plantation zone, an eerie expanse of flatland covered by mile upon mile of rubber trees planted in endless files. The driver pulled to a stop, engaged the clip in his submachine gun, and checked the safety to ensure that the jolting ride would not cause the gun to fire.

"Pas bon," he explained, indicating the surrounding landscape. "No good, many Viets." He drove off the main road onto a laterite trail, churning up a cloud of rusty dust. We were passing among the rubber trees now. I was thankful for their shade. Even though I was wearing a bush hat, the sun had become searing, the air thick and heavy.

We came upon a group of Spahis clustered around a half-track. The driver spoke to them in Arabic. After much discussion and pointing he swung the jeep off the track and we headed across country. About ten minutes later we found the Spahi command group. Three armored cars and two half-tracks were parked in a sun-dappled clearing. A group of French officers were gathered around an armored car with an unusually large turret. I climbed from the jeep and walked over to introduce myself, *ordre de mission* in hand. I was asked to wait. It appeared something was wrong with the turret traversing mechanism. From the banging within the turret I took it someone was making repairs. I used the time to look around. The wide lanes between the rubber trees stretched on into infinity. The ground was layered with fallen leaves that curled and cracked with the heat. The Spahi troopers were wearing baggy fatigues, leather cartridge pouches, and turbans on their shaven heads. Their dark skins had taken on a strange coloration from the russet dust. Some of them were armed with the old bolt-action MAS rifle, others were carrying submachine guns. Their steel helmets were hung on the half-track like a row of pots in a kitchen.

Finally an engine roared into life, followed by a metallic grating as the heavy turret began to pivot. After a few more trials the engine coughed into silence. A dirt-smeared Frenchman lifted himself out of the hatch and jumped to the ground. He was stripped to the waist and had a grease-smeared towel around his neck. A hurried conversation, some gestures in my direction, and the erstwhile repairman walked toward me wiping his hands on the towel. He was the captain of Spahis in charge of the "plantation sweep" and visibly unenthusiastic about my presence. He was a handsome man with a prematurely lined face. He read my *ordre de mission* carefully and accepted its contents with a shrug. Grudgingly he offered a quick briefing, "as we are already behind schedule."

The captain pulled on his shirt while another officer produced an acetate-covered map and spread it on the jeep's hood. The captain explained that a reinforced company of Vietminh Regionals had been operating in the area. Two nights ago they had attacked the plantation tapper's quarters and murdered a foreman and his family. Today's operational plan called for the Spahis to move forward in a large arc, driving the marauding Regionals toward a stream where a Colonial Infantry battalion was waiting in a blocking position. Although the captain had sent on the bulk of his force, the jammed turret had cost him precious time. He was now anxious to make it up. In a sudden rush of quick French and frenetic activity the captain handed me my rucksack, took over the jeep, and shot off in a cloud of dust with *my* driver. I was left with a smiling young lieutenant who suggested I ride with him in the armored car with the faulty turret.

I had seen too many burnt-out armored vehicles in Normandy to be at ease in them, but I had no choice. Everyone was watching the strange foreigner as I clambered up beside the lieutenant. He explained that the other armored cars were newer and American made. This one dated from the postwar British presence in Indochina, and the French had acquired it in 1946. He said the turret was much too heavy, causing the vehicle to tip over on hills or rough terrain. With this reassurance, he slipped into the turret first, indicating a cramped space for me behind the turbaned gunner. The engine started, sending its vibrations through the metal. The noise was deafening as we lurched forward. At some point there must have been strategically placed padding on the hard surfaces to protect the crew. It was now long gone. Every sway and jolt threatened a major bruise until I wedged my knees against a stanchion and braced my arms against the turret wall. When the gunner activated the turret mechanism to sweep his heavy machine gun over the terrain, it sounded like a giant running his fingernail down a blackboard. A combination of engine heat and the sun had turned the vehicle into a mobile oven. The open turret provided no relief. Perspiration was dripping off my nose and burning my eyes. I suddenly understood why grimy towels had replaced the traditional white cotton scarf of the Spahis.

Mercifully we pulled to a stop about fifteen minutes later. The lieutenant was listening on his radio headset. He handed me the earphones as he squirmed up to the open turret hatch. I tried to make sense out of the grainy, static-filled radio traffic. The code names meant nothing to me but there seemed to be a lot of cursing. Someone—I guessed it was the captain—was definitely unhappy. The lieutenant reappeared to reclaim his headset. He spoke a few cryptic sentences into the mouthpiece, signed off, and suggested I take my turn at the fresh air. From the open turret I could see the other armored cars spaced out and immobile at some distance. The plantation appeared as peaceful and silent as ever.

We spent the rest of the morning grinding through the laterite or crunching over the leaves, stopping for unknown reasons for long waits under the increasingly vicious sun. By now the confined interior of the armored car had taken on the aroma of a garbage truck. Heated engine oil, body odors, old food scraps, sour wine, and sweat-stained leather had produced a unique stench. We had rolled to another stop. I was looking forward to another gulp of fresh air when a sustained burst of firing made us all start. The whiplash rip of automatic weapons is impressive enough when you're expecting it. It's doubly impressive when you're not. It tends to produce a hollowness in the stomach, a tightening of the sphincter muscle, and a rush of adrenaline. I suddenly had no desire to go near the turret hatch. Another rattle of firing and the lieutenant was back to his headset. It was all taking place at some distance, but our gunner had tensed over his weapon.

Then the lieutenant began to laugh. It was a strange reaction. I waited for him to finish with the radio and explain.

"We don't have the *baraka* today," he finally said. "No luck, no Viet, no action." I asked him about the shooting. He chuckled and explained. The captain had come upon some Vietnamese riflemen from the blocking force when he'd led the forward armored cars to the stream. They had not been in position and prepared to stop a fleeing enemy. They'd been swimming! The captain had decided to teach them a lesson and ordered one of his gunners to fire a few bursts into the water. The Spahis were now holding several rifles and some clothing left behind by the fleeing swimmers. The lieutenant shook his head.

The Colonial Infantry was officered by Frenchmen and he could see trouble in the offing.

We left our wheeled torture chamber and stretched our legs.

Each rubber tree had the old keloids of previous bleedings, and new incisions were feeding a slow drip of rubber sap into small, circular cups attached to the trunk. The Spahis began gathering wood for a fire, and a grizzle-headed old soldier produced a dented brass pot from the half-track for their mint tea. The captain returned in a pall of dust, shouted some orders from the jeep, and waved for me to join him. The operation was finished, we were going to have lunch at the plantation, and he suggested I bring my haversack.

The entry gate to the main plantation buildings was guarded by a sinister-looking band of armed irregulars wearing black blouses and trousers resembling pajamas. For a few seconds I thought we'd driven directly into a Vietminh ambush, but the captain greeted their leader by name and he grinned, replying with an exaggerated, splay-fingered salute. Most of the irregulars had brush-cut hair and very dark skin. They were armed with a mix of weapons: an old Thompson submachine gun, a few Mauser rifles, American carbines, and a German Schmeisser. The gates were opened and we rolled up the long drive toward a three-story, mustard-colored building surrounded by palms.

The captain explained that the irregulars at the gate belonged to the private army of the plantation manager. They were Cambodians from the Sangke region, just over the border. The plantation manager found them trustworthy, ruthless, and anti-Vietnamese, useful qualities for countering Vietminh infiltration of the plantation. As we pulled up before the colonnaded porch of the main building, the captain predicted I would find the manager "very interesting."

A servant led us to a shaded patio where our host was waiting. The manager was a short, balding man with a deep tan and dark rings under his eyes. He was wearing a well-tailored white bush jacket and trousers—almost a uniform— and sipping a pastis. A colorful parrot, climbing around its perch, paused at our arrival and cocked its head, watching us. Introductions were made, the plantation manager chided the captain for being late, and we were shown to a large, tiled bathroom where we washed the laterite off our face and hands. We had a hurried pastis and entered the airy, fan-cooled dining room where the table was laid with silver and crystal. The movement of the armored car was still with me, like the aftermath of a rough sea voyage, but my full attention was devoted to the food. I had suddenly become very hungry. We ate our way through deviled crab baked in its shell, beef and sautéed potatoes, salad and cheese, and a delicious crème caramel. We drank a Corsican rosé and finished the meal with cognac and short Dutch cigars.

There was a dreamlike quality to this interlude. The plantation seemed an oasis in the middle of a hostile environment. The shuffle of the silent servants, the buzz of the fans, and the occasional whistles from the parrot created a false sense of security. It was hard to imagine that the ranks of distant rubber trees constituted a battle zone. I had also noticed that the manager had been speaking around me throughout the meal. It was as if I didn't exist. My few attempts to engage him in conversation had been met with curt replies. I'd been content to eat, drink, and listen. The captain and the manager had discussed the morning's unproductive operation. The manager had decried the use of the Spahis' armored cars. He'd told the captain that if informers among his workers hadn't already warned the Vietminh, the sound of the revving engines had carried for a long distance, giving the Regionals plenty of time to fade into the jungle. The captain had recounted the swimming incident. The manager hadn't laughed. He'd delivered a long harangue about the uselessness of regular troops and complained that they caused him almost as much trouble as the Vietminh.

"Come," he finally said to the captain, "I'll show you the cold meat." We left the table and the house, walked over a weed-infested expanse of lawn, and arrived at a long, low building guarded by an earthen observation post shaded by palm fronds. Three piratical Cambodians armed with a French automatic rifle manned the position. They rose to their feet in a parody of military attention as the manager unlocked the building's steel-braced door. We entered a cool room with a beaten earth floor. It was the plantation's armory. Two long tables held the parts of field-stripped weapons, oiling cans, rags, magazines, and a variety of gunsmith's tools. The manager turned on an overhead light and we could see a full rack of rifles secured with a chain and padlock. A .30 caliber Browning machine gun sat on its tripod in a corner of the room, and there were ammunition crates piled halfway to the ceiling along one wall.

"In here," the manager said, pushing open another door. A new odor suddenly dominated the armory's smell of Cosmolene and cleaning fluids. The two dead men were lying facedown on the mud floor. They were so small that I first thought they must be children. Then I saw that one of them had gray hair. They were wearing mud-smeared black pajamas. The gray-haired man was naked to the waist, and a jagged exit wound under his left shoulder blade was crusted with black flies. There was something unusual about the other corpse, and it took a while before I realized what it was. Half the skull was missing. What remained lay flat on the ground like a hairy, sliced melon. The manager's little surprise had caught me unprepared. The lunch churned in my stomach and I had to fight to keep it down. The captain had obviously known what we were to be shown. I resented the fact he'd given me no warning. The dead men had been Vietminh couriers. They'd been tracked and killed by the Cambodians. The manager handed the captain what looked like a leather school sack and the small Japanese pistol one of the couriers had been carrying. The captain delved in the sack, examining its contents, and looked pleased. The manager explained that they had come a long way and that he thought the older man may be more than a simple courier. The bare feet of the dead men were rimmed with yellow calluses. They already appeared to be a part of the earth under them. I didn't realize it at the time, but it was a phenomenon common to Vietminh dead I was to notice during future military operations.

"Are you taking your American guest to the Holy See?" the manager asked the captain as we prepared to leave. The captain checked his wristwatch and said that although he couldn't take me to the Cao Dai capital of Tay Ninh, my driver could find his way there. He warned that we wouldn't have much time to linger if we wanted to reach Saigon before the roads were closed. My knowledge of the Cao Dai was limited. I knew they were members of a religious-military sect allied with the French against the Vietminh. The captain was already giving orders to the driver. He was to stop briefly in Tay Ninh so I could see the Cao Dai temple. I shook hands with the manager and thanked him for the lunch. He smiled without warmth.

"Perhaps you have guessed?" he asked. "I am sorry, but I detest Americans." Caught completely off guard, I watched him turn and walk into the house. Red-faced with anger and the frustration of not having had a ready reply, I said goodbye to the captain, whose own jeep had finally arrived. It was only when my driver had reached the main road for Tay Ninh that I realized I'd not once offered to break open my bottle of scotch. All things considered, it was just as well.

I made a feeble attempt to countermand the captain's orders, suggesting that we forget Tay Ninh and the temple and drive directly to Saigon. It was a waste of time. Spahis followed orders and the driver had his. I was to see the temple whether I wanted to or not. The drive to the plantation, the ordeal in the armored car, the heat, the heavy lunch with wine and cognac, the armory interlude with the corpses, and the manager's insult had drained me. I was not really prepared for my first encounter with the Cao Dai.

Their religion, founded in 1919, was an uneven blend of Asian beliefs and Christianity steeped in spiritualism. The Cao Dai rites were colorful, imaginative, and reminiscent of an illustration from a "lost planet" work of science fiction. This religious façade only partly hid the reality of the sect's power. The Cao Dai "pope" and his generals commanded a loyal army of approximately 17,000 men, many of whom had been trained and equipped by the Japanese during their World War II presence in Vietnam. French Intelligence had stepped in following the Japanese departure to finance the Cao Dai and mold their army into an anti-Vietminh asset. By 1952 the Cao Dai controlled the important region of Tay Ninh and certain sectors of the Mekong Delta.

The Cao Dai temple at Tay Ninh was a large rococo building of cream stucco with blue and orange trimming. Its tall tower dominated the surrounding flat-land, and a high wall protected the administrative and housing area. After being waved on by some well-armed Cao Dai guards in mustard-colored uniforms, the driver left me at the temple entrance. A shaven-headed Cao Dai monk received me, suggested I remove my boots, and bowed me into the tile-floored, open-sided center of the Cao Dai universe. I asked him about the brightly colored, personalized wall murals near the entrance. He told me they depicted the "saints" of the Cao Dai: Jesus, Buddha, Victor Hugo, Sun Yat-sen, and Joan of Arc. He volunteered the information that Winston Churchill was in line for sainthood once departed from this earth.

The elaborate altar was raised on a dais at the far end of the nave. It was dominated by a huge blue ball dotted with silver stars. An all-seeing eye looked out of its center. The monk spoke on in a whisper of slowly enunciated French. He told me about past and present popes of the Cao Dai, the nuns of the church, the vegetarianism practiced by the priests, and the search for universal peace. My brief visit ended with an invitation. I was to come and spend a few days of meditation with the monks, but I must be sure to notify them in advance. On my way to the jeep I passed some "nuns" dressed in loose-fitting white robes. They were uncommonly young and attractive and broke into frivolous giggles once they'd moved on. I was to learn later that the friendly monk had been selective in his facts. He'd totally ignored the secular history of the Cao Dai, including its private army, its wealth, power, skill at political intrigue, and wartime alliance with the Japanese. I found the driver squatting Vietnamese-style by the side of the road enjoying a glass of coconut juice from an ambulant vendor. We shared the oranges I'd brought and headed back to Saigon as a scarlet sun backlit the palms.

Much later that night I decided to eat at the Bodega, a small restaurant near the Continental noted for its good food. After such a full day I should have been content with an early night. As it was, I wanted to get out, to be around people, perhaps share some of my experiences. I was trying to analyze what I'd seen. If Captain Gardes considered the plantation operation "the truth" about Indochina and the war, God help us! It had been my first contact with colonial troops. Despite their failure to flush out the enemy, the Spahis had impressed me as professionals. But after being with them for only a few hours I'd found myself wondering at the depth or sincerity of the camaraderie, tempered by obvious paternalism, between the French officers and their North African troopers. I couldn't help but wonder if the Moroccans, Algerians, Tunisians, and black Africans of the Expeditionary Corps weren't taking part in some huge charade. What were they really thinking, fighting under the tricolor so many thousands of miles from home? I'd heard the Vietminh had already zeroed in on France's colonial troops as prime targets in their propaganda campaign and wondered how effective it had been.

All these grave thoughts were shelved on arrival at the Bodega. It was crowded but I managed to find a small table for one. The pickup was playing Piaf, there were bright flowers on the sideboard, and a great deal of conversation and laughter. I ordered a pastis and took my time with the menu, appreciating the large number of attractive French and Vietnamese women in the dining room. I was admiring a stunning brunette in the white uniform of an army nurse as she raised her glass of wine to touch that of her escort. Only then did I recognize the Spahi captain from the plantation. He was immaculate in dress whites complete with campaign ribbons, hardly comparable to the bare-chested, oil-spattered ruffian of that morning. We exchanged quick nods of recognition.

Later, when the nurse had gone to the rest room, the captain came to my table, *digestif* in hand, and we shook hands. He sat down heavily and yawned before speaking about the plantation manager. The captain said he was worried about him. The manager had become obsessed by his own private war with the Vietminh to the detriment of the plantation's production. The captain explained why. The manager's wife was Vietnamese. The year before, he'd taken his wife and children to Saigon during the holiday season, leaving his aged Vietnamese mother-in-law at the plantation. The Vietminh had mounted a heavy attack during his absence with the complicity of some Vietnamese house servants. A number of Cambodian guards had been knifed while they slept. The old mother-in-law had been dragged before a captive audience of plantation workers, where she'd been vilified, dishonored, and badly wounded by a number of slashes from razor-sharp *coup-coups*. She had then been beheaded and her head placed on a mound of earth in the middle of the driveway. When the manager returned to the plantation with a relieving force and sped through the gates, his headlights illuminated his mother-in-law, who appeared to be buried up to her neck. He rushed forward to help her and the severed head rolled off the mound. Ever since he'd been devoting most of his energy to killing Vietminh. The story didn't go too well with my rare steak. The captain said goodnight and went back to the beautiful nurse. I ordered a cognac and resolved to go to bed. It was indeed a strange war.

The image of the two Vietminh couriers stayed with me for some time. I tried to imagine where they had come from, what their mission had been, and wondered if those who had sent them would ever learn of their death. It was difficult to match their half-clad corpses with the portrait of the uniformed Vietminh in my mind. I was still thinking of the Indochina War in Western terms. Official communiqués spoke of the movement of battalions and divisions. General Giap was said to have at least six regular divisions numbering some 75,000 men, plus 35,000 Regionals and 50,000 members of the "people's militia" in Tonkin alone. To me, even the latter term had conjured up an image of a uniformed, organized force.

I had been ignoring an important lesson. The large-scale Vietminh offensives and attacks were tactically important, but in a revolutionary war they were only the tip of the iceberg. While Giap's main force divisions hit and ran, inflicting losses on the French and the Vietnamese and keeping them off balance, Vietminh political cadres, agents, and clandestine guerrillas were hard at work in so-called secure areas. They were maintaining old networks, building new ones, recruiting members, eliminating or terrorizing individuals who posed a threat, collecting taxes, and building their own infrastructure in the villages and hamlets nominally under Franco-Vietnamese control. This, in effect, was the "real war," the continuous, meticulously planned sapping of a shaky society—a dependable tactic that was to be inherited and improved on by the Vietcong during the 1960s.

CHAPTER 3

Les Amerloques

The corrugated metal fuselage of the venerable Junkers trimotor was easy to spot among the dun-colored operational aircraft on the military side of Tan Son Nhut Airfield. It was shortly after dawn and the stucco control tower gleamed like marzipan in the first light. I parked my press section jeep beside the two French Army sedans and walked over to introduce myself to the young officer watching his men load the Junkers. It was to be my first leaflet drop. I was curious and a bit nervous. Curious to see how things worked and nervous because we'd be flying over "enemy territory."

There had been a number of changes in the months following my visit to the plantation. Gene Gregory had been evacuated with infectious hepatitis and I'd become the mission press officer. I now supervised the press section of USIS, acted as first contact for newsmen seeking information or interviews, and contributed to the drafting of the ambassador's rare speeches or statements. I had also been asked to attend meetings of the Franco-Vietnamese psychological warfare planning committee as a U.S. representative. New to Indochina and with only a vague founding in the complexities of psywar, I had nevertheless begun to wonder about the efficacy of the Franco-Vietnamese propaganda effort.

The officer from Captain Gardes's psychological warfare staff wore heavy-framed glasses and chained-smoked cigarettes. He gave the impression he'd be much more at home teaching at the Sorbonne or sitting on the terrace of a Left Bank café. His men were slinging bundles of leaflets to two Senegalese soldiers aboard the Junkers. I greeted the officer, he glanced at my *ordre de mission* and told me we'd be leaving in half an hour. I drifted over to a stack of leaflets and eased one out of its wrapping. A gray photograph took up two-thirds of the sheet. It depicted a French soldier armed with a submachine gun

27

standing over a Vietminh corpse. The text, in Vietnamese and French, was direct. "Surrender now," it warned, "or this will be your fate." The reverse side was a safe conduct pass allowing the holder to surrender and ordering French and Vietnamese troops to honor the document. It didn't take a master's degree in psychology to imagine the counterproductive effect of the leaflet's theme. It was the type of effort a Vietminh mole would readily approve, knowing its blunt message would infuriate Vietminh troops and probably ensure an influx of new recruits.

The cargo was finally loaded and the officer waved me aboard. I asked how old the aircraft was. He told me it had once served the Luftwaffe. Judging from its condition, it could well have been flown in the Polish campaign of 1939. Most of the isinglass windows were missing. Those remaining were cracked, holed, or yellowed with age. The crew chief handed shovels to the Senegalese and directed them to the rear of the aircraft. There were no seats, so I followed the officer's example and grabbed hold of the overhead static line, placing myself well clear of the open cargo door. The pilots arrived in a battered weapons carrier. They were wearing khaki shorts, sleeveless shirts, and tinted aviator's glasses. One of them had a holstered Colt .45 slung low on his right hip. Both looked like they'd had a very rough night on the town.

Our takeoff was worthy of a comedy-thriller. The three ancient radial engines coughed smoke as they started one by one. The fuselage shook and vibrated. The undercarriage squeaked as we taxied down the strip. A full roar from the engines sent us bouncing along the tarmac with a noticeable side-to-side sway. We finally lifted off with an ominous thump, traveling at an unusually slow speed, and cleared the trees with little room to spare. We climbed higher, making a long, slow swing and steadied on a course that would take us close to the Cambodian border northwest of Trang Bang. The psywar officer lit another cigarette and went forward to check his map with the pilots.

A sudden pain made me wince and grab my forearm. I thought I'd been stung until I saw the glistening black spots. Hot oil from the radial engines was blowing back into the aircraft through the broken windows. I sought shelter against the cockpit bulkhead. The sun had appeared in a clear sky and its heat was already warming the fuselage. After a noisy, unsteady half hour the three-man drop crew—two pushers and a kicker—manhandled the first large bundle of leaflets to the door. They seemed undaunted by the lack of safety lines and the void so close to their feet. The officer was studying the ground with binoculars. A shiny, serpentine river cut through the green landscape, and wisps of light clouds drifted by. One of the pilots shouted from the cockpit. The officer nodded, slung his binoculars, and told the drop crew to get ready.

We lost altitude in a series of stomach-wrenching swoops until we could see the bushy tops of the gray-trunked trees. The pilot dropped us even lower and cut back his engines.

"Allez!" the officer shouted. "Go!" The kicker sent the first bundle tumbling into the slipstream. It cracked open with the sound of a pistol shot, the leaflets fluttering toward the forest in a sunlit cascade. I craned my neck at one of the open windows, examining the ground. This particular forest was dominated by the Vietminh. If the French wanted to enter, they had to muster a sizable force and they didn't stay long. I strained my eyes for some sign of life or movement, but the jungle reflected only a multitude of flickering greens and yellows. The fine tracing of reddish footpaths or deserted roads appeared rarely and were quickly swallowed up by the foliage as we passed overhead.

The pushers and the kicker were hard at work; the bundles continued to crack open as we laid a swath of leaflets in our wake. The drop crew were not the only hard workers. The two Senegalese troopers were also busy. The slipstream was blowing a surprising number of leaflets back into the aircraft. The Senegalese were shoveling them out as fast as they could, beads of perspiration gleaming on their foreheads.

Watching our cargo diminish, I wondered what effect the leaflets might have. It was obvious that many would land on the highest trees and stay there. I tried to imagine what might happen to those that eventually hit the ground. Would some Vietminh soldier hide a leaflet under his shirt, read it in secret, and set off the next day to surrender at the nearest French post? It seemed unlikely. From what I'd seen since my introduction to the mysteries of psychological warfare, the practitioners seemed to be operating in a vacuum.

The few psywar meetings I'd attended in Saigon had been revealing. Although a Vietnamese official from the Ministry of Information was in the chair, there was little doubt that a French colonel was in charge. A few of the colonel's staff seemed to know their business, and lobbied for more imaginative approaches, but the majority appeared to have little interest in their assignment. It didn't take long to realize that psywar, considered a waste of time by most commanders, had become a dumping ground or transitional assignment for officers relieved of more important tasks or those soon to be repatriated to France. The newly proclaimed independence of the Associated States of Indochina (Vietnam, Laos, and Cambodia) within the French Union had added a new dimension to the struggle for hearts and minds. Some French psywar operatives pushed hard to make the independence issue a salient point of their campaign. Their simplified message was, "Why are you fighting and dying for something already achieved?"

Unreconstructed colonial officials and officers were cool to this ploy. The word independence was still anathema to them. Military victory was their goal, and the troubling question of independent status was something to be arranged with great care over a long period of time—after the Vietminh had been defeated. The Vietminh, past masters of agitprop procedures, countered the independence issue with increased use of the label "puppet" in all references to the French-backed Saigon government. With French officials and military officers still in obvious control down to the hamlet and village level, it was not difficult to convince both city dwellers and peasants that their proclaimed "independence" had a hollow ring.

The Vietminh version of "hearts and minds" featured the steel-fist-in-a-velvet-glove approach. Vietminh detachments shared their meager rations and medicine with people in the countryside, made a show of paying for needed supplies, spent long hours lecturing the population on their goals—often presented in reference to Vietnamese legends and history—and exploited every excess of the French Expeditionary Corps and the newly formed Vietnamese National Army. At the same time, the Vietminh chipped away at the Franco-Vietnamese establishment by assassinating local officials, police officers, teachers, "collaborators," and anyone they took to be a threat to their war effort.

The last packet of leaflets had gone out the door and the ponderous Junkers banked into another slow swing, heading back to Saigon. The crew chief broke out some lukewarm bottles of Kronenbourg beer and ham sandwiches. By the time we bounced down on the runway at Tan Son Nhut it was almost noon. The entire drop had been an anticlimax, more of a daily milk run than a wartime operation. I'd been prepared to see villages flying Vietminh flags and half expected some ground fire to come our way. But we hadn't seen a living creature—except for some egrets that had been flushed from the trees. What if we had? How do you identify the enemy? Without fully realizing it, I'd had my first lesson in the vagaries of guerrilla warfare. Before leaving the Junkers I stuffed a few leaflets into my pocket. I was sure of one thing—that particular masterpiece of propaganda had not been cleared by the planning committee.

In mid-1952, since the beginning of the American military aid program in 1949 and the establishment of a Military Assistance Advisory Group (MAAG) at Saigon in 1950, over 200 ships had delivered U.S. war matériel to Indochina. By 1951 approximately $50 million worth of U.S. military assistance had been received and the figure had climbed toward the $60 million mark in 1952. One important stipulation of the Franco-American agreements required the French to accelerate the formation of a viable Vietnamese national army to confront the Vietminh and rob them of their exclusive label as the only true nationalists. Although the French High Command had the final word on the distribution of military matériel, the MAAG Mission, in its advisory role, was allowed to make suggestions. More important, the MAAG was charged with performing "end-use" inspections in the field to see how the American-supplied equipment was being maintained and used.

Both the State Department and the Pentagon were under pressure from Congress to report on the progress of the Military Aid Program. At the same time Washington was anxious to publicize the program's scope and effectiveness in the United States and abroad. This latter objective became the responsibility of my office. I had already covered the arrival of military aid shipments on the Saigon docks, but crated cargo and lashed-down tanks were less than inspiring as news items. Even the few journalists representing American agencies had failed to appear and were content to lift a few figures from our press releases to flesh out their stories on actual operations received from French military briefers.

Black Jack Pickering decided to try a different tack. He sent me to see Brig. Gen. Thomas J. H. Trapnell, the newly arrived MAAG commander. I was to obtain his permission to accompany the end-use missions and return with photos and copy for Washington and local press distribution. I knocked on the screened door of General Trapnell's villa with some trepidation. As a World War II GI, my contacts with generals had been nonexistent. But my concern was unwarranted. "Trap" Trapnell greeted me at the door, offered me coffee, and listened with interest to my proposal. He was a lean Gary Cooper type with a ready smile. He'd fought the delaying action in the Philippines, been captured by the Japanese, and spent the rest of the war in their infamous prison camps. During this period he'd survived the sinking of a Japanese prison ship by Allied aircraft. Trapnell, who now wore a parachutist's wings, had been saddled with a difficult task. By December of 1952, Secretary of State John Foster Dulles would be complaining to Jean Letourneau, French minister for the Associated States, that General Trapnell was "not getting much, if any, information" from the French in Indochina. That frustration was yet to come the day Trapnell agreed to find a place for me with his end-use teams and sent me off with a list of upcoming inspections.

Thus began what were soon called the "end-use charades." The MAAG visits were to be arranged after a minimum of one month's notice. This time often stretched to two or three months due to "operational requirements" signaled by the French. Granted, they were fighting a war and there was no reason to expect them to drop everything to accommodate the American visitors. But we supposedly shared the same objectives, and we expected they wanted to show there had been progress in forming a Vietnamese national army, that Vietnamese units were in action, and that American arms and equipment were both welcome and well used.

I enlisted the help of photographer Robert Giraud, a former French commando, and we joined a number of end-use missions that took us to the Mekong Delta and central Cambodia. A certain pattern soon developed. We'd fly out of Tan Son Nhut early in the morning aboard the MAAG C-47 and arrive at our destination to find that "due to security reasons" the inspection would be limited to service and support units. If we were lucky enough to reach a Vietnamese or Cambodian battalion in a static position, our arrival inevitably coincided with the lunch period. A sumptuous mess table would have been laid for us. The meal would be preceded by generous glasses of pastis, the four courses would be washed down by white and red wines and terminated by cognac toasts offered by the senior French officer present. When we finally emerged, poleaxed, into the bright afternoon sun, it would be too late to visit the outlying posts.

The MAAG officers did make valiant attempts to inspect U.S.-supplied equipment and were occasionally rewarded by the sight of a unit's vehicles drawn up in spotless array with heavy weapons and small arms laid out on canvas groundsheets. One such inspection planted the germ of suspicion among us. A MAAG officer asked a Vietnamese half-track gunner to demonstrate his ability to disassemble a .50 caliber Browning machine gun. It was soon obvious the grinning but embarrassed trooper did not know where to begin.

Lunches with heavy alcoholic content worked both ways. It may have kept us in easily controlled, happy groups but it also loosened the tongues of our French and Vietnamese allies. It wasn't long before some of the French officers assigned to Vietnamese units or newly commissioned Vietnamese officers vented their frustrations. In some cases American matériel meant for the Vietnamese was being shortstopped and supplied to French units, which then willed their worn castoffs to the Vietnamese. The long delays in our visiting schedules were sometimes used to return equipment to a Vietnamese unit due for inspection, the same equipment being reclaimed by the French after our departure. Equipment may not make the soldier, and French combat troops were in more daily contact with the Vietminh than the fledgling Vietnamese National Army, but this situation automatically cut the effectiveness of the Vietnamese and had a deleterious effect on their morale.

It also exacerbated Franco-American tensions at a time when cooperation and coordination were called for. French obstructionism spread as the end-use inspections increased. Jeeps assigned to pick us up at 0700 hrs. arrived after 1000 hrs. Drivers unexplainably lost their way. Flight clearances were delayed and battalions on the inspection schedule would suddenly be involved in hurried operations. The flowery mess toasts may have referred to "our gallant American allies," Lafayette, and the Normandy landings, but to a majority of the French, both military and civilian, we were "les Amerloques," a derogatory slang phrase for "crazy Americans." They felt we were muscling in on their territory, spreading wild ideas about freedom and independence among the local population, and showing a dangerous tendency toward criminal naïveté in a region we knew little about.

This sensitive situation was not improved by the fact that many American officers and civilian officials in Indochina were World War II veterans who, despite the heroism of the French Resistance and the performance of de Gaulle's Free French Forces, retained a negative image of France's war role. Add to that the average American's distaste for postwar colonialism and you had a built-in tension and mistrust that did not contribute to good Franco-American relations. Ed Gullion, Ambassador Heath's deputy, had shaken Washington with a number of informed, no-holds-barred reports on the French performance in Indochina. He'd also made no secret of his view that Washington would have to put pressure on the French to do more about real Vietnamese independence if the war was to be won. Gullion, who was to become an outstanding ambassador and dean of the Fletcher School of Law and Diplomacy, left Saigon for another assignment shortly after my arrival.

The undercurrent of Franco-U.S. tension sometimes exploded into minor incidents. One night I was sitting at the upstairs bar of La Tour d'Ivoire, a popular dance hall on the Boulevard Galliéni. The small combo led by Larry, a Hungarian sax player, was belting out a noisy tune, the Vietnamese and Chinese "hostesses" were waiting for customers, and the barman had just refilled my gin and tonic. All seemed right with the world until a loud group of Foreign Legion officers swept through the door. Their leader was a tall lieutenant colonel with a weather-beaten face and short-cropped gray hair. They moved to the bar in a phalanx, the colonel in the middle. Most of them were obviously loaded. There was adequate room at the bar for all, but my presence seemed to be a hindrance. A junior officer exerted enough pressure to push me off my barstool. I could have laughed it off but I didn't. I pushed back. This was the first of two mistakes I made that night. I was suddenly pinned against the bar by the Legionnaires. Only the colonel's intercession saved me some teeth. I remained hemmed in by the colonel's entourage. Larry tried to help by volunteering that I was an American official. This prompted some unprintable comments featuring the word *Amerloque* and a lot of hilarity.

But it was the colonel's night to be magnanimous. His courtiers allowed me some space and he insisted on buying me a drink. The period of rapprochement was short-lived. The colonel loosed a barrage of barbed questions that raised my boiling point. Why were the Americans in Indochina? What did we think we'd accomplish? How much time had I spent in Vietnam? Did I know anything about the country? My replies, slowed by alcohol and heated by a growing fury, were not models of clarity. This pleased the colonel. His baiting of the *Amerloque* was entertaining his entourage. Then he went too far.

"Do you know why the Americans landed in France?" he asked. Before I could organize a reply, he answered for me. "To take over Michelin tires and the Renault auto works!"

It was too much. I swung on the colonel without weighing the risks or the possible consequences. My blow was easily blocked by one of his aides and I found myself hustled toward the door.

"I recommend you do not return tonight," the aide said, releasing my arm. "We wish you no harm."

Larry found me on the stairs pondering a defiant return. He strongly recommended I leave. He asked if I realized how brash I'd been. "That man is the legendary Colonel Gaucher of the Legion's 13 demi-Brigade. Few people raise a hand against him and walk away!"

I made a point of finding out more about Gaucher in the next few days. He was definitely a legend, a sort of latter-day centurion. He'd been in Indochina since 1940, ranging the mountains and deltas at the head of his Legionnaires. They'd fought the Japanese, the Vietminh, and bands of tribal smugglers. Near a small mountain village in the T'ai country of northwestern Vietnam called Dien Bien Phu, Gaucher had held off marauding Chinese Nationalist troops, depriving a warlord of the local opium harvest. The more I learned of the colonel and his band, the more I realized how lucky I'd been. Black Jack Pickering found it all very amusing. As I measure only five foot four and a quarter inches, there was a certain black humor to the incident. Colonel Gaucher and I were to meet again in North Vietnam under much different circumstances.

Growing French resentment of the American presence in Saigon became a corrosive mix of suspicion and mistrust. Anti-Americanism was nothing new to the French who had passed the war years in Indochina or the officials appointed by de Gaulle who had arrived to "liberate" the colony after the war.

French officials in Saigon, relieved at the withdrawal of the British troops under Maj. Gen. Douglas Gracey after the Japanese surrender, were alarmed at the influx of more "Anglo-Saxons." Through their eyes the MAAG Mission was seen as a possible threat, and the many civilians in the embassy, the Aid Mission, and USIS were often suspected of being intelligence agents with dark designs on French sovereignty. In sum, the French needed our financial and material support but they would have preferred receiving it without our presence. The fact that we were offering suggestions and advice on military, political, and economic matters often put them in a white-hot fury.

This built-in paranoia was fueled by the presence of many "not-so-quiet" Americans on the streets of Saigon. We patronized the restaurants, bars, and nightclubs, roomed our transients in the hotels, and moved through the streets in large black sedans and new Jeep station wagons. The American officers and secretaries from the Information Sections of USIS and the Aid Mission met for pre-lunch beers daily on the terrace of the Continental Hotel, a symbol of the old colonial Indochina. We were a boisterous group, playing the match game for drinks and laughing loudly at inconsequential jokes, well aware of the disapproving *colons* who left a *cordon sanitaire* of empty tables around us. In retrospect I can understand some of the French resentment. Bill Lederer had not yet coined the phrase "ugly American," but there were moments when we came dangerously close to that description.

One unintentional accident, involving Black Jack Pickering and myself, almost created a diplomatic incident. Pickering had brought a black Cadillac sedan to Saigon as his personal vehicle. Its impressive bulk was distinctive in the city. It had already created problems. Ambassador Heath's official car, a battered Packard, had seen better days. On one occasion, when Pickering had driven up to the portico of the prime minister's palace to attend a reception, the honor guard had rendered him full honors. When the ambassador arrived a short time later, the honor guard had already dispersed. From that moment on it was agreed that Black Jack's Cadillac would arrive at official functions well after the ambassador's Packard.

Pickering was a happily married man with an attractive, charming wife, but he had a newsman's curiosity and a leader's sense of responsibility. One evening, in the middle of a particularly boring cocktail party for a visiting French general, he decided it was time he inspected Momma's bordello. He'd never been there, but the tales he'd heard from his own staff and various newsmen had piqued his curiosity. The rainy season had begun and we drove to Momma's in a torrential downpour. The warm pavement steamed under the deluge, and sections of the road were already flooded. I suggested we park directly in front of Momma's to avoid slogging through the mud.

Pickering swung the wheel, pointed the black hood of the Cadillac at the door, and reached for the footbrake. The damp rubber sole of his shoe slipped off the brake pedal with a thunk. We glided majestically and irretrievably forward. The bordello's door buckled, splintered, and ripped from its hinges; a table crunched under our wheels and split; a supporting beam in our path snapped; and the roof came down in slow motion to rest on top of the Cadillac. Our dramatic entry sent everyone—French officers in mufti, hard-eyed Sûreté agents, and Momma's voluptuous staff—scrambling over tables and clambering up the antigrenade netting like chickens threatened by a hungry fox.

As the dust settled and the last hunk of loose roofing clunked down, Momma launched a tirade worthy of a Vietnamese funeral lament. Her shouting and howling quickly drew an audience. Cyclo-drivers, street vendors, French soldiers on their way to the Parc aux Buffles, and ancient Chinese *amahs* crowded around. A shaken French officer appeared, hurriedly buttoning his trousers. He took one look at the crowd of spectators and retreated back to the cubicle he'd just left. Two skinny Vietnamese policemen in white shorts and pith helmets arrived on the scene, decided that since the Cadillac was off the street it was no longer within their jurisdiction, and walked off, relieved. Momma was finally placated, reparations were made, the roof shored up enough to extract the Cadillac, and we withdrew with what little dignity we could salvage. Another horror story about *les Amerloques* was added to the repertoire. Pickering's Cadillac was never seen in that particular neighborhood again, but for quite a while—out of his hearing—Momma's was referred to as the only drive-in bordello in Saigon.

As French requests for aircraft, armored vehicles, arms, and ammunition increased and more U.S. economic aid was channeled into the country, the number of high- and middle-level American visitors doubled. In the last five months of 1952, Chester Bowles, the U.S. ambassador in New Delhi, flew into Tan Son Nhut on a fact-finding visit. Adm. Arthur Radford, commander in chief, Pacific Fleet, arrived with his staff for consultations with the French High Command. He was followed by Assistant Secretary of Defense Anna Rosenberg. Henry Luce, the Time-Life director, passed through Saigon long enough to appear at a press conference and lecture the Vietnamese on the evils of "attentism," or fence-sitting, in the struggle engulfing their country.

Each of these visits called for careful handling in regard to media exposure. Some of the VIPs had something to say and wanted to say it. Others would have been overjoyed not to have seen a journalist during their entire stay. I was experiencing the trials and pitfalls of being an embassy press officer. The newsmen and women clamored for interviews or press conferences, the visiting VIPs wanting no exposure or arbitrarily selecting some favored journalist for an exclusive "chat." I was often caught in the middle, trying to retain the friendship of the in-country press while meeting the requirements of the visitors and their own press advisers.

The hazards were many. Coordinating policy in the early 1950s was even more difficult than it is today. The embassy's view from Saigon and that of the visitors sometimes differed considerably. Pre-departure decisions made in Washington were not always relayed in their entirety to Saigon, and some of our views and priorities had received cursory consideration in Washington. It was therefore of particular importance to ensure that official statements and speeches regarding the U.S. role in Indochina were properly presented and interpreted. We had to bear in mind the sensitivities of the French and Vietnamese and the U.S. administration's need to explain its policy and actions to both the American public and a world audience. We also had to be alert to any leak, slip, or verbal banana peel that could make disastrous international headlines on the other side of the world while we slept.

Diplomats of any nationality are not particularly at ease with journalists. U.S. diplomats, despite our free press traditions, are no exception. Those Foreign Service officers who believe they can "handle" the press through calculated leaks, preferential treatment, or mutual back-scratching often find they are mistaken. With few exceptions it's usually the press that does the handling. The first months in Indochina taught me a lesson. In the eyes of the State Department some journalists were more equal than others. The policy line and influence of a publisher, agency, or network, the general tone of a correspondent's copy or commentaries, his or her membership as an insider of the Washington "old boy/girl network," all helped to guarantee an official welcome in Saigon.

My exposure to this unexpected facet of public diplomacy came early one morning through a call from Ambassador Heath. Joseph Alsop had arrived at the residence and the ambassador was asking me to come over for breakfast. I soon learned that the famous syndicated columnist had been picked up at the airport by the ambassador's chauffeur, that he would be a guest at the residence, and that my invitation to breakfast was based on Alsop's need to have someone run his copy to the cable office. All of us who'd known the acerbic Alsop over a number of years had varying degrees of respect for the curmudgeonly columnist. But that particular morning, as he stood in his silk bathrobe, giving me orders, he was not my favorite journalist. Leaving the residence with his copy in my pocket, I passed an officer from Captain Gardes's section hurrying toward the door. He was rushing to deliver a new set of camouflaged jungle fatigues for Alsop to wear in the field. Things weren't the same on Alsop's next visit. The ambassador was absent, so there was no room at the official inn. When Joe called my office for a press section vehicle to deliver his copy, I was able to tell him none were available for such tasks and suggest he try calling a cab. Other correspondents, including Pulitzer Prize–winner Marguerite Higgins, aspired to VIP rank and were often cosseted and wooed by U.S. officials. Fortunately, my first encounter with Alsop inoculated me against the "red carpet" virus. From that moment on, any sign of journalistic pretension or requests for special treatment rang a mental alarm bell and raised my professional hackles.

With more American correspondents adding Saigon to their itineraries, Vietnamese officials of the French-run Bao Dai government found themselves on the receiving end of requests for interviews. Wary of the freewheeling U.S. press and accustomed only to rare, well-orchestrated media exposure, the officials and their French advisers turned to us for help. Giving a crash course on American journalism and the power of the press was impossible. The important point I had to make was the linkup between satisfactory coverage in the U.S. media and the continuance of American military and economic aid. If some Vietnamese officials schooled in the ways of the Mandarinate failed to see the connection, their French advisers usually did.

This briefing task took me to the office of Prime Minister Nguyen Van Tam, a small man with a deeply wrinkled face, steel-brush gray hair, gold-capped teeth, a missing finger, a stutter, and a seemingly perpetual smile. Tam sat on the edge of his chair, feet barely touching the floor, and listened with infinite patience to what I had to say. It was the first experience I'd had in advising a high Vietnamese official. As I brushed a rapid picture of the media's importance and influence in America, sped on to the technicalities of "on-the-record," "off-the-record," "background," and the subtleties of cushioning a "no comment" reply, I saw my first example of the glaze-over syndrome. The prime minister's smile was still in place, but his eyes betrayed the fact his mind was far away. I am not sure this capacity to switch off was a hereditary mechanism the Vietnamese had developed in self-defense over many years of exposure to foreign advisers or a foolproof way to end an audience. Whatever the origin, it was effective.

When I left the prime minister, he asked me if I could accompany American journalists who came to interview him. I promised to help and for some time thereafter found myself sitting through a number of interviews. The scenario seldom varied: the quasi-ceremonial entrance to the prime ministerial palace; the offer of soft drinks, green tea, and cigarettes; the wait; and the entry of the tiny, beaming prime minister. Tam had been well briefed by his French advisers and fielded pointed queries with long discourses on planned reforms, progress in the war, and Vietminh reverses, his Cheshire-cat smile ever present. One unforgettable bit of unplanned farce involved the prime minister's interview by Homer Bigart, the top war correspondent and veteran reporter of the New York *Herald*. It was immediately apparent that Bigart and Tam had something in common. They both stuttered. Translating Bigart's questions into French and the prime minister's responses into English could be compared to operating two faulty Telex machines in tandem. I came away perspiring, certain that some key points had been lost or confused. Bigart, blithely unconcerned, considered it a "good" interview.

Many official and unofficial American visitors who met the soft-spoken prime minister left the palace with the opinion that he was an unimpressive but "nice little guy." In reality, Nguyen Van Tam, "the Tiger of Cailai" or "the Executioner," was a brutally efficient security expert. In 1940 he had crushed a Communist-led peasant uprising in his native village of Cailai in the Mekong Delta, allegedly executing some of the instigators personally. In 1945 he was captured and tortured by the Kempetai, the Japanese secret police. Not long afterward he was imprisoned by the Vietminh when they seized Saigon before it was retaken by French troops. His intransigence earned him more torture, resulting in the loss of his finger. The Vietminh also killed two of his sons. Prior to his appointment as prime minister, Tam had evened the score. Serving as chief of the Sûreté in Saigon, he wiped out the principal Vietminh cells in the city with a violent campaign that left numerous corpses in the gutter. Placards around their necks labeled the dead as Communist assassins executed for their crimes. There was definitely a dark side to the "nice little guy."

CHAPTER 4

North to Hanoi

The last days of the rainy season in 1952 brought sluicing down-pours to Saigon. They were heralded by flashing lightning and the cannon crack of thunder. The rain fell in solid, perpendicular sheets, overloading the city's drains and flooding the streets. Taxis stalled, cyclos moved slowly through the rising water like small, canopied boats, and shoeshine boys put aside their boxes to splash and cavort in the gutters. Drinkers on the terrace of the Conti-nental Hotel retreated from the terrace to the open-arched inner bar that looked onto the street. From there they could still observe the heartbeat of the city: the portly Franchini saying a fond goodbye to a shapely French mistress after a satisfying *sieste* in the Continental's annex apartments; the ebb and flow of the Corsican Mafia at their tables near the dining room; the French wives of officials and bankers hurrying into Givral across the street to pick up ice cream and pastries; and the innocent sexuality of passing Vietnamese girls with trays of sliced pineapple balanced on their heads, rain-soaked blouses molded to their young breasts.

Official receptions and dinners brought the staff officers of the High Com-mand out into the downpour in their white dress uniforms. The crews of patrol boats and monitors moored near the Naval Headquarters on the Saigon River rigged their sun awnings to channel off the rain. Heavily armed Binh Xuyen shock police wrapped in ponchos patrolled the streets in green jeeps, alert to Vietminh interference in their protection collections, while the incongruous Iberian rhythms of the paso doble issued from the wide, open doorway of the Croix du Sud.

An indefinable tension existed under this façade of apparent normality. You didn't have to be a student of Clausewitz to know that the dry season inevitably heralded increased military action. General Giap's great victories in 1950 had begun with the end of the rains. The Vietminh 308th Division and the 209th Brigade supported by four battalions of Chinese trained and equipped artillery had rolled up the French garrisons along the Chinese border one after the other. This had ensured direct access to their Chinese training and supply bases. It had also cost the French close to 7,000 men and huge quantities of arms and matériel, including 2,000 tons of munitions and 4,000 submachine guns, still in their crates, abandoned when Lang Son was evacuated.

Now, leaks and rumors from official French sources indicated that Giap, smarting from his setbacks in the Tonkin Delta, was preparing an offensive toward the northwest and the mountains of the T'ai region. This strategy appeared eminently sensible. It would threaten the thinly garrisoned French posts, pose a direct menace to Laos, force the French to commit troops held in reserve to protect the Delta, extend the tenuous French lines of communication, and force them to fight in mountain and jungle terrain where the effectiveness of air support would be reduced.

These leaks and rumors, based on solid intelligence reports, proved to be correct. In late October French radio intercepts identified the presence of Giap's elite assault divisions, the 308th and 312th, in the T'ai region. Agents and observers confirmed enemy troop movements on the Red River near Yen Bay and reported close to 20,000 coolies in support of the Vietminh forces. Within weeks, after bloody fighting in the eerie, fog-shrouded mountains, the Vietminh had overrun the important post of Nghia Lo. General Salan had ordered the commanders of other isolated strongpoints to fall back toward the old, French-held airstrip at Nasan.

It was against this backdrop that I suddenly found my press officer role expanded. I graduated from being a tagalong on end-use missions and assumed the role of USIS war correspondent. This was not a complete innovation. USIS had put correspondents in the field in Korea to report on the war for the Voice of America and the official, worldwide International Press Service (IPS). The reports on the MAAG end-use visits I'd Telexed to Washington had been dismally tame and repetitive. Somewhere, out there beyond Saigon, Washington was sure there were Vietnamese troops in action using American-supplied equipment. Both VOA and IPS needed newsworthy copy on the Vietnamese National Army and its performance in battle.

Lee Brady and Black Jack Pickering agreed that it was time I traveled north to Hanoi. I had carte blanche to cover any military operations that looked promising, familiarize myself with our small office at the consulate, and make contact with officials and journalists, both Vietnamese and French. My accreditation as a correspondent had to be approved at a high level, but the issuance of the press card was handled by Captain Gardes's office. Although the approval was only a formality, and the French were in no position to object to my new role, they were suspicious of my motives. Those officials and officers who had taken so much trouble to limit the scope of our end-use visits were particularly unenthusiastic about my ranging the northern battle zone as a "correspondent."

This can be attributed to the "psychosis of intelligence" prevalent at the time. It did not take great imagination to realize that I would be reporting officially on what I'd seen and heard in addition to the press copy I was filing. That's what the Foreign Service is all about. You don't have to be a CIA officer or agent to go after facts or trends and make predictions. Every diplomatic service in the world depends on such reporting, be it political, economic, or military. A diplomat spends more time drafting messages than he or she does pushing cookies. Admittedly, under the circumstances, my position was unusual. Most embassy officers, when they did travel outside of Saigon, followed well-beaten paths. French officials liked to know exactly where their American counterparts were and what they were doing. My metamorphosis into a war correspondent might not have caused sleepless nights in the upper echelons of the High Command. They had more important things to worry about. But it did cause some wariness and suspicion at the working level of the military information service and the intelligence services with which it was linked.

Fortunately, this didn't apply to Captain Gardes. He seemed to think that the more Americans saw of the real war the better. Although I'd be using the USIS house in Hanoi as my base, Gardes called the officer in charge of the Army press camp in the city to confirm my imminent arrival and make sure I received a proper reception. A few days later I left the press section in the able hands of Dinh Le Ngoan, my Vietnamese assistant, and under the overall supervision of Black Jack Pickering, bid goodbye to Saigon, and took an Air Vietnam flight to Hanoi. I was carrying a rucksack containing warm clothes, two bottles of duty-free scotch, a Rolleiflex, film, two boxes of Manila cigars, and my Colt revolver. A hastily fabricated shoulder tab identified me as a "correspondent de guerre, USIS."

Hanoi was the opposite of Saigon. A cold wind was rattling the hangar doors of Gia Lam Airfield when our flight disembarked. One immediately sensed the proximity of a shooting war. The guardpost and machine gun positions in the South had been softened and disguised by lush foliage, scattered flowers, and verdant paddy fields. Here they jutted out of the landscape, utilitarian and grim, with cleared fields of fire surrounded by double-apron barbed wire fences. Mud-spattered military vehicles moved with an urgency not seen in Saigon. A Vietnamese driver from USIS Hanoi picked me up and inched his way into the backed-up column of trucks, overloaded buses, and private vehicles waiting to cross the Doumer Bridge, the long steel span over the muddy waters of the Red River. There was a two-way flow of foot traffic along the narrow walkways on each side of the bridge. I had the impression that the Europeanized façade of Indochina exemplified by Saigon had been ripped away and I was seeing Asia for the first time.

The Tonkinese peasants shuffling past under the heavy loads of their balanced baskets were a compact human mass. They seemed to have stepped from an ancient Chinese print or the flickering newsreel coverage of mass movements during the Japanese invasion of Manchuria. But this unending crowd wasn't fleeing a rampaging army. They were engaged in basic commerce, scrab-

bling for a living in a region accustomed to floods, droughts, wars, and invasions. Most of the porters, both men and women, wore woven, conical hats.
Their teeth were blackened by protective lacquer and the betel nuts they
chewed and spat onto the roadway in sudden jets. They were carrying covered
baskets of squawking ducks and clucking chickens, precarious piles of green
onions and herbs, pole-slung piglets, deep paniers of coal chips, firewood, cases
of condensed milk, vegetables, and large, mud-smeared river fish. The whole
landscape and those moving through it were a study in gray. The lowering sky
was gray, the peasants' tattered clothing was gray. Gray mud lined the river-
banks, and the roiling water below was gray with a tint of ocher. Even the
Tonkinese faces that looked at us—and through us—with dull acceptance radi-
ated a gray light.

Hanoi appeared as a drab garrison city, reminiscent of newly liberated French
towns just behind the front lines in the winter of 1944. Military traffic was
heavy, and jeeploads of armed troops from combat units sped through the
streets. We passed a tank park on the outskirts of the city, where the walls of
private dwellings had been knocked down to shelter M-24 tanks, and grease-
smeared French mechanics were cooking food over an open fire. The city became more attractive as we reached its center. Tree-lined avenues, squares, and
cafés appeared, and the small electric trolleys unique to Hanoi rocked along on
narrow rails.

The driver dropped me off in front of the USIS house at the consulate complex, where I was shown to my room by a servant, and dutifully made my
presence known to the officer in charge. After a late lunch and an informal
briefing on local developments and relations with the consulate staff, I arranged
for a driver to take me to the French Army press camp. It was far from a
"camp." It was located in a tree-shaded, walled complex in the European residential area and housed in a peak-roofed colonial villa. The villa contained
several bedrooms, a dining room cum lounge where drinks and food were
served to accredited correspondents at reduced prices, and offices for the Army
information staff including the censors. The dining room and lounge doubled
as a briefing area where the daily communiqué was issued and Army press
officers fielded questions from the newsmen.

I was greeted with cool detachment by a young officer who had the bearing
and affectations of a graduate from France's military academy at Saint-Cyr and
introduced to a purple-nosed major sitting behind the military censor's desk.
The major checked my orders, welcomed me to the camp, and offered to buy
me a drink. I accepted, although I had a strong suspicion that I was merely
providing a good excuse for him to return to the bar. Two cognac-sodas and a
cigar later, the major was called back to his office and the resident correspondents began to drift in to compare notes before the evening briefing. General
Giap's offensive had drawn some of the Saigon-based newsmen, and I recognized a familiar face. Lucien Bodard of *France-Soir* and one of the Continental's
regulars examined my war correspondent's tab with obvious distaste, as if he'd
encountered some form of human chameleon, and gave me a limp handshake.

I introduced myself to Larry Allen of AP, a thin, laconic American considered the unofficial doyen of the press camp. Allen, to whom the French would later award the Croix de Guerre, was a legend in Hanoi and a fixture of the camp. He had good contacts among the French military. While other journalists were rushing from province to province seeking action, Allen put his stories together with a few telephone calls and discreet inquiries over a few drinks at the Hôtel Métropole or the Café Normandie. When he did venture into the field, his sources had already assured him the displacement would be worthwhile.

Reassured that the new Yank would be no competition, Allen welcomed me to the fold and suggested we take our seats for the briefing. The young officer I'd seen earlier arrived with some papers in his hand. An enlisted man helped him arrange a blackboard and wall map. The correspondents gathered around, bringing their drinks, and settled down to listen. The officer read off a list of minor engagements in various locations, posts attacked, assaults repulsed, mop-up sweeps by armor-supported *groupes mobiles*, weapons recovered, and casualty reports. The latter were primarily lists of enemy losses, a preview of the "body count" procedure U.S. forces were to adapt in the future. It was a dull litany and few of the newsmen took any notes. There was a slight rise in interest when the officer revealed some details of the 6th Colonial Parachute Battalion's fighting withdrawal from Tu Le, one of the abandoned posts near Nghia Lo. A certain Major Bigeard had led his men through seventy kilometers of jungle, carrying their own wounded, while under constant enemy pressure. It had the makings of a modern military odyssey. Allen confirmed that a number of Bigeard's paras were Vietnamese. I made a note of it for future reference.

The questions began when the formal briefing ended. The knowledgeable newsmen posed their queries like bowmen aiming for the vulnerable points of a cornered quarry. You could almost hear the shafts striking home. One journalist pointed out that since a large number of arms had been *recovered* near Point X, it would be of considerable interest to know what unit originally lost the arms and why and how they'd been lost. Had a post been overrun? A convoy ambushed? Had there been many French and Vietnamese casualties in such an action? The briefing officer tried to explain that the arms were probably collected or stolen over a long period of time, and no one incident or action had put them in the hands of the enemy. His response was greeted with sotto voce grumbling and exclamations of disbelief. Before he could recover, another verbal arrow sped in his direction. He was asked if it was true that a certain Vietnamese battalion in the Delta was suffering from a high rate of desertion. The game continued until the press lost interest. The questions petered out and the perspiring officer left, promising to follow up on specific requests for information and probably looking forward to the day he'd once again face the enemy and not a roomful of journalists.

I shared a table that evening with the denizens of the press camp, listening to their cynical insiders' comments and projections on the war. The consensus was that something was shaping up at Nasan, where General Salan had ordered the fortification of the terrain surrounding the airstrip. Rumor had it that he hoped to draw Giap out of the jungle, tempting him to launch an attack in the open where his forces would be vulnerable to French artillery and air strikes. The table soon split into two argumentative camps. One group was certain the Vietminh would make a major effort in the Delta south of Hanoi, the other was convinced the clash would come at Nasan. The problem was to be at the right place at the right time.

Professional rivalry made it unlikely that anyone receiving a solid tip on an upcoming battle would rush to share his information with a colleague. Larry Allen told me of his foolproof method for sniffing out the truth. A small team of Army combat photographers and cameramen shared a room in the press camp. They were inevitably tipped off in advance on major operations and slipped out of the camp well before any official announcement was made to their civilian counterparts. Allen kept a weather eye on these young sergeants. Any sudden absence on their part would send him down to the motor pool for a quick chat with the duty driver. The driver, having driven the team to the airfield, usually had a good idea of their final destination. Allen would then spend some time confirming the tip with his higher-ranking contacts. Ordering a last scotch before retiring, Allen informed me the combat cameramen and photographers were already at Nasan.

I spent the next morning putting in an urgent request for an *ordre de mission* that would take me to Nasan. It was then a question of waiting. I spent a minimum of time at the consulate. The two USIS officers stationed in Hanoi were busy with their small operation and the consul, Paul Sturm, was preoccupied with his reporting task. Only recently, thanks to the Freedom of Information Act, was I made aware of the heavy volume of cable and dispatch traffic he was supplying to Washington and the embassy in Saigon. Our occasional meetings in Hanoi were correct, if cool. He obviously would have been happier if I'd remained in Saigon. As it was, I spent much of my time at the press camp waiting for my travel to be approved and trying to learn more about the war.

I'd already done considerable cramming on the genesis of the Vietnamese National Army and the end-use visits had given me some first-hand insights but I still had much to learn. Press camp opinion on the VNA was clearly divided. Army press officers were ready with statistics and quotes of praise from French generals to show the VNA was a dependable, growing military asset. Veteran correspondents had their own favorite horror stories about VNA incompetence and corruption. Seeking a middle ground was difficult. A decision had been made in 1948 to establish a national army, but actual implementation had not begun till 1949. Official French figures put the VNA strength that year at 25,000. By 1952 it had reached approximately 80,000 officers and men and was under the command of Gen. Nguyen Van Hinh, a Vietnamese of French citizenship who had been a pilot with the French Air Force during World War II. General Hinh also happened to be the son of Emperor Bao Dai's diminutive Prime Minister Nguyen Van Tam, who had promoted the young lieutenant colonel to general and named him chief of staff of the Army.

The VNA drew much of its strength from the old colonial regiments of the

French Army, and its units were cadred by French officers and noncoms, veteran Vietnamese noncoms, and Vietnamese graduates of the French officers' schools at Dalat and Thu Duc. Until the Indochina War, the Vietnamese had been considered more apt to serve in supply and service units. Even some of the old French Indochina hands, who had led Tonkinese or Annamite riflemen, tended to promote tough Cambodians into the noncommissioned ranks in preference to the Vietnamese. To many French officers, the idea of a fighting Vietnamese national army was a grim joke. Ironically, few of them seemed to recognize that the relentless Vietminh who had managed to defeat some of the best French units in set-piece battles were themselves Vietnamese. This attitude had another serious effect: French commanders, ordered to recommend officers and noncoms for service in Vietnamese units, often hoarded their best men and picked the least effective for the task. Fortunately, there were French officers who had commanded Vietnamese troops in combat and knew how capable they could be if properly motivated and well trained. But, from its very inception, the VNA was to bear the stigma of its "colonial" origins. The bravery or skill of individual units, officers, and men, and all the propaganda or psychological warfare techniques in the world would never change that basic fact.

I still hadn't learned this lesson as I cooled my heels in the press camp. I did hear rumors that any Vietnamese with 50,000 piasters could buy himself out of military service and that the sons of prominent families, having graduated from the military schools, actively sought noncombat assignments. I was also told that the Vietminh command, well aware of the psychological and political dangers of an effective VNA, had directed both their Regular and Regional forces to overrun VNA positions and set deadly ambushes for the untried troops.

The French Expeditionary Corps was easier to analyze but no less complicated. Without fully realizing it I was about to witness the twilight of one of the world's last colonial armies. The FEC numbered 200,993 in 1952, including 69,513 Frenchmen, 20,082 Foreign Legionnaires (Germans, Poles, Hungarians, Spaniards, etc.), 52,323 Africans and North Africans, and 59,075 Indochinese (Vietnamese, Cambodians, Laotians, and tribal peoples). A typical operation in the Tonkin Delta could include a French tank unit; Moroccan, Vietnamese, or Senegalese infantry; a Legion mortar company; and French Navy gunboats from the Riverine Force.

The officer corps was a strange amalgam from an army that had suffered severe trauma during World War II. There were officers from the colonial units of the *Armée d'Afrique* who, after opposing the Allied landings in North Africa, had joined the Allied effort to fight in Italy and land in Southern France with General de Lattre's First French Army; the *anciens d'Indo* who had remained in Indochina, surviving the long-distance directives of Vichy, the Japanese occupation, and the first Vietminh insurrections; the Gaullists, veterans of the Resistance and the heady days of the Liberation; and a new generation of officers, recruited following the Liberation, who had experienced their baptism of fire in Germany just prior to the Nazi collapse.

In an earlier century the FEC would have been a solid professional army, a finely honed tool for military adventure and colonial conquest. In the 1950s it was already archaic and vulnerable in a new age of revolutionary warfare and political evolution. Protests against the war and the use of conscripts were mounting in France, the hot wind of independence was sweeping Africa, and each military reverse in Indochina shook the foundations of traditional political balance in Paris. The FEC's racial and religious mix was in itself a potential political problem. The Vietminh had been quick to exploit this Achilles' heel. Non-French prisoners, particularly those from the French colonies in North and West Africa, were separated from their French officers and noncoms for "reeducation" by Vietminh political cadres or previously captured countrymen who had proven cooperative. Subtle psychological methods of privation and reward, a drumfire of lectures on the evils of French colonialism, and continued exploitation of the prisoner's homesickness often resulted in changed loyalties. Under the circumstances it was surprising that so many colonial troops did remain loyal to their officers, their regiments, and to France. But those who did not were to form the indoctrinated, dedicated cadres of such revolutionary groups as the FLN in Algeria during the twilight of French colonial rule.

The high morale and hope that General de Lattre had brought to the FEC had faded. The chain of fortified concrete bunkers he had ordered built to act as a barrier to Vietminh infiltration of the Delta *and* a base for aggressive offensive action had degenerated into a second Maginot Line. These isolated fortresses, buttoned up at night, had engendered a psychology of defense that spread like an infection. Before his death de Lattre had come to see the war as one of movement and surprise, with special emphasis on the use of commando and parachute units. But he had underestimated the allure of thick, dry concrete walls, relative security, and the understandably human tendency to make a nasty war as comfortable as possible.

Gen. Raoul Salan, de Lattre's successor, known as *Le Chinois* or *Le Mandarin*, was a Saint-Cyrien who had fought in World War I, been wounded in Lebanon in the early 1920s, and served as a young officer in Indochina from 1924 to 1938. He'd then directed the intelligence service of the Ministry for the Colonies. He'd returned to Indochina in 1945 after commanding two infantry divisions during World War II. His knowledge of Vietnam designated him as a principal actor in the drama of Indochina. He had traveled to the abortive Fontainebleau conference in 1946 with Ho Chi Minh. When the conference collapsed and the Indochina war began, he returned to Vietnam as the commander of French forces in Tonkin. When de Lattre came to Indochina in 1950, he'd named Salan as his deputy.

I had met Salan officially and fleetingly in Saigon and observed him at receptions. He was an unimpressive, gray-haired man with a slight paunch, or *oeuf colonial* (literally "colonial egg"), the mark of a long-serving officer of the Colonial Infantry. He wore his four stars and five rows of ribbons with ease but he seemed almost shy and there was a sad, distant quality to his eyes. The bamboo telegraph had it that Salan's first love was the "great game" of intelligence, a pursuit his past experience in Asia had proved essential to military success. It was also said that his long service in the Chinese border region and Laos had introduced him to the soft pleasures of opium and that his own collection of opium pipes was not purely for show.

The attacks on Nasan began the night of November 30. A strongpoint to the northeast of the airstrip held by T'ai tribal irregulars cadred by Moroccans was overrun by Vietminh infantry led by sappers with bangalore torpedos. A heavy mortar barrage supported the assault. The next morning at dawn a counterattack *à la fourchette* (with fixed bayonets) by the 3rd Colonial Parachute Battalion retook the position. More attacks followed but the details were sketchy. I renewed my request for orders to Nasan and vented my frustration by familiarizing myself with Hanoi. I had admired the *Petit Lac,* a park-bounded small lake with a pagoda and slow-moving carp, walked along the Street of Silk, sipped an apéritif at the Normandie, and eaten a sumptuous Chinese lunch. Meanwhile my orders had come through. As I walked into the graveled driveway of the press camp, the purple-nosed major was waving at me from the balcony.

"Bon Dieu!" he shouted. "Where have you been?" I had missed a flight to Nasan. The major, after a conciliatory drink at the bar, promised to put me on the manifest for the next day. That night, with the help of the press camp barman, I prepared a bedroll with a borrowed wool blanket and groundsheet, checked the items in my rucksack, and went to bed early.

The flight to Nasan took about fifty minutes. It was a cold, uncomfortable experience. The C-47, loaded with ammunition, bucked through gray clouds, the noise of its straining engines rising and falling. My fellow passengers, a Legion captain and three enlisted men, were sprawled in their bucket seats, wrapped in blankets and fast asleep. Far below, the rough, mountainous terrain appeared sinister and hostile. I tried to sleep but couldn't. The thought that the aged C-47 could easily suffer engine failure and pancake down to a forced landing in the middle of a Vietminh division crossed my mind. If that occurred, the uniformed passengers would immediately become prisoners of war. What would happen to the *"correspondent de guerre, USIS"* with the holstered Colt under his jacket? At the very least he would have some fast explaining to do. I pushed that depressing thought aside and leafed through my notebook. I had been told there was a Vietnamese battalion at Nasan, the 55th, under the command of Capt. Pham Van Dong. I had also been instructed to make contact on arrival with Lieutenant Colonel Fourcade, the chief of staff of the Nasan commander, Colonel Gilles. The aircraft banked steeply, the engine pitch changed, and we dropped low to do a pass over the fortified airstrip. Below us the earth seemed to have been worked by a massive mole. The summits of the surrounding hills were scarred and marked by excavated defensive positions linked by the tracings of zigzag communication trenches. Smoke from the strongpoints that had been under attack rose straight into the still air. The strip was half hidden by a hanging cloud of dust.

Our pilot put us down lightly. We rattled and bumped along the strip and swung in an arc to clear it. The crew chief explained that one loaded C-47, or Dakota, was landing every ten minutes and the strip had to be cleared quickly. He opened the cargo doors and waved us out. We jumped to the ground and cleared our gear just as an empty truck backed up to the aircraft to begin unloading the cargo. The cool mountain air came as a shock as we jogged toward a grouping of vehicles on the edge of the strip. A howitzer fired nearby, the loud report like a giant's hammer blow, and a perfect smoke ring rose above the gun emplacement.

Nasan resembled the set of a Cecil B. De Mille extravaganza. We were surrounded by activity. A column of mules loaded with cased artillery shells and led by North African troops was climbing toward a nearby hilltop position. Green and white cargo parachutes were blossoming overhead from aircraft not scheduled to land on the strip. French parachutists, stripped to the waist, were manhandling jerri-cans full of water into a weapons carrier. Barbed wire glinted on a nearby slope like a silver blanket. Nasan was a busy, bellicose, human beehive and the prevailing urgency underlined a sense of imminent threat.

My flight companions were greeted by comrades and drove off to their units. I dropped my bedroll and rucksack to approach a group of officers hunched over a field telephone. I asked if one of them might be Lieutenant Colonel Fourcade. They turned to me as if I had been a man from Mars or a tourist who'd taken the wrong turn on his way to the Paris Métro. A hurried explanation convinced them I did have business at Nasan and a call was put through to the command post. Lieutenant Colonel Fourcade arrived in his jeep fifteen minutes later, braking to an abrupt stop in a cloud of dust. He was a tall, rugged man with broad shoulders, premature flecks of gray in his dark hair, and the physical ease of someone in top physical condition. Wearing a camouflage jump jacket, boots, and para's red beret, he could have stepped out of a recruiting poster.

Fourcade gave me a quick briefing as he sped along the edge of the strip. He told me about the night attacks, the tenacity of the enemy, the rows of Vietminh dead found in the morning. I asked him if they'd return. Was an attack expected? Fourcade shrugged and increased our speed. We stopped near the sandbagged, canvas-covered entrance to the command post dugout. Its roof was studded with radio aerials. On a slight rise not too far away a red cross flag flapped over the field surgical unit.

Fourcade asked me if I'd ever met Colonel Gilles. When I told him I hadn't, he raised his eyebrows and smiled. He told me to wait and ducked into the CP. A small group of men were sitting on the rim of a sandbagged slit-trench nearby. They were a singularly unsoldierly-looking bunch. Most of them were bareheaded and wore baggy jump jackets. They were smoking cigarettes and passing around a large bottle of beer. It wasn't the type of gathering you'd expect to see on a commanding officer's doorstep. Then I noticed the Rolleis and the hand-held movie cameras. I'd found the team of combat cameramen and photographers that Larry Allen had found so useful as an operational weathervane.

Fourcade reappeared, motioning me into the CP. I followed, dragging my rucksack and bedroll. The cavelike dugout was cold and damp. The earthen walls and thick log beams glistened with moisture. It was a busy place. A long trestle table supported an array of field telephones and radio receivers. Maps were fixed to the walls and displayed on easels. Staff officers were sending and receiving messages, reading reports, and tracing the progress of patrols on the maps. The hum of electronic equipment and the crackle of radio static filled the narrow space. I was led farther into the labyrinth, past some screening blankets, to a long table in the center of a sandbagged room. A grinning Senegalese soldier with tribal scars on his cheeks poked his head out of an alcove. Lieutenant Colonel Fourcade shouted something I couldn't understand and within seconds I was served a steaming canteen cup of black coffee. Fourcade left after explaining that he had work to do and someone would soon come to show me my sleeping quarters.

I settled down to wait, lit a Manila cigar, and sipped the strong coffee. The howitzers went into teeth-jarring action again and dirt sifted from the dugout ceiling. I felt like an actor in a World War I film. A few minutes later the hanging blanket was pushed aside and a stocky parachute officer with heavy black eyebrows stood glaring at me.

"Who are you?" he demanded, as if the wrong answer could have dire consequences. I stood up to explain my presence and noticed his rank. I was in the presence of the redoubtable, one-eyed, *Père* Gilles, the commander of Nasan. He listened to my flustered reply with obvious impatience. When I'd finished he muttered a grudging "*Eh bien*" and withdrew, flicking the curtain shut behind him. The blanket did little to mask the tirade he loosed on his staff officers. What was an *Amerloque* doing in his CP? What idiot in Hanoi had sent him to Nasan? Didn't the colonel have enough to worry about with the Viet sniffing at the defenses? There was a marked lack of response but things moved very fast thereafter. A supply officer appeared to lead me out of the CP to a nearby dugout where I was assigned a bunk belonging to an artilleryman who was on night alert and slept during the day. I was shown the latrine, the location of the water-filled lister bag, and told I'd be eating at the CP mess.

Once settled in, I left the dugout to take a good look at Nasan. I found a raised vantage point behind the CP and tried to orient myself. The briefing officers in Hanoi had described Nasan as a direct threat to the rear of Vietminh forces menacing the Kingdom of Laos. The fortified camp was approximately ninety miles from the frontier of Communist China. The military briefers had compared the surrounding mountains to "impenetrable walls" advantageous to the Franco-Vietnamese defenders. Watching the last of the C-47s touching down before sunset, I had the uneasy feeling an argument could be made that the dark heights dominating the airstrip could also pose a threat. Another column of North African infantry with slung rifles was moving over the open ground below. They wore the distinctive striped burnoose and tightly rolled turban of the Goumier, riflemen from the Atlas Mountains with a reputation for ferocity who had made life uncomfortable for the Germans during the campaign of Italy. Far across the valley a heavy machine gun began a baritone chopping, the gunner tapping out rounds as bright tracers arced through the gathering darkness and ricocheted off a distant hillside.

Luckily I had thought to take one of my bottles of scotch to the CP that evening. It changed my introduction to the assembled officers from a stiff formality to an almost jovial occasion. Pastis and rum went untouched as the scotch was passed around. By the time Colonel Gilles made his appearance with Lieutenant Colonel Fourcade, I was being called "Sim-son" by most of his staff and was under intense questioning on subjects ranging from why I had come to Nasan when I didn't have to, to details of California living. Père Gilles took in the scene with his good eye, accepted a jolt of whiskey, and sat down at the head of the table. I was allotted a seat at the far end, and Gilles's Senegalese orderly began serving the dinner. It was surprisingly good for a campaign mess. The only ration cans in sight contained jam. We were served a cold *salade russe* followed by meat, potatoes, and chicory lettuce. The bread was not fresh, but the *pinard*, a heavy army red wine, flowed freely.

I learned more about the fighting during the meal. The staff officer estimated that the Vietminh 308th and 312th divisions had taken heavy casualties. Close to 500 dead had been found in front of the French positions. I was feeling my way in an entirely new environment. I wanted to ask these officers about their own casualties but I decided it could wait till the next day. Considering Colonel Gilles's reaction to me, I'd need all the allies I could get if I wanted to remain at Nasan. The colonel frowned in my direction from time to time. At one point I sensed that he and Fourcade were discussing my presence. It appeared that Fourcade was arguing my case, but I couldn't be sure. When the dinner ended, most of the officers left the table to return to their duties. I then witnessed a brief ceremony that had become a tradition at Gilles's table. He asked the staff meteorologist for a reading on the outside temperature. The meteorologist was prepared with a reply that verified how cold it had become since nightfall. Once Gilles heard the report, he shouted to his orderly, who brought hot coffee and a bottle of dark rum to the table. We were all entitled to a tot in our coffee as a nightcap. Winter in the T'ai mountain country of North Vietnam can be extremely cold. There were few nights the fortifying rum didn't appear.

The night was a mix of pyrotechnics and potential menace. Multicolored tracers from the defensive positions hosed into the darkness periodically. Was it a new attack or the reaction of a nervous gunner? Illumination flares dropped from C-47s threw a ghostly, temporary light over the barbed wire. Cryptic messages from perimeter listening posts reporting real or imagined enemy movement could start the 105mm batteries thumping, their rounds gurgling up out of the valley and slamming into the hills. Daylight brought a tenuous relief, and clear skies meant a continuation of the sky bridge from Hanoi.

I visited the position of the 55th Battalion of the Vietnamese National Army the day after my arrival. Captain Dong, the commander, was a Nung—a professional soldier and member of the warrior tribe from the Chinese border region. The heavy smell of death flooded my nostrils as I climbed to the 55th's CP. Work parties were still burying enemy dead from the previous attacks. It was no easy task. Few of the corpses were in one piece, and fleshy fragments hung from the wire. I found the captain squatting near a field radio, shoveling steaming noodles into his mouth with chopsticks. His high cheekbones, aquiline nose, and brush-cut black hair gave him the appearance of an American Indian.

Dong's battalion was still cadred largely by French officers, but he was definitely in command. He insisted I accept some *pho* soup in a dented enamel bowl. One of his men wiped two chopsticks on his pants leg and handed them to me. I forced myself to eat, despite the stomach-wrenching stench and the horrors on the wire. Dong told me of the attacks with a disarming simplicity. The Viet had made a special effort to overrun his battalion. Led by suicidal sappers who were stripped to the waist and carrying satchel charges and bangalores, the enemy regulars had breached the wire in several places. Dong, seeing his losses grow, had ordered his supporting howitzers leveled, loaded with fragmentation rounds, and fired point-blank at the oncoming attackers. The gamble had worked and his men were still cleaning up the result. I spent the day with Captain Dong, talking with him and interviewing some of the young Vietnamese officers under his command. Then I said goodbye to Dong to return to Gilles's CP. It was only the first of many meetings between us and the beginning of a long friendship.

I borrowed a typewriter from one of Gilles's staff and, struggling with the French keyboard, managed to knock out a detailed story on the battle performance of the 55th Battalion. I addressed the copy to the major at the press camp with full instructions for filing to USINFO and VOA in Washington. An Army Information Service noncom taking film to be processed agreed to hand-carry the story on to Hanoi.

The days I spent at Nasan were a mix of impressions: the incongruous sound of a German marching song rising along a mountain trail as a Legion para battalion returned from a reconnaissance on Son La; the Chinese-style padded jackets that made already swollen Vietminh corpses look like Michelin men; the little-boy-lost look on the face of a French casualty with a fatal chest wound as they loaded him aboard a Medevac C-47; the pungent, acidy aura of *nuoc mam*, the fish sauce staple used by all Vietnamese troops; and the deathly silence of the surrounding landscape in contrast to the bustle and clatter of the French strongpoint.

As the days passed and patrols from Nasan ventured farther from the perimeter without making contact, it became clear that General Giap had pulled back his divisions. The nervous tension of expecting another assault gave way to a certain frustration palpable at the CP mess. Colonel Gilles was particularly testy. His parachutists were not trained or conditioned for defensive warfare. To him, each day the paras spent inactive in the trenches and dugouts was a waste of a prime operational asset. Even the battalion-size sweeps they were conducting outside the perimeter were proving useless. He wanted his paras out of there, and his arguments with Hanoi headquarters were not improving his temper.

It was time for me to return to Hanoi. I rolled my bedroll, left what remained of the scotch with the CP mess officer, said my goodbyes, and found space aboard a Bristol transport as it was warming up on the strip. Before long I would realize that Nasan had been a dress rehearsal for Dien Bien Phu.

CHAPTER 5

Delta War, Shadow War

They came down the hill in a well-spaced single file, barely distinguishable in the sifting mist. They were dressed in black pajama uniforms with cylindrical rice sacks slung over their shoulders. Some men wore the woven helmets of the Vietminh; others had soft black berets cocked over one eye. A few had tied a headband around their forehead. Some were French and some were Vietnamese. The weapons were also varied: French MAS submachine guns, a battered Thompson, Chinese assault rifles, and a scattering of German Schmeissers. Ammunition pouches bulged at their waists, and one man was laden with a haversack full of grenades. They moved slowly and silently, their muddy sneakers sinking into the soft soil—a strange parade of sinister pirates. I was seeing the *Commando d'Indochine* for the first time.

It had been decided that I'd stay in the North over the Christmas holidays. Washington had been happy with the copy I'd sent and wanted more. Pierre Schoendoerffer, one of the Army's combat cameramen, had suggested I spend Christmas at Phat Diem, a stronghold of Vietnamese Catholicism in the Tonkin Delta. He'd explained that the Delta war was much different from the mountain campaign I'd witnessed at Nasan.

The sprawling town of Phat Diem, sixty-five miles south of Hanoi, with its bishop and ponderous cathedral had become a symbol of Catholic resistance to the Communists. Vietminh regional forces had launched several strong assaults on the town in early December, hoping to smash the Catholic militia and gain both a military and psychological victory. The fighting had been hard, with the Vietminh gaining footholds inside the defense perimeter, but the stoic militiamen, supported by French artillery and light armor, had dislodged the Communists. The Vietminh had faded back into the patchwork paddies and limestone hills. Now, watching the commandos slip unobtrusively into Phat Diem a few days before Christmas, I had a premonition that something interesting was about to happen.

I was quartered in a shell-pocked house, occupied by three French artillery officers. When I returned to the house two of them were decorating a scrawny casuarina tree with tinfoil and colored paper. The food and drink they'd received in Christmas packages from France was arrayed on a collapsible table. My mention of the commandos was greeted with raised eyebrows, shrugs, and silence. Their reaction only deepened my interest.

Later that day I went in search of the commando billet. It was cold in Phat Diem. There was the far-off thump of artillery from the northwest in the direction of Ninh Binh, and the tin can tops hung from the barbed wire to signal enemy infiltration tinkled in the strong wind. I located the commandos in an abandoned Chinese shop that had been partly destroyed in the earlier attacks. A sentry asked my business and led me inside. The interior was smoky and smelled of rancid rice. A cooking fire burned in a corner of the room.

A group of commandos was sitting on the floor cleaning their weapons. The captain, who appeared to be a *métis*, was sipping tea from a mess cup, an opened map on his knees. He seemed young but I noticed the streaks of gray in his short-cropped hair and the deep lines under his dark eyes. He offered me some tea and asked what I wanted. He was surprised to learn I was an American. The friendly atmosphere changed when I posed my first question. The captain frowned and suggested I request a briefing from the Army press office in Hanoi on the activities of the *Commando d'Indochine*. I was not offered a second cup of tea. There was an awkward moment when two mud-smeared commandos appeared in the doorway. It was obvious they had been on a reconnaissance and had returned to make their report. It was also obvious the captain was waiting for me to leave. I thanked him for the tea and departed. It was my first glimpse of the special units directed by various French intelligence organizations that were fighting their own type of counterguerrilla warfare.

Later, when I became known and trusted by a number of commando and parachute officers, I learned exactly what the captain had been doing in Phat Diem. Waterborne weapons and ammunition had been slipping through the sector to regular enemy units putting pressure on the regional headquarters at Nam Dinh. Classic daylight operations mounted by the French *groupe mobile* had failed to produce results. The commandos were there to do the job. Each day, small commando patrols ranged the dike paths and villages, gathering information on the Vietminh. They had temporarily incorporated a number of selected militiamen into their unit as guides and scouts. At dusk, a section of commandos would leave their billet, making enough noise to ensure their departure had been noticed by the local residents. This section would continue in the same direction until nightfall, then double back to meet and join forces with another section that had slipped out of Phat Diem under cover of darkness.

They would set up ambushes at a spot where the sluggish canal met the river. They would lie in the muddy rushes throughout the night—waiting, investing their professional skill and patience in what the captain had decided was a worthwhile tactic. At the first sign of dawn, they erased all traces of their presence and drifted back into Phat Diem in small groups and from different directions.

Schoendoerffer had been right, the war in the Delta *was* different. It was a "people's war" in the worst sense of that overused term, and the people were often the primary victims. The few days I spent in the field with the 18th Vietnamese Infantry Battalion introduced me to a sinister environment of lowering skies; flat, muddy landscapes; and sawtooth mountain ranges. The drama of violence, suffering, and brutality played against this backdrop had a Goya-like quality.

It was a war of villages and hamlets, some of them occupied and defended by the Vietminh. It was therefore a war of burning villages and civilian casualties, a war of attrition. The air was always thick with stinking smoke and cinders. Certain images remain indelible: the badly burned sow, still alive and squealing in agony in a deserted village square; the lower half of a male infant lying on some corrugated iron sheeting partly covered by a straw mat; the legless Vietnamese rifleman, mutilated by a landmine, staring up at the sky with wide eyes as a cursing French medic tried to staunch the flow of slippery, thick blood; the file of mud-smeared Tonkinese males rounded up as "suspects" moving slowly along the top of a dike, connected to one another by a choke rope looped around their necks, their hands tied behind their backs; the crow-like figures of black-clad, hard-faced Vietnamese members of a special intelligence unit resting on their haunches, calmly smoking cigarettes while the unmistakable gurgle and gasp of someone undergoing the water torture issues from a nearby hut; a Catholic militiaman surreptitiously removing a rosary from around the neck of a Vietminh corpse as if to deny that any Catholic could have succumbed to such a godless cause. And there were always the tears of the peasant women, welling from their eyes, running down their worn cheeks, and dripping off their chins in a troubling silence.

The commander of the 18th Battalion, a forty-year-old Vietnamese major, was thin, wizened, and seemed to subsist principally on tea. Although his unit was part of the sector's *groupe mobile* under the command of a French colonel, the major was allowed a certain leeway in planning small sweeps and operations under the watchful eye of the French advisers assigned to his headquarters. He worked closely with the Catholic militia and praised their mastery of guerrilla warfare. The French colonel at sector headquarters didn't share the major's enthusiasm and considered the militia more of a useless rabble than a military asset. One evening, after some militiamen had delivered three dead, trussed Vietminh and one live prisoner to him, the major had turned to me, smiled wanly, and said, "You see, our colonel does not understand this war."

The field headquarters of the 18th Battalion had been set up in a deserted Buddhist pagoda near Phat Diem. It was there, paradoxically, that I received my first real introduction to Vietnamese food. The inventiveness of the battal-

ion's cooks was unbelievable. Never before had I seen so few do so much with
so little. A few scrawny chickens, some limp vegetables, dry rice noodles, onions and garlic would produce a nourishing soup. Spiked with *nuoc mam* sauce
and macerated hot chili peppers it served as a breakfast eye-opener and a forti-
fier against the cold at dinnertime. The cooks had set up their kitchen in the
open courtyard of the pagoda, where they worked from dawn to dusk, chopping and frying, stewing and boiling. Long tables were covered with bunches
of herbs: mint, lemon grass, coriander, and wild watercress; and with pots,
pans, knives, and enamel dishes filled with meat chunks of doubtful origin and
bony river fish. A haze of slow-moving flies hung over the worktables. The
busy cooks hawked and spat on the slippery stone floor, where doomed ducks
foraged for scraps. A chorus of scrawny crows perched on the ceramic dragons
decorating the tiled roof of the pagoda, waiting to vie with the ducks for their
share of the scraps. Off-duty soldiers gathered in small groups to gamble or
wrapped themselves in ponchos and slept.

Two days before Christmas I was standing on a sandbagged revetment smoking a pipe and reflecting on how nice it might have been to spend the holiday
season in Saigon when I heard the unmistakable sound of female laughter. At
first I thought it must be a radio, but a second burst of hilarity convinced me
it was both real and nearby. Curious, I headed for the source. Two large tents
had been pitched in a dry paddy. They were surrounded by a thin barbed wire
fence and the entry was guarded by a tall Senegalese sentry. Drawing closer, I
could see a group of women in brightly colored clothing gathered around two
oil drums of steaming water. They were doing their laundry. Most of them were
young, heavily made up, and raunchily sexy. Their bright-red lipstick con-
trasted with the blue facial tattoos on their foreheads and chins. My knowledge
of Momma's in Saigon helped solve the puzzle. I'd stumbled onto a BMC—a
bordel militaire de campagne—a military field bordello, staffed by professional
prostitutes of the Ouled Nail tribe from North Africa.

As I stood gaping, a stout older woman minced toward me swinging her hips
in a parody of sexual invitation, jingling her bracelets and rolling her kohl-
rimmed eyes. She shouted something I didn't understand, beckoning me
toward the tent. Her companions burst into uncontrolled laughter. Even the
Senegalese sentry flashed a broad grin. A frowning French sergeant appeared
to inform me the bordello would not be open until later in the day. Red-faced,
I beat a hasty retreat.

Later, one of the artillery officers told me more about the BMCs. It was a
French Army tradition, he explained, to provide decent food and passable sex
to men whose life span might be drastically shortened at any time by a well-
placed mine or a stray mortar burst. The mobile BMCs were strategically placed
to service various sectors and were continually on the move. The Phat Diem
sector had been lucky enough to draw such a visit for Christmas. He told
me that the staffing patterns varied. Some BMCs were primarily made up of
Vietnamese or Cambodian women. Some contained a preponderance of North
African or black African prostitutes. Although the BMCs were primarily for

enlisted men, he hinted that he had spent some unforgettable moments with a Laotian professional attached to a BMC near Savannakhet.

Suddenly serious, he sketched a depressing picture of the prostitutes' existence and related some horror stories of the facial and sexual mutilations suffered by Indochinese prostitutes captured by the Vietminh. He also praised the courage shown by individual members of a BMC who pitched in as stretcher bearers and untrained nurses during the bloody siege of an isolated outpost.

Christmas Eve morning broke over the Delta with a steel-gray light. To the north the mountains floated above a heavy ground mist, and the stars of colored paper hanging from the cathedral were ripped and battered by the wind. My housemates had worked out a duty schedule that assured their howitzers were manned while providing adequate off-duty time for themselves and their men. They seemed certain an unwritten truce would prevail during Christmas. A convoy of Dodge trucks had ground its way into Phat Diem loaded with holiday supplies. It brought cases of wine, beer, pastis, *vin mousseux*, fresh poultry, beef, Christmas sausages, tinned biscuits, cheese, apples, oranges, chocolate, and tobacco. One truck was packed with clothing for the Catholic militiamen and their families, including several large sacks of red and blue berets for the children. Within minutes the drab town was dotted with spots of bright color as the children donned their new acquisitions.

Christmas mass in the cathedral was a unique celebration. Huge pillars of black hardwood supported the cathedral's high ceiling. A crèche had been set up not far from the elaborately decorated altar. The figures in the nativity scene had Asian features, and the infant Jesus looked like a tiny Buddha. Candles threw a flickering light on the tall walls. The hobnailed boots of the militiamen acting as altar boys protruded from their white robes as they knelt on the altar steps. Other militiamen and their families crowded into the cathedral beside local merchants, rice farmers, and government officials. The colonel and his staff appeared in crisply ironed uniforms complete with their military decorations. Some off-duty girls from the BMC were also in attendance, their bright head scarves covering most of their faces. They watched the service as if it were a rare, special entertainment. A male choir of militiamen and soldiers, their black hair slicked down tight and shining, sang Vietnamese versions of the old hymns while the cadaverous bishop and his priests filled the cathedral with puffs of perfumed incense.

The dinner at the headquarters mess featured tinned foie gras as the first course of a hearty meal lubricated by Alsatian wine, Burgundy, and beer. There were toasts and songs and generous dollops of cognac to go with the strong black coffee. As in any wartime Christmas, there was an undercurrent of sadness. Men thought of their families, the war, the dead, and wondered about their own future. On the surface it was all bonhomie, jokes, and laughter. A rubber-legged young officer who had overindulged had to be carried to his quarters. Most of the Vietnamese officers present were flushed by the unaccustomed heavy doses of alcohol and I wondered how they'd be able to drive back to their units.

Early the next morning, while it was still dark, the sudden pop and rip of small-arms fire could be heard to the northwest. It was followed by three dull thumps that could only be exploding grenades. The firing intensified and a single tracer arced into the sky. By the time I arrived at the ambush site with the support group it was all over. Two pirogues floated bottom-up among the reeds, and a raft with a heavy mortar and crates of ammunition lashed to it had been beached nearby. Six dead Vietminh lay in a row at the water's edge, covered with mud and blood. A single prisoner crouched, shivering, by the raft. The commando captain seemed neither elated nor triumphant. He had helped his men retrieve the bodies and was soaked to the skin. When I lit my pipe to get the smell of death out of my nostrils, he looked at me in the flickering light of the match. "I knew they would come this way," he said quietly.

I arrived back in Saigon in time to file my copy before New Year's Day. Saigon seemed unreal after Tonkin. I had the strange impression that I had entered an entirely different world. For the first time I realized my position of privilege. I was able to "drop in" on the war and leave it as I chose, unlike those who were risking their lives on a daily basis. I knew I couldn't be accused of voyeurism but I did experience a twinge of guilt.

On January 2 the USS *Rochester* visited Saigon to show the flag. I accompanied a delegation of MAAG officers to Cap Saint-Jacques (later Vung Tau) to board the cruiser for its sail up the Saigon River. There was something surreal about the exercise. The muddy Saigon River loops and twirls its way to the sea through mangrove swamps and jungle. Small, thatch-roofed fishing villages appear unexpectedly around sharp bends. In the first days of 1953 some of these villages were secure while others were controlled by the Vietminh. The sudden appearance of the *Rochester*, its steep flanks and antenna-cluttered masts towering above the palms, was like a visit from outer space for the local inhabitants.

French river patrol boats formed a waterborne security escort, and detachments of Vietnamese infantry had been placed in "hot" zones where enemy action might be directed at the American ship. Sailors armed with M-1s were posted on the *Rochester's* deck, and watch officers scanned the riverbank with binoculars. But the only reaction came from skinny dogs barking at our passage and bands of bare-bottomed village children waving and shouting from the shore. There was little doubt that Vietminh agents and members of their regional forces were also watching our progress, but it must have been difficult for them to relate the significance of the *Rochester's* floating firepower to the type of guerrilla war they were fighting. In reality, the cruiser's presence was aimed more at impressing the Vietnamese government and the inhabitants of Saigon with America's political and military support than any attempt to intimidate the Vietminh.

It was a long, slow journey. At times the river was so serpentine that we appeared to be headed back to the sea. Mudbanks near some of the bends had us going astern and swinging the *Rochester's* bow perilously close to the bank. The cruiser's powerful screws churned up soupy brown swirls of mud, the ship's filters began to clog, and it was obvious the commanding officer was having second thoughts about the logic behind the visit. Even after the spire of the Saigon cathedral and the docks came into view it took a long time to point the *Rochester*'s bow downstream. The skipper finally had to ram the cruiser's sharp prow into the soft mud of the bank to gain enough space for the turnaround.

The official visits began once the *Rochester* was lying alongside the docks. The original visiting schedule was in tatters due to our late arrival. Sleek sedans were depositing French and Vietnamese officials at the foot of the hastily rigged boarding ladder and there was great confusion over boarding precedence. It was a protocol officer's nightmare. The fact that no protocol officer was present to take responsibility only made matters worse. The captain and his staff knew what honors were due to French naval officers; they had a pretty good idea of their obligations when it came to Army visitors; but they were totally in the dark about unidentifiable civilian officials. In desperation they turned to the only State Department man aboard—myself.

My knowledge of protocol at the time was extremely limited. It didn't go much beyond the diplomatic fact that an American ambassador was addressed as "Mr. Ambassador" by his staff. Now I found myself on deck with the captain under a tightly stretched canvas awning, trying to assess the ranking importance of each visitor. The crux of the matter appeared to be the number of side boys to place as an honor guard at the head of the boarding ladder. In times of crisis the easiest solution is often the best. When in doubt I hedged my bets by suggesting the maximum honors. The bosun's pipes squealed, the side boys saluted, and I was reassured when the visitors smiled with satisfaction. Toward the end of the ordeal I recognized a leading member of Saigon's Rotary Club emerging from his chauffeur-driven sedan. He was a local Pakistani merchant, a very tall and impressive figure, accompanied by three of his sons. Without hesitation I suggested six side boys for his reception. It obviously made his day. For months thereafter, whenever I encountered him at a reception or passed in front of his shop, he smilingly pressed a Havana cigar on me, a recurrent offer I could hardly refuse.

After writing some classified reports for Washington on my trip to the North I fell back into the pattern of Saigon life: a routine of office work, staff meetings, psywar conferences, VIP arrivals, and media visits. I had moved to a top-floor apartment just off the Rue Catinat, a short three-minute walk from the office and the Hotel Continental. I took my breakfast in the fading cool of the morning at La Pagode, a café that served some of the best croissants and coffee in Saigon. During the grenade attacks in the late 1940s the Pagode's tiled floors had been stained with the blood of its staff and customers more than once, but its managers had never installed anti-grenade screening. Sitting at one of the Pagode's low tables under the revolving ceiling fans in the early 1950s was still an act of bravado practiced by local French residents and the wives and children of French officials.

I often lunched or dined at Le Papillon, a Corsican bar-restaurant run by Yvonne, an attractive *métis* whose customers—police officials, shady Corsican entrepreneurs, and Vietnamese operators—shared a fondness for pastis, highly spiced cuisine, and heavy wines. I found Le Papillon both congenial and interesting. After an initial period of suspicion, when my arrival caused an abrupt end to conversation, the new *Amerloque* became an accepted client, shared the rounds of pre-lunch pastis, was initiated to the Corsican sausage *figatelli*, savored the strong *Patrimonio* wine, and was allowed to hear some of the inside gossip about what was *really* going on in Saigon.

The time I'd spent in the field had automatically enhanced my status among my Saigon-bound colleagues, the foreign correspondents, and certain Franco-Vietnamese officials. Whatever they thought of me personally, I had been where the action was. That fact alone opened more doors and made me, in a limited sense, an insider.

It also made a particular difference in my dealings with the military. The brief encounter with the *Commando d'Indochine* had raised a number of questions. Who were these tough professionals who had taken the symbol of the black panther for their beret badge? Where were they from, who had formed them, and for whom did they work? It wasn't difficult to come by this information. It only took some time and patience. My friends in Captain Gardes's office filled me in on the basics, veteran French correspondents shared their behind-the-scenes knowledge, and a few MAAG officers contributed to my education.

The commandos I'd seen at Phat Diem were only part of a major effort to win a crucial war in the shadows every bit as important as the classic day-to-day operations mentioned in the official communiqués. It included special commando groups, guerrilla and counterguerrilla warfare, infiltration of enemy territory, deep-penetration raids, detailed reconnaissance missions, psychological warfare, sabotage missions, organization of partisan groups, and the kidnapping or elimination of Vietminh cadres.

Since the beginning of the Indochina War the SDECE (*Service de Documentation Extérieure et de Contre-espionnage*), France's CIA, had established its Southeast Asia headquarters in Saigon. But, as so often happens with intelligence operations, it had not been easy. On their return to Indochina in 1945, representatives of the wartime intelligence organizations under de Gaulle's leadership had a difficult task asserting their authority in the wake of the Japanese surrender. Old colonial intelligence operatives jealously guarded their own turf, and new organizations, both military and civilian, had sprung up as the Franco-Vietminh conflict spread. By 1950, when SDECE was finally given authority to cap all French intelligence activities in Indochina, the various organizations included: Military Security; the *2ème Bureau*, military intelligence; the *5ème Bureau*, reporting to the High Command; the SRO (*Service de Renseignement Opérationnel*) under the authority of the commander in chief; the Sûreté, the police security service; and other smaller units such as those charged with collecting political intelligence and the *Bureau Technique de Liaison et de Coordination* located in the offices of the French high commissioner.

All of these organizations had jealously guarded their prerogatives and often vied with each other operationally, submitting conflicting reports and wasting precious time on internal competition. However, by 1951 the *Service Action* was amalgamated under the title of the *Groupement de Commando mixtes Aéroportés* (GCMA). These shock troops were meant for special operations under the direction of SDECE, and the high commissioner represented by the French commander in chief in Indochina. Many of the officers who made up the original cadre of the GCMA were veterans of special operations in Europe and the Far East during World War II. Some of them were Southeast Asian experts, having served in Indochina earlier in their careers. A majority of the rank and file were selected Vietnamese, Cambodians, Laotians, or tribal peoples drawn from Colonial Parachute Battalions, special units, or irregular forces.

By 1953 the GCMA, although still treated as a clandestine organization, had made a name for itself through a number of impressive successes. GCMA sections were active in organizing tribal minority resistance groups, including the Meo, the Yao, the Lolo, and the White, Black, and Red T'ai tribes, to fight the Vietminh. Their task was made easier, not because the tribal peoples were anticommunist or had any idea of the global politics involved, but because they had a well-founded mistrust and dislike of the Vietnamese—any Vietnamese. This situation was mirrored in the 1960s when the U.S. Special Forces worked with some of the same minority groups under the direction of the CIA.

Ironically, the CIA had offered to help the French organize their *Service Action* with funds, equipment, and advisers for Ty-Wan, the special operations school at Cap Saint-Jacques, in the early 1950s. Col. Edward G. Lansdale, the American who had masterminded Philippine President Magsaysay's victory over the Communist-led Hukbalahap rebels, had made the offer and it had been rejected. Nevertheless, Lansdale, who became the model for the lead character in Graham Greene's *The Quiet American* and William J. Lederer's and Eugene Burdick's "Colonel Hillendale" in *The Ugly American*, didn't throw in the towel. General de Lattre had finally accepted an American liaison mission to work with SDECE in Saigon.

The Americans weren't the only outsiders involved with the development of the French action teams. French wartime links with the British SAS, now operating against the Communist-inspired insurrection in Malaysia, ensured an exchange of officers, techniques, and useful information. A small number of Chinese Nationalist specialists from Taiwan also contributed to the training process at Ty-Wan.

GCMA commandos ranged the Vietminh rear gathering intelligence, carrying out sabotage, setting ambushes, and making life generally uncomfortable and dangerous for Ho Chi Minh's troops and officials. Special commando groups, operating off the Vietminh-occupied coastline in disguised, well-armed junks, seized shipments of arms and landed to blow up enemy installations. Others played a grim game of cat-and-mouse with enemy patrols near the Chinese border, keeping tabs on the movement of supplies and the Vietminh divisions going to or coming from their training centers in China.

More irregular groups linked to French Intelligence operated in and around Saigon. The husky chief bartender at the Majestic Hotel, a former parachutist, would fold his apron twice a week shortly after midnight and leave to join a covert pirogue patrol along the Saigon River and its many canals. This small Franco-Vietnamese force, moving in silence during the early-morning hours and acting on informers' tips, took a heavy toll among Vietminh couriers, agents, and sappers trying to infiltrate the Saigon-Cholon area. Civilian members of the French Information Services responsible for psychological-warfare programs occasionally donned black pajamas to join their military counterparts in covert "armed propaganda" (paramilitary) operations.

The SDECE effort to enlist dependable allies among minority groups extended to the religious-military sects in South Vietnam. French intelligence operatives worked with the Cao Dai, the Hoa Hao, as well as the Binh Xuyen, providing funds, arms, and advice in exchange for their help against the Vietminh. This often demanded a closed-eye policy regarding corruption and the use of force for personal gain. Special funding changed loyalties overnight and professional, black-clad assassins were used to reverse the local balance of power in the semifeudal fiefdoms of the Mekong Delta. The resultant quagmire of double-dealing, clandestine violence, and freelance initiative created a unique environment of suspicion and mistrust.

Trafficking in the illegal exchange of piasters was bringing millions of francs regularly to French and Vietnamese businessmen, bankers, and officials in Saigon and Hanoi. Some of these ill-gotten gains were augmented by the clandestine sale of arms to the Vietminh through second and third parties or "cutouts." The chance discovery of a huge shipment of wire cutters on the docks of Haiphong and a subsequent investigation showed the tools were meant for delivery to the Vietminh for breaching the barbed wire of French outposts. Another investigation found that the director of the Banque Franco-Chinoise was also serving as the French treasurer for the Vietminh. A Secret report from the U.S. embassy, released under the Freedom of Information Act, reveals that a French transport company was passing a substantial amount of their cargo to the Vietminh in exchange for ambush-free passage on the Hanoi-Haiphong road. Many of these reports, passed to Paris by intelligence operatives, were ignored or buried by the French governments in power.

Operation X in early 1953 was an example of the realities and necessities of revolutionary war in Asia. If the French-sponsored partisan war against the Vietminh was to be successful, SDECE had to secure the cooperation of the independent, warlike Meo tribe that occupied the mountain regions of northwestern Vietnam. The Meos are traditional opium harvesters and live by the opium trade. When asked by the French to work with the GCMA in establishing guerrilla operations in the Vietminh rear, the chief of the Meos posed one condition. The French would have to assist him in selling the opium harvest.

In the past a number of forces had scrambled to get their hands on the product of the Meo poppy fields. The French, the Chinese Nationalists, and the Vietminh were well aware of the huge profits involved. It was only in 1945 that opium was declared illegal in Indochina, a move that drove the trade underground, increasing the prices. Maj. Roger Trinquier, the GCMA officer responsible for Operation X, estimated that the Vietminh could arm a new division each year if they got their hands on the opium profits.

The problem of finding a buyer was settled quickly. Bay Vien, the Saigon vice lord, friend of Bao Dai and "general" of the Binh Xuyen river pirates, now doubling as the shock police of Saigon, was the man. The GCMA arranged a special flight from Saigon to the French controlled Plain of Jars, a flat plateau area spotted with ancient stone urns, in Laos, where the opium was loaded for the trip back to Tan Son Nhut. A detour put the aircraft down on a secret airstrip near the commando base at Cap Saint-Jacques. Trucks rushed the high-quality raw opium to Bay Vien's headquarters near Cholon for processing, and the DC-3 returned in all innocence to Saigon. From that moment on the French were able to count on the support of the Meo, who formed one of the most effective partisan forces of the Indochina War.

Vietminh intelligence operations benefited from many years of clandestine experience. The very survival of Vietnamese Communists, radicals, national-ists, and anti-French agitators had long depended on the careful organization of small operational cells, multiple pseudonyms, and innocent-appearing agents planted in government offices, commercial establishments, and military instal-lations. Vietminh infiltration of the police and civil service was an acknowl-edged fact that the French had to live with. Their counterintelligence opera-tives did their best to keep it to a minimum, but it was a difficult task and there were always new Vietminh agents to fill sudden vacancies. The Vietnamese had perfected the art of survival over many centuries and many invasions. The defeats dealt to the colonial powers by Japan, the Japanese occupation of Indochina, and Japan's subsequent surrender had only underlined the imper-manence of outside political and military power. Many Vietnamese families had sons serving with the Franco-Vietnamese forces as well as with the Vietminh, or "the resistance" as they preferred to call it, and some cautious Vietnamese government officials maintained a discreet link with the "other side."

Except for a small number of OSS veterans and rare specialists, Indochina was a new world to the majority of American officials assigned to Saigon. Many had been sent to Indochina because of their knowledge of the French language or previous service in France. They often brought with them a number of mis-conceptions about Southeast Asia and Vietnam in particular. These miscon-ceptions were sometimes accompanied by a naïveté that affected their day-to-day effectiveness. Few newly arrived Americans realized the extent of the in-trigue going on around them. This made them vulnerable to misinformation and falsehoods spread by French and Vietnamese contacts who were only too glad to feed the newcomers what they wanted to hear or what the contacts hoped would be included in the next dispatch to Washington. The thought that the sociable Vietnamese official or business contact an American may have met at a reception or dinner might be a Vietminh agent took some time to develop and impress.

I might not have been completely naïve when I'd stepped off the plane at Tan Son Nhut, but I knew precious little about Indochina. Fortunately, Vietnam's school of hard knocks was an accelerated learning process. The first lesson to retain was that things were never what they seemed. Once that was absorbed, and you understood that every doubt was reasonable, your education was on the right path. This orientation would prove to be important. Nevertheless, eleven years later, I was destined to share an office with a Vietnamese colonel who has since been given a hero's burial by the Communist regime as one of their prime agents in the South.

Whatever the extent of Saigon's seething intrigue, the year 1953 was to see policy and personnel changes at the American Mission in Saigon, a reshuffle of French officials involved in the conduct of the war, and a new strategy in the war itself.

CHAPTER 6

A Year of Change

The composition of the American embassy in Saigon underwent a considerable change in the early months of 1953. Robert McClintock, a career Foreign Service officer, arrived as chargé d'affaires. With Ambassador Heath's departure on a long-delayed home leave, McClintock became acting chief of mission. George M. Hellyer, the new chief of USIS, had also come to Saigon with orders to develop a more active information and psychological warfare program in Indochina. McClintock and Hellyer were doers, willing to take risks, and they worked well together.

Rob McClintock was mustachioed, dapper, and worldly, with a strong streak of nonconformism. He had no illusions about the local French attitude toward U.S. policy and Americans in general, but he had the requisite culture and personal charm to play the game of diplomatic chess with skill. He also understood the importance of press contacts, or what is now known grandiloquently as "public diplomacy." Within days of his arrival McClintock had begun a series of pre-lunch drink meetings with newsmen, both American and foreign. He knew he had a lot to learn from them, and they were pleasantly surprised to find an American diplomat apparently so relaxed and frank in his comments.

George Hellyer, a pipe-smoking former tea planter from Taiwan who had served as a Marine Corps captain with British general Orde Wingate's Chindits during the World War II Burma campaign, was a gung-ho senior officer with a son serving in the Corps in Korea. He had little interest in the cultural side of USIS or diplomatic niceties, particularly in the wartime atmosphere of Vietnam. Hellyer, like McClintock, spoke perfect French and knew the French well.

He also had a broad knowledge of world history coupled with practical experience in the Far East.

A third newcomer was Lt. Gen. John "Iron Mike" O'Daniel, the new chief of the MAAG Mission. General O'Daniel had been the hard-driving commander of the 3rd U.S. Infantry Division during the European campaigns of World War II. He and General de Lattre de Tassigny had crossed swords on tactical matters during the drive north from the Allied landings in Southern France. Now the French were faced with this tough old campaigner in his new role as MAAG commander and watchdog of U.S. military expenditure in Indochina. In Ambassador Heath's absence, the new team gradually added an addendum to the "French are fighting the good fight" policy. If put on paper it would have read, "but they could be doing a hell of a lot better."

I met Col. Ed Lansdale for the first time during this period. Despite the cold shoulder the French had given his earlier offer to assist in forming their *Service Action*, he was soon to become a Saigon regular. Uncle Sam was paying a large portion of the war's cost—the 250th shipload of U.S. military aid had arrived in March 1953—and the new Eisenhower administration expected to have more say in the conduct of the war, particularly the search for a nationalist third force, neither Communist nor colonialist. Lansdale's visit included a long closed-door conference with George Hellyer. When it was over, Hellyer introduced us. I showed Lansdale some of the psywar material we were producing, and he questioned me in detail about my experiences in the field with the Franco-Vietnamese forces. We also discussed the Saigon press and the editorial tendencies of various newspapers. Lansdale, as the CIA's top counterguerrilla expert in the Far East, was laying the groundwork for the insertion of his Saigon Military Mission, a small group of intelligence operatives destined to play a key role in the installation of President Ngo Dinh Diem in 1954.

In 1953 USIS moved out of the State Department to become an independent entity, the U.S. Information Agency. Serving officers, like myself, greeted the move with enthusiasm. We had always felt fettered by the State Department hierarchy, particularly the traditional diplomats, who still considered "information" a dirty word and viewed all such programs with an ingrained suspicion. Although the ambassador and the embassy's political section still held the policy reins, we now had a bit more leeway in planning and carrying out our day-to-day tasks. One immediate change was the merging of the U.S. AID Information Program with our own and the setting up of a joint photolab under the direction of "Dixie" Reese, a talented photographer. The tall, bespectacled Reese soon earned a reputation for giving dusk-to-dawn parties at his apartment overlooking the Rue Catinat. *Tout-Saigon* showed up for his extravaganzas, including high-ranking French and Vietnamese officers, Vietnamese artists, foreign correspondents, U.S. officials, intelligence operatives, foreign embassy officials, and some of the most beautiful women in Saigon. The wine flowed, the food trays were refilled, the music blared, and for a few hours the war seemed far away. Dixie ran his lab with talent and precision, but his great desire was to become a combat photographer in the mold of Robert Capa.

In late March word reached us of a major military operation in the Ninh Binh sector of the Tonkin Delta. Operation Hautes Alpes was of interest to us because a Vietnamese-led *groupe mobile* would be participating. It was of particular interest to me, as the commander of the GM was Pham Van Dong, the captain I had met at Nasan, now promoted to the rank of major. I also learned that the operation was under the command of the brusque Gilles, who had been promoted to general following the battle of Nasan. George Hellyer enthusiastically endorsed my request to cover the operation and I rushed to procure an *ordre de mission*.

A few days later something happened that changed my life. I had been drinking a noontime beer under the fans on the terrace of the Continental Hotel when I was introduced to a newly arrived secretary of the U.S. AID Mission. Mary Alice Turner was short, slim, vivacious, blonde, and intelligent. She also had the most striking green eyes I had ever seen. It wasn't what the French would call a *coup de foudre*, but something had definitely clicked. Without knowing it I was about to enter an unplanned, rollicking period of courtship that would end with our marriage in June 1954.

Prior to my departure for Tonkin, Black Jack Pickering showed me a telegram announcing the imminent arrival of former Illinois governor Adlai Stevenson, who had been an unsuccessful Democratic candidate for president in 1952. Pickering, having cut his teeth on Chicago newspapers, knew Stevenson personally. He'd heard informally from one of the governor's aides who had asked for ideas for Stevenson's fact-finding trip. During our discussion I suggested the governor ask his French hosts to see the war at first hand and I mentioned Operation Hautes Alpes as a possibility. I told Pickering about Major Dong and typed out a list of possible questions Stevenson might want to ask during his visit.

Forty-eight hours later I was on a bad-weather, wing-waving flight from Hanoi to Nam Dinh in an old de Haviland bimotor. I reached Ninh Binh by road convoy late in the evening. I was back in the land of mud, blood, and chilling cold. Operational headquarters consisted of a number of tents clustered on the banks of the Day River. A pontoon bridge supported the heavy traffic of combat vehicles, jeeps, and trucks, their passage signaled by the rattling of the unsteady roadway, as if a child were running a stick along a fence. Artillery and mortar positions encircled the command post. Some gunboats and a small naval monitor were moored in the river, the red pompoms on the sailors' caps incongruous in the inland setting.

On the other side of the river the "Rock of Ninh Binh," a scrub-topped pinnacle of granite, rose out of the flat landscape like an error of nature. It was here, in an earlier operation, that de Lattre's son Bernard had been killed in action. Ninh Binh had always been a "dirty" zone for the Franco-Vietminh forces. The Vietminh, both Regulars and Regionals, infested the area, striking hard at selected targets and fading away before French reaction could be effective. Hautes Alpes had been designed to inflict punishment on the enemy, reestablish security along the Day, and exact revenge for past losses.

I came incredibly close to killing General Gilles accidentally at Ninh Binh. The general had greeted me with his usual lack of enthusiasm, but after I'd spent a few days with Major Dong's 2nd Vietnamese Mobile Group the wind seemed to have changed. Gilles had become almost cordial. One afternoon, following a well-lubricated lunch, he invited me to join his inspection of a newly laid, temporary airstrip for observation planes. After the general had congratulated the engineer officer in charge and stamped on the perforated metal to test its solidity, he asked to see the revolver he knew I was carrying. I handed him the loaded Colt. He examined it carefully, made a lighthearted comment about the "Wild West," and suggested I give a firing demonstration.

The heavy mess wine I'd had at lunch, combined with the sun that had broken through the clouds, and the mention of the Wild West, inspired me to do something exceedingly stupid. I tried to impress my audience by fanning the hammer of the Colt in the manner of a Western gunfighter. Unfortunately the hammer tip on the Police Special was very sharp. It punched into the flesh of my hand, the revolver tilted upward and fired, the bullet clearing the general's beret by inches. The color drained from his face. In the shocked silence that followed, one of his aides stepped forward to take the Colt from me while the general turned on his heel and left.

Over time the mind tends to delete embarrassing memories, but I recall clearly that I was not the most popular individual at Ninh Binh. If the muzzle of the Colt had tilted a bit more, the French would have lost the commander of their Airborne Forces in Indochina, inexplicably "assassinated" by an American official. The incident was never mentioned again by Gilles or any of his staff. Even the officer who returned the Colt had nothing to say. Only the imminent arrival of Adlai Stevenson and his party rescued me from my pariah status. The general and Colonel Fourcade, who were to play host during the visit, wanted to know all about Governor Stevenson. I spent a long afternoon trying to answer their questions while a sputtering radio relayed program changes and demands on the Stevenson visit from Hanoi headquarters. Fortunately for General Gilles, Operation Hautes Alpes was winding down and he was able to concentrate on the preparations.

By the time the Stevenson party arrived, dusty and out of place in their seersucker suits, the Ninh Binh sector was particularly calm. After a flurry of greetings, during which he was introduced to Major Dong, the governor was ushered into the command post for a briefing. It ended just before noon and everyone adjourned to the mess tent for a pre-lunch aperitif. We were just raising our glasses when a terrific blast shuddered the tent poles. It was followed by another—and another.

"My God!" a Stevenson staff member gasped. "What the hell was that?"

"Howitzers," I told him, still a bit breathless myself. "Interdiction fire probably."

More thunder from the nearby battery knocked a vermouth bottle off a table and raised dust from the dirt floor. I edged over to Colonel Fourcade, who was sipping his pastis as if a howitzer concert was a normal lunchtime occurrence at Ninh Binh.

"What's going on?" I asked.

"Orders from Hanoi," he replied, winking. "We're supposed to show him the war." This put me in a difficult position. I didn't want to play the informer or ruin Gilles's day, but the short-lived barrage was so patently phony I had to be sure the Stevenson party harbored no illusions about its origin before their departure. But the governor had figured things out for himself. I only had to confirm his suspicions.

In April of 1953 General Giap's troops began an invasion of northern Laos. The 304th and 325th Vietminh divisions were reported moving on the strategic town of Xieng Khouang, while other forces headed for the French posts at Sam Neau and Muong Khoua. The much touted "hedgehog" defensive position of Nasan, intended to block any enemy move on Laos, had proved a costly illusion. The Vietminh simply moved through the jungle around it to attack the small, isolated mountain garrisons manned by French-officered, Laotian Chasseurs. Some of these posts were evacuated and their personnel fell back to the Plain of Jars, where a hurried French airlift had landed troops and supplies to set up another defensive position.

The Laotians are basically gentle, easygoing people whose calendar is full of festivals, both national and local, with piquant sexual overtones. Their Buddhist faith is linked with a strong belief in a world of spirits: spirits of the water, spirits of the trees, spirits of the stones and flowers. These "*phi*" are mostly benevolent creatures, but they must be mollified by offerings and veneration. Death-dealing and violence are to be avoided, particularly as the *phi* of someone killed will return to haunt whoever was responsible for the death. Such beliefs, while exemplarily humane, do not produce the ideal soldier. Although some Laotians fought well in costly delaying actions, others expended their ammunition by firing into the air before abandoning their positions.

General Giap's ability to move large forces through territory considered impassable by the strategists in French headquarters was the result of practical experience and detailed logistic planning. Rice and porters were two of the essential ingredients of Vietminh tactics. Giap's Regular troops were allotted 800 grams of rice a day and his Regionals 750 grams. This, with salt, and *nuoc mam* sauce for protein, provided the basic diet. The fighting *Bo Doi*, with his sausage roll containing four days of rice rations, was the spearhead of a complete popular mobilization by the Vietminh. The rice paddy had become "the battlefield," the hoe and plow were "weapons," and the workers had become "soldiers." Rice from Annam, often from French-"controlled" areas, was spirited north to the Vietminh zone by teams of porters. Other shipments came all the way from the Mekong Delta via junks and sampans, despite the French Navy's attempts at blockade. Some of this rice, plus opium from north Tonkin and Laos, and pepper from Cambodia, were exported by the Vietminh to obtain foreign currency. Income from the sales was used to purchase arms, radios, drugs, and equipment in Hong Kong, Singapore, and U.S. Army surplus in the Philippines.

Thousands of workers, both men and women, toiled at keeping the jungle trails and roads open for the passage of Giap's troops. Special companies of porters were equipped with bicycles reinforced to carry from sixty to one hundred kilos of supplies. Others carried heavy loads suspended from traditional balancing poles or strapped to cumbersome back harnesses. Camouflaged way stations provided rest stops where medical personnel rationed out the meager supply of drugs to fight malaria and other endemic infections. Fresh teams of porters replaced the exhausted new arrivals. Nighttime movements to avoid French air-reconnaissance and bombing took place under the thick jungle canopy, lit by myriads of small candles. Log bridges were built just under the surface of mountain streams to hide them from airborne eyes. A special medal was struck for the "heros of portage," and official communiqués lauded the exploits of the laborers, elevating them to the status of combatants.

Giap's spring offensive in 1953 threatened Luang Prabang, the Royal Capital of Laos, where the elderly King Sisavong Vong was in residence. A blind monk and respected local soothsayer had already predicted that the Vietminh would never reach Luang Prabang, although a post only forty kilometers distant had fallen. The king, despite French urging, refused to leave his capital. Had not the blind monk also stated the Vietminh would never cross the Nam Suong River? It was a period of high anxiety, hurried military planning, and troop shifts. Despite constant air reconnaissance and the efforts of GCMA scouts, the French were not sure exactly where the enemy was and where he was heading, nor did they know the exact strength of his varied forces.

After returning to Hanoi from Ninh Binh I was ordered to Laos to cover the "coming battle for Luang Prabang." I flew to Vientiane, the administrative capital, where I caught a flight to the Plain of Jars in a Moraine observation aircraft. The pilot, an insouciant French lieutenant wearing an American-style baseball cap, gave me a beginner's course in aerial snooping and artillery spotting. Jockeying his fragile craft low over the mountainous terrain, he seemed determined to explore each wooded ravine, every dip in the land, or wisp of smoke from a tribal cooking fire. By the time he'd set us down on the small strip at the Plain of Jars and cut his overheated washing machine of an engine, I was badly in need of a drink and prolonged treatment for motion sickness. My mood wasn't improved by the greeting I received when I climbed unsteadily to the ground.

"You flew with him?" a Legion officer asked, dumbfounded. "But he's absolutely crazy!"

Nothing was happening at the Plain of Jars. Officers flying in from Luang Prabang confirmed that the same vacuum of action existed there. Boredom is a staple of warfare, but there is no need to endure it when it's unnecessary. I made my way back to Vientiane Airfield—where I was asked to talk down a U.S. Air Force "Flying Boxcar" transport by the non-English-speaking control tower crew—and returned to Hanoi aboard an Air Vietnam flight. By the time

I reached Saigon the expected "battle for Luang Prabang" was no longer being mentioned. A week later intelligence reports confirmed a general Vietminh withdrawal from Laos. General Giap was rumored to have ordered his divisions back to their bases before the heavy rains. The blind monk, in his own mysterious universe, had seen what French aerial reconnaissance and long-range patrols had failed to discern. The Vietminh had not reached Luang Prabang, nor had they crossed the Nam Suong River.

The major change of the year for the French and all those involved with them in Indochina occurred on May 19. Gen. Henri Navarre, the new commander in chief, arrived in Saigon to replace Gen. Raoul Salan. Salan's overdue departure marked the true close of the de Lattre era. The last of de Lattre's "marshals" left with him. Only Gen. René Cogny, a former member of de Lattre's general staff, who had become a specialist of war in the Tonkin Delta, remained to serve with Navarre.

Saigon was buzzing with rumors about the new commander in chief. Most of them were negative. He was cold and effete. He knew nothing of Asia or Indochina. He had tried to avoid the assignment. The government had had to pry him away from his previous post as chief of staff to Marshal Juin at NATO. The few positive comments were categorized as wishful thinking. He was coming to Vietnam with a positive plan designed to take the initiative from the enemy. He believed in offensive warfare. He had a brilliant analytical mind. The fifty-five-year-old cavalryman, veteran of two world wars and service in Lebanon, Morocco, and Algeria, now faced the daunting task of restoring the confidence of the Expeditionary Corps and shifting the French war effort out of neutral.

The morning of General Navarre's arrival a long, continuous file of official vehicles took the road to Tan Son Nhut. It appeared every major and minor French and Vietnamese official and officer had decided it was absolutely essential to appear at the airport. The same was true to a lesser degree for the American mission and other friendly embassies in Saigon. Black sedans jammed the parking areas, and officials in tropical whites crowded the VIP reception area, vying for position according to rank and influence. The front ranks of the reception committee glinted with general's stars and kepis trimmed with gold oak leaves. The less colorful civilians in places of honor represented the wealth, influence, and power of Indochina. If the Vietminh had seen fit to loose a suicide section of determined sappers at Tan Son Nhut that day, the Franco-Vietnamese war effort would have been decapitated.

It was particularly hot and humid. As the noon hour approached, sweat spots darkened the well-pressed suits and uniforms and the two battalions drawn up on the tarmac as an honor guard sweltered under the fiery sun. The ordeal was prolonged for forty-five minutes, waiting for an aircraft from Hanoi to arrive with Jean Letourneau, the French high commissioner. Letourneau had to be on the ground to greet Navarre in the interests of protocol.

When the Constellation finally taxied to a stop before the reception committee, the relief was almost audible. The press photographers and cameramen were released from their holding area. I took advantage of my role as embassy press officer to move to a better vantage point. General Navarre appeared at the aircraft's door to a drum and bugle fanfare. The general acknowledged the salutes due him, shook the extended hands, and moved closer. He was impeccably uniformed and groomed, like a man who had just stepped from a barber's chair. I found myself trying to equate this spotless, precise military manikin with officers like General Gilles, Colonel Fourcade, Major Dong, and the captain of commandos I'd encountered at Phat Diem, or imagine him understanding the guerrilla warfare going on in the paddies and mountains. Somehow he seemed out of place, a military figure from another age in search of the wrong war. A veteran British correspondent summed up the general feeling in one pithy comment.

"Christ," he murmured as Navarre was ushered to his waiting sedan. "I think we've all got a problem."

Some time later Chargé Rob McClintock summoned me to his residence to meet the American photographer David Douglas Duncan. Duncan's coverage of the Korean War for *Life* magazine had been published as *This Is War* by Harper & Brothers in 1951, one of the finest books of combat photography ever produced. McClintock introduced us and explained that Duncan had come to Indochina to do a special report on the war for *Life*. He said Duncan's time was limited and he couldn't afford to waste it on fruitless contacts, abortive operations, or official obstructionism on the part of the French. He asked if I'd be willing to accompany Duncan on his trip to the North and help him get the war coverage he was seeking.

The question was really an order but I had no objections. Duncan was famous for risk-taking, but I admired his work and had formed a positive first impression of him. McClintock asked me to remain after Duncan had left. He explained that Duncan's coverage in *Life* would be important and influential both in the United States and internationally. He made my part in the project abundantly clear.

"Show him the truth," McClintock said forcefully. "Show him what's going on."

In the following weeks the tall, soft-spoken ex-Marine and I formed a "Mutt and Jeff" combination, covering Tonkin from the Delta to the Chinese border area. French officials, aware that *Life*'s publisher, Henry Luce, supported France's efforts in Indochina, were unusually cooperative in providing transport and facilitating Duncan's work. They did *not* realize that Duncan was a photojournalist with his own ideas and an aversion to toeing any editorial line. With the experiences of "No Name Ridge," Seoul, and the fighting retreat from the Changjin Reservoir fresh in his mind, Duncan viewed much of what he was seeing with sensitivity and a critical eye. It wasn't long before his coverage began to take on the aspects of an exposé.

A light plane put us down at Lai Chau, traditional capital of the regional T'ai tribes and a key French post in the mountains of northwestern Vietnam. The small town nestled in a story-book setting on the Black River, surrounded by jungled peaks. Slim T'ai women wearing traditional tight white bodices, long black skirts, and wide-brimmed woven hats were washing clothes at the river's edge. It was early in the afternoon when we made our way to the headquarters, seeking out the regional commander. A sleepy soldier, roused from his siesta, led us to the commander's office. Neither the commander nor any of his staff were anywhere to be seen. This was a region under constant threat from the Vietminh, and Lai Chau was only thirty-five miles as the crow flies from the Chinese border. It seemed unbelievable that such an important installation would go unmanned at any time of the day. After we'd cooled our heels for half an hour, Duncan unlimbered his cameras and shot a series of photos including several of the empty desks under a wall clock showing the time as 3:00 P.M.

We dined with the commander that night and he apologized for not greeting us earlier. He had been ill and his staff had been in the field. His story would have been easier to believe if a T'ai orderly had not responded to our query on his earlier whereabouts by repeating "*sieste, sieste*" and miming the act of someone laying his head down.

In Hanoi some officers of the U.S. AID Mission unloaded their frustrations and grievances, giving Duncan an earful. I wasn't present when they told their story of local corruption, payoffs, and disappearing supplies, but I did accompany Duncan to the provinces to check on one of their complaints. A refugee center financed by U.S. funds had been constructed under the aegis of the governor of North Vietnam. It had been inaugurated a few weeks earlier with considerable ceremony, including refugees waving Vietnamese and U.S. flags, an honor guard, and official speeches. It was to be a model for other such installations, providing crude but basically livable and secure quarters to refugees from the battle zones.

We arrived at the center in a drizzling *crachin*, the cold rain that comes down from the north, to find the housing area semi-abandoned in a sea of mud. A few young and lightly armed militiamen provided the only protection. Many of the poorly constructed houses had already been stripped of plumbing and sections of roofing. The few miserable families that remained complained of their lot and begged us to help them. They were short of rice, the children were ill, and the inhabitants of the nearest village were hostile. The government had told them they must stay; the Vietminh had ordered them to leave. As Duncan's camera clicked on, I began to wonder just how far my mandate to show him "the truth" extended.

Duncan returned to Saigon with his bags full of exposed film. I came back with my first attack of dysentery. He proceeded to complete his coverage in Saigon. I wrote a brief report on our voyage, threw a supply of Enterovioform tablets in my bag, and went off to the coastal town of Nhatrang for two weeks of leave. Nhatrang seemed like paradise after the North. The sun-bleached town on the South China Sea, with its white beaches, palms, and cool offshore breezes was quiet and restful.

I stayed in a small seaside hotel run by a swashbuckling Frenchman with a

Vietnamese wife and many children. Once my dysentery had subsided I accompanied him on early-morning fishing expeditions aboard his motorized junk. After we'd anchored in a likely spot, one of his Vietnamese crew would dive in and scout the clear water near the junk for schools of fish. When fish were spotted, he'd indicate their position and swim swiftly back to the junk before his skipper arced a concussion grenade—supplied by the hotel's French military clients—into the sea. It was hardly sport, but the hotel owner was feeding a number of families beside his own and he preferred to return to the beach quickly to avoid complications. He had an unwritten agreement with the Vietminh occupying some of the offshore islands. A percentage of his catch was turned over to one of their local representatives in exchange for "fishing rights." The Sûreté frowned on this arrangement but they had never been able to prove its existence, although the hotel owner had spent some time in jail for "suspected traffic with the enemy." He was constantly alert for approaching patrol boats whose commanders had been ordered to discover the source of the grenades.

It was a pleasant interlude marked by early-morning breakfasts of *saucisson*, fresh bread, red wine, and black coffee; spearfishing for sand sharks; leisurely lunches of grilled fish or cracked crab, garlicky salads, and rosé. Afternoon siestas and reading were followed by Vietnamese dinners and late discussions under the stars with the sound of the surf as a backdrop. Only the thump of distant artillery or bugle calls from the nearby Foreign Legion headquarters jarred the illusion of life in a resort town.

I returned to Saigon sunburned but rested to find that all hell had broken loose. Duncan's coverage had made the cover of *Life* and the shock waves were continual. By one of those rare and unexpected quirks of journalistic fate, Henry Luce had been absent from his editorial offices when the issue went to press. His explosive reaction to the "anti-French" coverage had broken over Duncan's head. Luce had followed up with an apologetic editorial supporting the French effort in Indochina. The French authorities had printed a rebuttal to Duncan's piece. Now, according to them, the officer in Lai Chau had been absent on a long patrol during our visit. The *Journal d'Extrème Orient*, Saigon's leading French-language daily representing French interests, had published a vitriolic editorial accusing *Life* and the U.S. government of working together to undermine France in Indochina. If Luce and the French had been furious, the State Department was apoplectic, particularly when it learned that Duncan had been guided and escorted during his travels by the press officer from its embassy in Saigon.

George Hellyer called me to his office and handed me a copy of the *Life* issue including the controversial story. I saw the photos of the empty office at Lai Chau and the semideserted refugee center. I read the testimony of the disgruntled AID Mission officials. I also noted that Duncan's additional coverage included shots taken in a Vietnamese military cemetery near Saigon. The accompanying text questioned the validity of Vietnamese dying for the French cause.

Ambassador Heath had returned from his home leave in the middle of this brouhaha. I was told that my immediate departure from Saigon had been under consideration during an embassy staff meeting. The support of McClintock and Hellyer, plus my providential absence at Nhatrang had averted the banishment. Hellyer suggested I stay clear of the ambassador for a few more days till the storm passed. I followed his advice. The official freeze didn't last long, but until it became obvious the ambassador had welcomed me back on the team, a number of embassy officers I encountered in the course of the working day seemed inordinately busy and eager to part company.

CHAPTER 7

General Navarre's Plan

A glittering reception was held for General Navarre at the Continental Hotel shortly after his arrival in Saigon. The hum of conversation and the pop of corks carried to the Rue Catinat, where the shoeshine boys and the barefoot street vendors watched, mesmerized by a world that would never be their own. It could have been the Hollywood set of some 1940s colonial classic starring Claude Rains or Paul Henreid, a gathering of white sharkskin suits, white dress uniforms, expensive European gowns, and silken *ao dais*. Guests sipped champagne and helped themselves to the hors d'oeuvres. The diplomatic community was present in force, eager to size up the new commander in chief and absorb additional information that might flesh out their reports. The Americans were easily recognizable by their Brooks Brothers summer suits, rep ties, and a tendency to group together.

George Hellyer had come to the reception bearing a gift for General Navarre. He presented it to the general during a brief conversation as we passed through the receiving line. It was a copy of *Prisoners of Hope* by Brig. Gen. Michael "Mad Mike" Calvert, an account of Gen. Orde Wingate's campaigns behind Japanese lines in Burma, in which Hellyer had participated. During his presentation Hellyer intimated there were lessons to be learned from the narrative that might dovetail with Navarre's professed interest in offensive action. The general's reaction was understandably cool. He said he was familiar with Wingate's operations and passed the book to one of his aides without looking at it. Hellyer's initiative was definitely unsubtle, but it did reflect the thinking of many of us in the American Mission, including Rob McClintock and General

O'Daniel. How could there be a possible military solution unless the French left their fortified posts and pillboxes to take the war to the enemy?

Following a series of visits to the field to get a feel for the new, unfamiliar war he'd inherited, Navarre launched his plan. "One can only win by attacking," he wrote in his first open letter to the Expeditionary Corps. The Navarre Plan called for reinforcements from France, the reintegration of static units into his mobile forces, and a buildup of the national armies of Vietnam, Cambodia, and Laos to free more French units for operations against Vietminh Regular formations. Keeping the enemy off balance by continued raids on his training areas and supply depots was also high on Navarre's list, as was the defense of Laos against another Vietminh attack.

Like many laboriously conceived French and American battle plans during the Indochina conflicts, Navarre's recipe was basically sound for a classic, European-style war, but the war was neither classic nor European, and the proper ingredients were lacking. Successive French governments of the Fourth Republic were going through a "musical chairs" period. The government of René Meyer had collapsed at the moment of Navarre's arrival in Saigon, leaving France rudderless for a period of thirty-six days. French politicians, government officials, and high-ranking officers considered the Indochina War an extremely hot potato known to burn hands and singe careers. Navarre's power base in Paris was therefore spongy and changeable. Crucial decisions were already being shelved, and requests for specific backup were to be ignored. The general's desire to draw French combat forces from defensive positions and replace them with Vietnamese units revealed the wide gap between readiness reports and reality. The actual strength of the Vietnamese battalions seldom matched the listed figure, the quality of the cadre was often doubtful, low morale and desertion were real problems. To trust key posts in the crucial Tonkin Delta to such a doubtful force would, at best, be a calculated gamble.

A proposal to form Vietnamese "light" battalions capable of carrying out security and pacification duties in the countryside had already been addressed by the French High Command and Gen. Nguyen Van Hinh, chief of staff of the VNA. On April 1, 1953, the first group of young Vietnamese draftees had passed through the gates of Quang Yen training camp, twenty kilometers from Haiphong, for ninety-eight days of intensive military training. Smaller training centers had been established near Hué in central Vietnam and at Quang Tre in the South. By December 1953 the Quang Yen camp was to have produced 40,000 recruits for the new 700-man light battalions. The basic idea was that these units, unencumbered by heavy equipment, would install themselves in contested areas, make continuous friendly contact with the hamlet and village population, root out the Vietminh agents and militia members, and conduct armed propaganda operations to win popular support for the government. The *Tieu Doan Kinh-Quan*, or light battalions, were designed to beat the enemy at their own game.

In principle, the American Mission and MAAG approved of the new initiative. It had the potential of weaning the Vietnamese National Army away from its Western orientation and dependence on the road grid, fortifications, and by-the-book artillery support. If the Vietminh operated and survived in the countryside without tanks, artillery, and air support, why couldn't these new light units of the National Army do the same? If the Vietminh won the hearts and minds of the peasantry by sharing their existence, helping with the crops, doling out medicine, and organizing propaganda lectures, surely the VNA—with U.S. funding—could match the enemy?

The basic scheme bore a striking resemblance to the tactics used by Colonel Lansdale and the Magsaysay government in the Philippines. The trainees who came out of Quang Yen were supposed to be well versed in guerrilla warfare, Vietminh tactics, and counterguerrilla methods. They were to have the ability to establish themselves in the villages, living the same life as the peasants, and win the friendship of the rural population. They were to be "the image of the new nation they represent in the face of Vietminh ideology." They were expected to go forth to vanquish the enemy "a guitar under the left arm, a submachine gun under the right."

From what I had seen so far during military operations, the Franco-Vietnamese forces had a long way to go before they would gain the confidence of the population. Although unit commanders in the field had done their best to keep me away from "incidents" involving the civilian population, I had seen enough to be troubled. In one village of the Tonkin Delta I had blundered on a group of Vietnamese soldiers interrogating a suspect while his wife and grandchildren wailed with fear. The shivering old man had been beaten with bamboo flails and his chest cut in a perpendicular pattern with a sharp trench knife. His interrogators continued to pose questions alternating between a calm conversational tone and strident, angry shouts. The panicked suspect, who had wet himself, was insisting he knew nothing of local Vietminh activities.

I interrupted the session to ask what crime the man had committed. What naïveté! My question was greeted with hoots of laughter. I would later come to realize that the Vietnamese soldiers I'd confronted were not sadistic monsters. They were following an age-old behavioral pattern with no particular link to current ideologies. If captured, they could expect the same treatment, and a peasant suspected of collaborating with the government faced a similar fate. The noncombatants were the vulnerable filling sandwiched between the antagonists engaged in a "people's war." Word was soon passed to the company commander that the "foreigner" had appeared where he shouldn't be. I was hustled off by a frowning Vietnamese captain who insisted the old man "knows much" about the Vietminh and the village was full of "liars."

Each time I had come across evidence of mistreatment and torture I had reported it on my return to Saigon. But it was hard for people who had not seen it for themselves to imagine the scope of the problem. It was true—if one can be objective in discussing torture—that interrogation by torture was nothing new in an Asian guerrilla war and that among the parties involved, including the Vietminh, there were many skilled practitioners. But the Communist political cadres and intelligence officers habitually operated with discretion and in secret. Only when an individual had been condemned by a "people's court" or it served the Party's political purposes did an individual undergo public punishment.

As we prepared to assist the Psywar Section of the National Army in supplying the light battalions with pro-government and anticommunist matériel, I recommended the Franco-Vietnamese Psychological Warfare Planning Committee include an antitorture training session for the new recruits. If they were expected to reap a harvest of "hearts and minds," I argued, water torture, beatings, and the agony of "a thousand cuts" could only foster hate and produce more Vietminh. The existence of torture was something not mentioned in polite official circles, and my suggestion was greeted with a poignant silence. The Vietnamese looked embarrassed and shuffled their papers. The French colonel in the chair glared daggers at me and instructed the secretary to note my suggestion for future consideration. After the meeting he took me aside to offer some advice.

"In a war like this, *mon ami*," he confided, "one cannot make an omelette without breaking some eggs."

The promise of the light battalions seemed too good to be true—and it was. The young draftees who arrived at the camps were a heterogeneous mix of barefoot peasants and city-bred students. Some of them were delivered by the police after being tracked down in the streets of Hanoi, Saigon, or Hué. Others had been pressed into service in the provinces by Army "recruiters" with quotas to meet. All of them had two things in common: none were volunteers; none had previous military training. Ever alert to the nuances of political warfare, the Vietminh ensured that some of their tested agents were seeded among each draft to report on details of the training procedures, identify likely sympathizers, and foment dissent at the right moment.

The training, supposed to produce a professional and dedicated "nationalist" counterguerrilla with psychological warfare skills, was conducted by French officers and noncoms with the assistance of Vietnamese cadres from the Colonial Army. It was an impossible task, even for those French officers who might have believed in their mission. The fact that the backbone of the new light battalions, the junior officers and noncoms, were selected from the inexperienced ranks after such a short training period doomed the experiment from the beginning.

The armament of the light battalions contributed to the eventual disaster. It was no secret that an influential clique in the French High Command had been against the light battalion project, despite the new imperatives of the Navarre Plan, considering it a sop to American suggestions for a more flexible, all-Vietnamese response to the Vietminh. This group promoted the thesis that the light battalions were a purely American initiative and saw to it that their prime weaponry was of U.S. origin. This seemed reasonable and even generous under the circumstances. In reality, the distribution of the weapons left fatal gaps in the new units' firepower. Heavy World War II M-1 rifles and even heavier Browning automatic rifles (BARs) were doled out to the diminutive Vietnamese. Worse, whole platoons were supplied with M-1 carbines, a light weapon of doubtful efficiency. Heavy-weapons companies that were to support the light battalions were slow in forming and often had to wait before receiving their mortars and 57mm recoilless rifles. The light battalion scheme soon turned into a latter-day slaughter of the innocents as the unsteady, green troops were loosed on the countryside where battle-tested Vietminh forces waited for them.

I saw one of these light battalions undergo its operational baptism during a land-sea operation at Tuy Hoa on Vietnam's south coast. A Tunisian battalion and a combat team of Vietnamese parachutists had landed from amphibious craft to find Tuy Hoa semideserted, its streets empty under a scorching sun. The resident Vietminh Regional force was nowhere to be found. The Vietnamese light battalion arrived in the wake of the Tunisians and the paras. Its members came wading in through the tepid surf laughing and chattering like a group of young people on a seaside outing. Once established in its defense perimeter, the battalion sent its propaganda section into the town to troll for hearts and minds in the shadow of the ancient Cham temples on the nearby hills. By the time they had set up their psywar circus in the town square, a number of old people and children had appeared, drawn by the sound of guitars and the whine of a badly adjusted PA system. Tuy Hoa soon echoed to the discordant notes of Vietnamese songs extolling the government and vilifying the Vietminh and their Chinese allies. The audience listened blank-faced as nonsinging members of the propaganda section moved among them distributing blankets, condensed milk, paper flags, and propaganda tracts.

Later, walking through the town, I watched a jeepload of beer-swilling Vietnamese parachutists career down a street, crushing a number of bamboo paniers under their tires. The paniers had been filled with small red peppers set out to dry in the sun. Once the paras had passed, two old women emerged to painstakingly gather up the peppers and salvage the broken paniers. It was a small, nonfatal incident in a long, brutal war, but it illustrated the fragility of the hearts-and-minds syndrome. Luckily for the fledgling light battalion at Tuy Hoa, the Vietminh had decided to avoid contact and wait in the hills till the Franco-Vietnamese force had withdrawn. Other light battalions in the North had not been so lucky. An entire battalion had been annihilated near Bui Chu, others had been fed into the meat grinder of combat without adequate support or competent leadership. Horror stories began to seep out: companies in headlong flight leaving a trail of abandoned arms; group desertions; mass carnage in untenable, badly chosen tactical positions; deliberate denial of French artillery support; and defections to the Vietminh side led by enemy agents planted in the ranks.

But General Navarre had even more pressing preoccupations than the fate of these new Vietnamese units. His plan and espousal of an offensive spirit had to be followed by appropriate actions. On July 17, 1953, three French parachute battalions were dropped on the Vietminh-occupied town of Lang Son, near the Chinese border. Lang Son, abandoned by the French in 1950, had become a major reception center for Chinese supplies. The lightning raid destroyed the armament for three enemy divisions and a large stock of explosives. The paras then withdrew to link up with a French *groupe mobile* that had landed on the coast. Navarre was to present his plan to the government for final approval later the same month in Paris, and the successful Lang Son operation couldn't have come at a better time.

Lang Son caught the imagination of the French media and boosted the morale of the parachute battalions, the elite "warrior-monks" of the Expeditionary Corps. It appeared as an example of how the war should be fought with a mix of élan, subterfuge, and surprise. It was cited as a practical lesson in taking the war to the enemy, hurting him, and not attempting to hold on to useless real estate.

The euphoria over Lang Son tended to obscure the fact that Operation Camargue, launched eleven days later with the objective of clearing Highway 1 between Hué and Quang Tri, had been a monumental failure. Camargue had been a replay of the classic French tactics that had failed so often in the past. A large Franco-Vietnamese force, including a strong armored contingent, had jousted with shadows while the Vietminh Regionals disappeared into the hills. Navarre had pulled units out of the crucial Tonkin Delta, despite General Cogny's protests, for what he had been led to believe would be a major blow to the enemy. Instead, his troops had combed the coastal sands and marshes in a complete vacuum broken only by the occasional mine or booby trap explosion.

In mid-October, Operation Mouette, at Phu Nho Quan, inflicted considerable losses on the Vietminh 320th Division. Despite the comparative success of the operation, Navarre's classified report on the action was both realistic and gloomy. "Our infantry," he wrote, "shows certain deficiencies when operating over difficult terrain and when it has to react to unexpected combat. A few parachute battalions remain the only troops of superior value. Operation Mouette made this clear and it is the opinion of General Cogny, General Gilles, and myself that, when we send our infantry beyond a distance of ten kilometers, within which it is supported by artillery, if it clashes with Vietminh infantry . . . it will be defeated."

Such misgivings only increased the general's worries about the defense of Laos. The small pro-French kingdom was seen as the most vulnerable of the Associated States. A major threat to Laos by the Communists could predictably start the dominos tumbling in Southeast Asia. It could also undermine any confidence in France's ability to defeat the Vietminh and their Laotian allies, the Pathet-Lao, and facilitate Vietminh infiltration of southern Vietnam.

Shortly after his arrival Navarre had turned his attention to the background material and recommendations drafted by General Salan prior to his departure. Salan's report was based on his long experience in Indochina. It was not surprising that his replacement, with little knowledge of the region, would use it in working out the details of his plan. One of Salan's recommendations involved the occupation of Dien Bien Phu, a small administrative hamlet in a strategic valley of northwestern Vietnam abandoned to the Vietminh by the French in

1952. Salan had seen Dien Bien Phu, together with Nasan, as essential, mutually supporting strongpoints for blocking further enemy moves on Laos. He'd argued that Dien Bien Phu would also bolster Lai Chau and provide operational support to the GCMA teams working with the anti-Vietminh tribal guerrillas of the region, particularly the Black T'ai and the Meo. Dominance of the confluence of the Nam Youm and Nam Ou rivers at Dien Bien Phu would deny a precious transport asset to the enemy. Pirogues loaded to the waterline with 250 kilos of supplies and powered by outboard motors could reach Luang Prabang in less than three days.

As General Navarre's immediate staff secretly weighed the advantages and disadvantages of seizing Dien Bien Phu, they were influenced by the recurrent, hopeful vision of a major set-piece battle. Such a dream sequence had become part of the folklore of the French Expeditionary Corps. This best-of-all-possible-worlds scenario had Giap's divisions pouring from the forested hills onto the valley floor of Dien Bien Phu, where they would be blocked by the French wire, decimated by artillery and air strikes, and mopped up by tanks.

In August of 1953 Navarre ordered the evacuation of Nasan. The strongpoint had been sitting in stagnant suspension since the Vietminh attacks in November and December of 1952, an empty symbol of power ignored by the enemy and requiring constant resupply by airlift from Hanoi. To a commander needing every combat unit and aircraft he could muster, the evacuation made practical sense. But it removed a stanchion of Salan's tactical recommendation that projected Nasan and Dien Bien Phu as mutually supporting bases.

The valley of Dien Bien Phu, sixteen kilometers long and nine kilometers wide at its broadest point and dominated by jungled mountains, was no stranger to the clash of arms. It had long been a stopping point for invaders from the North seeking access to the upper Mekong. In 1888 a French column had camped at Dien Bien Phu during operations against the Siamese. It later became an administrative post manned by a small detachment of local troops under French command. In 1939 a small emergency airstrip was built to support the garrison at Lai Chau. From 1940 to 1945 the Japanese occupation forces avoided Dien Bien Phu, and the French used the strip for clandestine landings of agents and members of Force 136, an anti-Japanese resistance unit. When Japanese forces reversed their live-and-let-live policy toward French authorities in Indochina in 1945 and attacked French garrisons throughout Vietnam, Dien Bien Phu was used to evacuate French wounded to the relative safety of China. A heavy firefight during this period found a Foreign Legion company charging with fixed bayonets to retake the airstrip from the Japanese. The company commander was a certain Captain Gaucher—the same officer, now a colonel, I had confronted at the bar of the Tour d'Ivoire in Saigon.

Navarre's planning for Dien Bien Phu remained a closely held secret. The U.S. diplomatic and military establishment in Saigon was busy monitoring the Navarre Plan to see if it lived up to expectations. Secretary of State John Foster Dulles had publicly welcomed the plan. The U.S. military were more cautious. They had heard the same tune played before and were waiting for more operations like Lang Son before showing any real enthusiasm. Their caution was echoed in the French capital. Navarre's demand for more reinforcements had sent a collective shiver through French political circles. A poll in the fall of 1953 reflected the lassitude of the French public regarding the Indochina War. A full 58 percent of those questioned favored negotiations or showed a lack of interest in the problem. Only 15 percent still favored a military solution. Minority opinions suggested the UN or the United States should intervene or favored a decision to leave if more effort was impossible. A 15 percent slice of opinion supported outright abandonment and a return of all troops to France.

I was now spending more time in Saigon. The Navarre Plan had kindled new interest in the Indochina War, and George Hellyer needed me back in the press office to handle the increased visits from American officials and journalists. The tempo of life in the capital had quickened with the buildup in military activities. It was a "sow your wild oats while you may" atmosphere. The bars, restaurants, and nightclubs were full to overflowing. Bay Vien's gambling halls were packed, and the Pakistani merchants on the Rue Catinat were doing a thriving business changing American dollars at the black market rate.

The press corps in Saigon had grown in strength. Correspondents based in Hong Kong were regular visitors, and more cameramen and photographers had appeared. Graham Greene was in town as a correspondent for the London *Observer*, gathering the material destined to appear in *The Quiet American*. He was no newcomer to Saigon, having visited Vietnam in 1950 and 1951. During the latter visit he'd had a run-in with General de Lattre, who suspected him of working for British Intelligence. The aloof, dyspeptic Greene made no secret of his basic anti-American feelings and obviously viewed the increased U.S. presence in Indochina with misgiving. I had been introduced to Greene at the Continental and had expected he might contact me for an interview with Ambassador Heath or General O'Daniel, but it was not to be. Greene remained with his French and Vietnamese friends and contacts, observing the *Amerloques* at a disdainful distance.

Each passing month saw more U.S. involvement in the war effort. The AID Mission expanded, the embassy grew, and more USIA officers arrived. Members of the MAAG Mission, easily identifiable in their uniforms, sped about Saigon in their sedans, and visiting U.S. military transport aircraft were commonplace at Tan Son Nhut Airport. We worked hard and we played hard. I found myself escorting visiting American journalists to several interviews with Gen. Nguyen Van Hinh at the General Staff Headquarters of the Vietnamese National Army. Hinh was intelligent and likable, if devious, and he handled his own public relations with skill. His informal manner and mastery of figures made a good first impression on many correspondents. It was only after they had dug a bit deeper and spoken with more sanguine observers that they realized the optimistic picture Hinh had painted of the Vietnamese National Army was far short of the truth.

General Hinh and his attractive French wife were regulars at the Sunday whiskey-sour parties given by George and Meg Hellyer at the swimming pool of their villa in a walled compound of embassy housing on Rue Thevenet. These colonial villas had shaded terraces and balconies surrounded by tropical foliage and blossoming trees. Hinh's wife habitually wore a tight pullover with an eye-catching jewelry bee pinned exactly over the nipple of one breast. It was difficult for men to carry on a conversation with her without locking their eyes on that glittering insect. But these relaxed Sunday gatherings were more than social occasions. They brought together French, Vietnamese, British, Australian, and American officials and military officers; visiting VIPs; foreign correspondents of many nationalities; Vietnamese newsmen; resident "spooks"; and Hellyer's own staff and their wives. It was a perfect venue for expanding contacts and exchanging information. The potent drinks relaxed the guests. Generals and diplomats found it difficult to be officious or stuffy clad only in swimming trunks. Useful working friendships were forged to the clink of glasses and the occasional howl from Hellyer's pet gibbon watching the proceedings from his perch on a nearby tree.

Other social events in Saigon were not so convivial. Thinly disguised tensions sometimes rose to the surface. At one such reception I overheard Jean-Pierre Dannaud, chief of the French Information Service, exchanging derogatory comments about General O'Daniel with another French official. "Iron Mike," the commander of the U.S. MAAG, was a tough, diamond-in-the-rough combat commander with a stocky build and bulldog face. He was outspoken and far from a diplomat. I can't remember Dannaud's exact words, but his effete critique covered these traits. I reminded Dannaud that General O'Daniel and his division had liberated large sections of France at a high cost while many of Dannaud's compatriots had remained uninvolved. Future contacts between us were understandably minimal and strained.

Word reached us in late October of an impending visit from Vice President Richard M. Nixon and preparations began to receive him and his entourage. White House visits, as brief as they might be, were major productions entailing months of planning and special arrangements. The embassy's cable traffic doubled as messages flew between Washington and Saigon covering everything from who was to meet the vice president at the airport and which Vietnamese and French officials were to be guests at an official luncheon, to the placement of vehicles in the cortege and the housing for accompanying Secret Service agents.

The vice president's fact-finding visit was designed to express U.S. support of the Franco-Vietnamese war effort and confidence in the Navarre Plan. My office was charged with coordinating media coverage arrangements with the French and Vietnamese and pulling together the elements of a speech that Nixon would give while in Saigon. The press coverage arrangements were relatively simple, although we did have to fight to assure equal access for the local press with the White House press group accompanying the vice president.

The speech was another matter. The ambassador, the political section of the embassy, and the MAAG and AID Missions all had contributions they wanted included in the text. This was a virtual impossibility in such a short address.

As I struggled to condense the salient points and statistics into a cogent presentation, the White House and the State Department bombarded us with their own essential additions. It took us at least three drafts before we obtained a lukewarm official approval from Washington.

We then had to find a fitting location for the delivery. The French were not enthusiastic, expecting inevitable references to a free and independent Vietnam by an American vice president. Any offering of an official venue for the speech on their part was out of the question. The same applied to the French-sponsored government of Vietnam. We eventually turned to the Saigon chapter of the International Rotary Club as a sponsor. The agreed location was to be the top-floor restaurant of the Majestic Hotel.

In retrospect I would have been wise to seek the services of a Vietnamese soothsayer prior to the Nixon arrival. The first day of the visit proved to be a comedy of errors. The British contract cameraman for our AID Mission was assigned to shoot official arrival footage. His habitual working costume was a sportshirt and tropical shorts. As a veteran of steamy climes he shunned underpants as superfluous instigators of prickly heat. He was an aggressive practitioner of the visual media, adept at elbowing his way to the best vantage point. When the vice president's plane rolled to a stop, our cameraman was in the front rank of those set to record the arrival. Once Nixon had descended from the aircraft, the cameraman bolted up the debarkation ladder, draped one leg over the hand railing, and continued to shoot. Alas, weight, balance, and cloth tension combined to put him in a situation where the phrase "letting it all hang out" had never been more applicable. It was only later, when the agency photographers and network cameramen processed their exposed film, that the awful truth dawned. There was our cameraman in the near background, just over the vice president's shoulder, with his dormant manhood exposed. Only judicious retouching saved some of the exposed stock, the rest had to be destroyed.

The vice president was to speed off to the Majestic Hotel for his speech after the official formalities at the airport. I had given George Hellyer a number of copies of the approved text before we left for the airport. He would be riding into Saigon with the official cortege while I went on ahead to see that all was ready at the hotel. I found everything in order. The multiracial Saigon Rotarians were drawn up as a reception committee, the microphones were working, and the chef of the Majestic was presiding over a buffet of impressive scale. Police sirens heralded the arrival of the cortege at the hotel entrance.

George Hellyer and some Secret Service agents were the first out of the elevator. He was unusually pale.

"Do you have the speech?" he demanded.

"No," I replied, a sudden empty feeling in my stomach. "I gave it to you!"

My reply confirmed his worst fears. The folder containing the speech texts had been left on his office desk. We quickly agreed on a plan. He would stall the proceedings while I retrieved the speech. The USIA office was normally a ten-minute drive from the Majestic. I shot past the incoming vice presidential party and raced to my jeep. It was hopelessly blocked in the hotel's parking area. I tried to commandeer an embassy sedan but the driver was part of the cortege and couldn't budge. To make matters worse, the surrounding streets were blocked by police barricades. I sprinted to the bank of the Saigon River where a cyclomotor driver was relaxing in the shade of a food stall. A handful of piasters convinced him my mission was urgent and we roared onto the street away from the barricades, taking the long way to the office.

By the time I arrived back at the Majestic, soaked in perspiration with the folder under my arm, the unmistakable Nixon baritone was echoing through the dining room. I looked at Hellyer in surprise. He only shrugged. Throwaway platitudes thickened the air while the non-English-speaking Rotarians listened with polite smiles on their uncomprehending faces. I then realized this was an entirely different speech. The White House wordsmiths had given our version the deep six in Washington and substituted their own.

The vice president spent a minimum of time in Saigon. He was whisked off to northern Vietnam where, accompanied by Maurice Dejean, the French commissioner general, he visited a Vietnamese infantry unit at Cho Gan. Before leaving, Nixon obliged accompanying photographers by posing in a shallow slit trench under the puzzled gaze of some dusty Vietnamese riflemen. When he flew out of Hanoi a short time later, no one could have predicted that nineteen years later, as president of the United States, he'd be ordering B-52s to hit the city during the Christmas period in the most concentrated and controversial air offensive of the war against North Vietnam.

While we were keeping the White House press contingent happy, convincing the Secret Service there were no security risks among members of the Saigon Rotary Club, and fretting over the Nixon speech, General Giap's Regular divisions and General Navarre's Expeditionary Corps had taken the first steps that would put them on a collision course in North Vietnam. Their converging paths were destined to bring them together at the calm, silent valley of Dien Bien Phu.

CHAPTER 8

DBP Airport

By November of 1953 the Saigon rumor mill was grinding out a variety of contradictory leads. The correspondents in the Continental's terrace bar argued the merits of the Navarre Plan and tried to guess the general's next move. There was basic agreement that a large operation was brewing and the majority of newsmen were sure it would take place in the North. The telltale signs had appeared. Officers on leave from combat units were suddenly missing from Saigon's restaurants and bars, Army press officers were unusually tight-lipped, and the old Indochina hands had quietly packed their bags and left for Hanoi.

Under the circumstances it was decided I would change hats once again, revert to my role as a USIA war correspondent, and fly north. If Saigon's rumor mill had been busy, the bamboo telegraph in Hanoi was positively vibrating with uncertain information: General Cogny had been given the needed reinforcements to carry out a massive offensive in the Tonkin Delta; General Navarre, encouraged by the Lang Son raid, was planning a major operation on the Chinese border; a Vietminh division headed for Laos would be cut off and annihilated in a coordinated attack by ground and airborne troops. All of these theories had their champions and denigrators. The press-camp contingent in Hanoi sipped their cognac-and-sodas, sniffed at each rumor, evaluated every leak, and grilled the briefing officers unmercifully, hoping for a slip or an unplanned revelation. The massing of Dakota transport aircraft at Hanoi's military airfield was one immediately verifiable sign of impending action obvious to all, including the Vietminh. Where they were going, when they were going, and what their load would be were the unanswered questions. The fact that no parachutists were visible on the streets or in their favorite bars, and certain parachute commanders had been spotted rushing in and out of military headquarters at Hanoi's old, fortified Citadel, indicated the Dakotas were likely to be carrying a human cargo.

While the journalists dug and scraped for information, General Navarre's planning for an airborne assault on Dien Bien Phu had reached its final phase. Operation Castor was scheduled for November 20, 1953. General Gilles and a reduced staff had locked themselves in to complete the planning while Navarre pondered the objections already voiced concerning the operation. General Cogny had underlined his worries for the security of the Tonkin Delta and demanded reinforcements to replace troops scheduled to participate in Castor. Air Force general Jean Dechaux, responsible for tactical air operations in North Vietnam, had expressed his concern about providing adequate air cover. His fighter-bombers from the Delta could reach Dien Bien Phu and return only by using unwieldy belly tanks. He was also uneasy about maintaining the 280-kilometer airborne supply life from Hanoi tasked to deliver a minimum of eighty tons a day to Dien Bien Phu. This would be cutting his assets close to the bone. Dechaux went on record, stating such an operation would be possible only if no other demands were levied on his aircraft and crews.

My old nemesis, General Gilles, who would lead the assault, had specific misgivings. He had been impressed by the tenacity of the Vietminh attacks at Nasan, and openly questioned whether he would have time to prepare adequate defenses at Dien Bien Phu before the enemy counterattacked. He was supported in his skepticism by Colonel Bastiani of his planning staff, a serious thinker and tactician, who stuck his neck out by predicting that a new air supplied base on the scale of Dien Bien Phu would not stop an invasion of Laos. He predicted the Vietminh would simply contain and bypass any such installation.

Other preoccupations had surfaced among the planners. Would the Vietminh be able to move their artillery within range of Dien Bien Phu? If they did, would the French artillery be able to neutralize the enemy guns? The consensus was that it would be a virtual impossibility for the enemy to move his guns over long distances through the jungle and along narrow, slippery mountain trails. If he was to move them at all, it would have to be by road. This would expose them to air attack. If some guns managed to slip by, they would be destroyed easily by French counterbattery fire. Col. Charles Piroth, the one-armed artilleryman who was to command the French guns at Dien Bien Phu, had no doubts about this and had so informed his superiors. The possible devastating effect of bad weather on air support and supply hung over the planners like an unwelcome, unrecognized specter.

As the crucial details of Operation Castor were being worked out, the French were profiting from an intelligence advantage. They had obtained portions of a secret Vietminh operational code, and their radio intercepts were revealing the location and intentions of Vietminh forces. Two enemy regiments, the 176th and the 148th, were identified and thought to be fully occupied hunting down GCMA teams in the T'ai region. The 316th Division was moving toward Lai Chau but was still too far away to intervene. This intelligence bonanza was to be short-lived. Following the French assault on Dien Bien Phu, a number of press telegrams would be filed from Hanoi mentioning the movements of the 316th Vietminh Division. These reports, based on leaks from French military sources, would prompt General Giap to change his code, thus depriving General Navarre of a prime asset. Meanwhile, three other divisions, the 308th, 312th, and 351st, had received orders that would point them toward Dien Bien Phu. The 351st, a "heavy" artillery division, included the 367th Antiaircraft Regiment, a unit slated to play a significant role in the battle's final outcome.

None of this information was known to us as we compared notes, waited for the daily briefing, and complained about the press-camp food. I used my free mornings to complete an informal survey of the Vietnamese-language press in Hanoi, interviewing editors and sipping tea in dingy offices while sweating, half-naked printers shouted over the racket of ancient presses. Part of my job was to place USIS policy material in Hanoi's newspapers, but the long-suffering editors had prior demands on their space from the official Vietnamese and French information services. One editor, a bone-thin Tonkinese with enormous horn-rimmed glasses, showed me a pile of articles he had just received from the British Information Service and asked how he could possibly keep everyone happy. Later I discovered my visits had been monitored by the Vietminh. The Hanoi daily *Song Hong* would run a series of articles in 1955 purportedly recording my conversations and labeling me as "the American spy with the sly smile."

I rushed back to the press camp after my newspaper visits to question the staff officers about new developments and scan the posted communiqués. My anxiety increased when I noted that Schoendoerffer and Peraud, the combat cameraman and photographer, had left "on operation." I spoke with the major in charge of the press camp, reiterating my desire to be included in any upcoming "major" operation. His response was vague and hardly reassuring. When he offered to send me off on a mopping-up operation near Hung Yen, I sensed he only wanted me out of the way.

I decided to climb the ladder and take my case to Maj. Gen. René Cogny, the Commander of French Forces in North Vietnam. Cogny agreed to receive me in his headquarters at the Citadel. He was a tall, rugged artilleryman who had fought in the Resistance, been captured by the Gestapo, and deported to Germany. As one of de Lattre's "marshals" he maintained a certain theatrical aura. His accessories included a bamboo cane and an ever-present cigarette jutting from the corner of his mouth. His Patton-like predilection for a motorcycle escort during his movements through Hanoi had earned him the nickname *Coco la Sirène*. But Cogny was courageous in action, well thought of by his men, and had a reputation for treating the press fairly.

Knowing the general had little time to waste, I had rehearsed my plea during the walk to the Citadel. He listened patiently as I put my case, enumerating the operations I had already experienced, the worldwide facilities of USIA's Voice of America and International Press Service, and underlining as tactfully as possible the U.S. government's interest in on-the-spot coverage of the war. I concluded by requesting inclusion in *the* upcoming operation. His eyebrows went up at this obvious emphasis but he didn't pursue the matter. He promised to do his best. Towering over me, Cogny bid goodbye with a firm handshake and led me to the door. I returned to the press camp reassured and feeling a bit smug about having taken my case to the top.

I was wrong on both counts. The bombshell exploded two days later, on November 20, 1953. A special briefing was called to announce Operation Castor, a three-battalion airborne drop at an old, abandoned airstrip in the T'ai mountain area of northwestern Vietnam. The briefing officer spelled out the unfamiliar name. D-i-e-n B-i-e-n P-h-u. We rushed to the wall maps to locate the scene of the action. There it was—a small dot on the Nam Youm River, south of Lai Chau, approximately 100 miles from the Chinese border. Fighting was continuing with Vietminh Regulars, and more paras were going in. The initial phase of the operation had been successful.

While the briefing officer droned on about the tactical importance of Dien Bien Phu, I stuffed my notebook in my pocket and jogged to the Citadel. A heavy tropical downpour caught me halfway there. I arrived soaked to the skin, cursing my luck, and wondering what had happened to General Cogny's promise. The headquarters for North Vietnam was fully and understandably occupied with Operation Castor. Under the circumstances it was a miracle that I got as far as Cogny's outer office. One of his busy staff passed me on to a parachute officer who listened to my complaint, made some notes on a clipboard, and promised to call me. I walked slowly back to the press camp feeling left out and infuriated. My mood didn't improve that evening when I learned that Howard Sochurek, a *Life* photographer, and Arnaud de Borchgrave of *Newsweek* had covered the assault. Once again, I suspected, the French had chosen to keep the "official" war correspondent at arm's length.

The call came the next morning. I was cleared to go in on one of the first Dakotas as soon as the engineers finished laying the metal stripping on the airfield. Was there no quicker method? No. How about a helicopter flight? The few available were busy with Medevac chores. Swallowing hard, I proposed a draconian solution. Could I jump? Out of the question. By this time the officer's voice had developed a definite edge. It was time to leave well enough alone. I thanked him and put down the receiver.

Forty-eight hours later I was on my way to Dien Bien Phu, sharing a Dakota with a Foreign Legion mortar section and a mysterious Vietnamese in civilian clothes, wearing a Colt .45 in a shoulder holster. The flight was a replay of my journey to Nasan. In addition to my whiskey-heavy rucksack, bedroll, and revolver, a Rolleiflex hung from my neck. Dixie Reese had given me a quick course in its use and assured me that *even* a writer could produce decent prints with this simplest of cameras. Updrafts and downdrafts shook and jarred the aircraft as we passed over rugged mountains and jungled valleys. Cold air whistled through the fuselage as we huddled in the bucket seats. The Legion corporal next to me was reading a detective paperback, his feet braced against a mortar tube. At one point we seemed to be flying dangerously close to the peaks on both sides of a narrow ravine. The landscape resembled an old Chi-

nese print done entirely in varying shades of green. We finally rose over
another wall of mountains and dropped down toward the Muong Thanh Valley and Dien Bien Phu. As we banked to settle on our approach run, I could
see the far-off shimmer of metal fuselages pinpointing other military aircraft
flying over the valley. The crew chief tapped my shoulder and pointed down.

"Dien Bien Phu Airport!" he shouted in English, grinning at the only American aboard.

We landed and the Dakota jolted to a stop. I gathered up my gear and struggled past the Legionnaires and over the mortars to the open cargo door. I
jumped to the ground and was slinging my bedroll over my shoulder when I
heard the putt-putting of a gasoline engine. I turned to see Père Gilles approaching, bouncing over the perforated metal stripping, astride a small, collapsible
motorbike. In his squared beret, dark glasses, voluminous camouflage parachute jacket, and dusty boots he resembled a character from a surrealist film,
a Fellini-like apparition. Colonel Fourcade was trailing along behind the general
in a jeep. The motorbike coughed to a stop beside the Dakota and the general
glared at me.

"What?" he growled. "You here?"

I hadn't expected to come face-to-face with Gilles so soon. Considering the
Wild West incident at Ninh Binh, I could understand his lack of enthusiasm.
I expected him to ask if I was armed and confiscate the Colt there and then. I
quickly questioned him about his unusual means of transport. He grudgingly
admitted the motorbike was of U.S. origin, a gift from his American Airborne
colleagues at Fort Bragg. The subsequent awkward silence was broken by Fourcade's timely arrival. Ebullient and welcoming as ever, the colonel offered to
drive me to "the village" and help me get settled while the general wobbled off
to watch the arrival of more reinforcements.

The Airborne Engineers were still hard at work improving the strip with the
help of a parachuted bulldozer. The chutes of the first dozer dropped had failed
to open and it was half buried in the ground. Each hummock seemed to be
lined with shovel-wielding soldiers digging defensive positions. The valley was
long and comparatively flat except for some well-spaced, low hills. It was
bounded on each side by hazy ridges and far-off mountains. The airspace above
us was overcrowded and throbbing with activity. Dakotas were circling, waiting
for their landing clearance; stubby Bristol transports were passing low over the
strip; and requisitioned civilian airliners were taxiing for a takeoff after unloading their cargo of troops. At one point Fourcade jammed on his brakes and
pointed skyward. A lumbering C-119 Flying Boxcar was steadying on a dropping course. Suddenly a metallic cascade tumbled from its rear cargo door in a
spectacular free-fall.

"Barbed wire," Fourcade said as the impacting rolls sent dust geysers into the
air on the far side of the strip. "Very dangerous." He told me an unfortunate
Algerian infantryman had strayed under such a lethal drop. "Drove him into
the ground like a nail!" he explained, frowning.

"They're your people," Fourcade said, looking up as the C-119 gained altitude for its flight back to Hanoi. "Mercenaries." The C-119s were, in fact, flown by American contract pilots of the Flying Tigers. One of them was the legendary James B. "Earthquake McGoon" McGovern, a bearded, daredevil pilot and bonvivant of impressive girth.

We drove toward the village past an artillery battery and parachutists manning mortar emplacements. Burning brush cleared from the positions blotted out the sun and spotted us with ashes. We reached the first huts where a group of Black T'ai tribesmen dressed in black jackets decorated with silver buttons were surveying the scene with a studied neutrality. Their black berets were pulled low on their foreheads, and one old man was smoking an elaborately carved bone pipe. Shy village children smiled timidly from the leafy shadows. Dien Bien Phu was a typical tribal village, a clustering of stilted, peak-roofed huts built of thick bamboo and thatched with woven leaf. Pigs and chickens squealed and clucked under the huts. A group of women wearing long black skirts and turbanlike headdresses shuffled past carrying cans of water from the Nam Youm. Some of the huts had been destroyed in the fighting. The ruins were still smoldering.

Fourcade pulled up in front of a large hut that served as a temporary CP and offered me a beer to "open your throat." Three French fighter-bombers roared low overhead, sped on to a line of far-off hills, and pulled up abruptly like angry wasps. Seconds later a flash of yellow fire and billowing black smoke marked the explosion of their napalm drop. Surprised, I asked Fourcade if the Vietminh were *that* close. He said the survivors of the enemy garrison were still lurking in the hills.

My arrival at the CP was something of a homecoming. The officers and noncoms of Gilles's staff were the same men I had met at Nasan and encountered for the second time at Ninh Binh. They took time for the ritual handshake before Fourcade led me to a map board. I sipped a beer while he described the assault and the action that had followed. Major Bigeard's 6th Battalion had dropped directly onto a Vietminh company carrying out a training exercise. For some time it had been touch-and-go, with the paras dispersed over the valley in isolated groups and the confused enemy blundering into them without warning. By the 22nd of November there were six parachute battalions on the ground, including the 5th Battalion of the Vietnamese National Army, and Dien Bien Phu and its valley were in French hands. Over 100 Vietminh dead had been laid out on the banks of the Nam Youm River. The French had buried their fifteen dead in a small, temporary cemetery not far from the airstrip.

Fourcade indicated the locations of the nine strongpoints being established as interdependent islands of defense scattered throughout the valley. With a bizarre touch of French gallantry these positions were all code-named after women: Isabelle, Claudine, Françoise, Huguette, Anne-Marie, Gabrielle, Béatrice, Dominique, and Élaine. Their newly arrived occupants were working 'round-the-clock: filling sandbags, laying barbed wire, digging dugouts and trenches, cutting logs, clearing fields of fire, and stringing field telephone lines connecting them with the CP and neighboring strongpoints. Fourcade explained that General Gilles was once again anxious to get his paras out of the valley. They had done their job. He didn't want to risk having them bottled up in a defensive position, but they couldn't leave until their infantry replacements had arrived and were installed. The incoming battalions included Foreign Legionnaires and Moroccan, Algerian, and T'ai riflemen.

The briefing finished, Fourcade loaned me a mess kit and canteen, said there would be a place for me at the CP mess, and instructed a noncom to take me to my quarters. We trudged through the dust beside the Nam Youm until we reached a tall, stilted hut screened by a thick stand of bamboo. I thanked my guide and climbed up the notched pole that served as a ladder. Walking gingerly over the swaying floor, I staked my claim to sleeping space by throwing down my bedroll and rucksack. A thin-flanked, gray pig squinted up at me through the floor slatting. I lit a Manila cigar and squatted down to check the exposure on my Rolleiflex. The howitzers near the airstrip started thumping out interdiction fire, the sun slid behind the mountains, and the temperature plummeted.

A burst of raucous laughter heralded the return of my hut-mates. Schoendoerffer and Peraud, who had jumped with the assault force, welcomed me to Dien Bien Phu and broke out a bottle of kirsch. They described the drop and the fight for the strip. The forty-nine-year-old General Gilles had jumped with the second wave of paras, calmly bundling up his chute and slinging it over his shoulder before striding over the rice paddies to join his officers on the ground. With the kirsch depleted, I opened a bottle of Ballantine's scotch. It was soon too late to hike back to the CP mess, so we shared a meal of tinned rations: sardines, salty pâté, hard biscuits, and fruit cocktail washed down with a bottle of army *gros rouge*. We turned in early that night, fully clothed and wrapped in blankets as the pigs rooted and grunted below.

While Gilles waited impatiently to turn over the command of Dien Bien Phu to his replacement, General Giap and his staff were making a major move that would change the course of the war. Although still uncertain of French intentions, Giap had decided that the French occupation of Dien Bien Phu presented him with a "favorable occasion" to engage the French under advantageous conditions. He planned to deal a severe blow to the Expeditionary Corps. One of his Regular units was ordered to move on Lai Chau and wipe out its garrison. Another moved to cut the route between Dien Bien Phu and Lai Chau to forestall the sortie of a relief column. His commanders were also directed to begin the encirclement of Dien Bien Phu and prepare for the "coming battle."

I awoke early in the morning after my arrival, climbed unsteadily to the ground, and went off in search of a latrine. The sun had not yet cleared the mountains. There were veils of mist over the Nam Youm, and low clouds scudded over the valley. I followed my nose to the nearest slit-trench latrine. When I'd finished, I climbed a slight rise to watch the first aircraft of the day touch down on the strip. Someone else had arrived before me. A Legion officer wearing a kepi and combat uniform was leaning on a cane and surveying the valley as if he were the sole proprietor. My boot struck some loose rock and the officer turned. Lt. Col. Jules Gaucher, commander of the Foreign Legion's 13th demibrigade and senior Legionnaire at Dien Bien Phu, looked down with complete disbelief at the *Amerloque* he'd skirmished with at the bar of the Tour d'Ivoire in Saigon. Of all the bivouacs available at Dien Bien Phu, I had been sent to Gaucher's realm.

We shook hands and carried on a hesitant, desultory conversation. He asked where I was quartered. I told him I was sharing a hut with Peraud and Schoendoerffer. I asked if all his men had arrived. He told me they hadn't, swung his cane like a golf club to send a pebble skimming over the ground, and left. That night an unexpected invitation brought Schoendoerffer and myself to Gaucher's tent. We finished off my opened bottle of scotch while the colonel regaled us with tales of his previous adventures in the T'ai mountain country. We were told of opulent dinners with opium-seeking Chinese warlords whose role as hosts prevented them from slitting Gaucher's throat and decimating his ludicrously small escort of Legionnaires; of long treks through the jungle, where more men died from malaria and dysentery than enemy action; and of bloody hand-to-hand fighting with smugglers among the limestone cliffs near the Chinese border. Our evening ended when Gaucher tumbled unceremoniously from his camp stool and an aide announced it was time to turn in.

For three days I visited the various strongpoints, watched the flow of incoming troops and supplies, spent twenty-four hours with the officers of the 5th Vietnamese Parachute Battalion, and ate at Gilles's mess. The rum made its appearance regularly, and staff officers argued about Giap's intentions. For the first time I had the impression of being accepted and no longer felt like a complete outsider. I sent off copy and exposed film to Saigon via returning aircraft and put in a request to accompany a patrol outside the defense perimeter. There was a perceptible tension in the air. The intelligence officers had little to say in my presence, but snatches of conversation at the mess and comments made by returning patrols indicated surprise and uneasiness at the enemy's proximity and strength.

American-supplied Bearcat fighters were now based at the airstrip, and their strike missions increased. I couldn't claim expertise as a tactician, but to me the dark ridges of the nearby mountains seemed ominous and threatening. The French howitzers near the airstrip were in open revetments surrounded by knee-high circles of sandbags. Such a disposition might have served well in some distant colonial clash with a lightly armed, disorganized opposition, but everyone, including the war correspondents, knew the Vietminh had artillery and could use it. Hadn't they been trained by veteran Chinese gunners with long experience in moving their pieces great distances over rough terrain? The more I listened to the optimism of the French artillerymen, the more it seemed they were living in a dream world. They were certain that any Vietminh attempt to deploy their guns—*if* by some miracle they ever got them as far as Dien Bien Phu—would be spotted and dealt with easily. There was little talk of the "high ground" at Dien Bien Phu; it had already been ceded to the enemy by default.

My constant badgering of the long-suffering Colonel Fourcade finally paid off. I was summoned to the CP and told I could accompany Major Bigeard's 6th Parachute Battalion on a patrol. General Gilles turned from his maps.

"Satisfied?" he asked.

"*Oui, mon général!*" I responded enthusiastically, failing to attach much significance to his uncharacteristic smile or the unexpected invitation to an early breakfast of rolls and coffee before the 5:00 A.M. sortie.

I was prepared the next morning when Bigeard's headquarters group appeared in their camouflaged jungle fatigues and distinctive headgear. General Gilles motioned me forward, pointing to the tall, hawk-nosed Bigeard, who used his Resistance code name "Bruno" as his radio call sign in Indochina. I had expected to be introduced but there was no time for formalities. Bigeard acknowledged my presence with a curt nod and strode on, swinging his walking stick. The hero of Tu Le didn't believe in carrying a personal weapon. I was traveling light, with the Rolleiflex slung around my neck, and wearing a parachute jacket that Schoendoerffer had found for me, khaki pants, an army bush hat, thick-soled desert boots, and a full canteen. The holstered Colt .38 was under my jacket, but Bigeard's example troubled me. If he could go unarmed, what game was I playing?

I fell in behind the headquarters group as the battalion passed through a gap in the wire. Sleepy Moroccan sentries watched us pass in a silence broken only by the shuffling of feet and the thump of equipment. We headed north along the *Piste Pavie*, an old colonial road fallen into disuse. The battalion was moving fast, with some companies breaking into a jog to close the gaps. At first I thought Major Bigeard was in a hurry to clear the fortifications, but once we were outside the perimeter the swift pace continued. The village mongrels that had gamboled at our heels dropped behind and we entered a world of abandoned paddies, elephant grass, and eerie quiet.

The sun rose above the ridges to slash bright swaths of heat through the valley. Dien Bien Phu was suddenly far behind. Salty perspiration stung my eyes, and the Rollei seemed to increase in weight. It was rough country, cut by sudden ravines, jagged stones, hidden streams, and thick growths of bamboo. On our first pause I asked the bearded Catholic padre of the 6th Battalion if Bigeard always moved so fast. He chuckled and explained that the 6th was known as the "Zatopek Battalion," a name taken from the famous Czech long-distance runner. Bigeard believed in speed of movement and had often surprised the enemy by the swiftness of his marches. Leaning against a tree and feeling the first signal of protest from my feet, I suddenly understood General Gilles's approval of my request and the reason for his conspiratorial smile.

The rest of the patrol was a purgatory of fast movement, brief halts, and cautious probing. Seven kilometers out we came to a deserted village. It clustered on a slight rise, empty and menacing. Bamboo boles groaned and rubbed together in a sudden wind. The high elephant grass and sticky creepers were covered with dusty grasshoppers that popped into the air at our approach. White butterflies played in and out of the shadows.

"We're being watched," the padre murmured, eyeing the nearby hills. "You can bet on that!"

Major Bigeard hunkered down near his radio to speak into the mouthpiece and watch the progress of his scouts as they approached the village. I welcomed the moment to rest my feet and shoot some photos. It was reassuring to be in the company of obvious professionals; not a wasted word or movement, no superfluous noise. When we sprinted into the shade of the abandoned huts there wasn't a dog or pig in sight. The sweating scouts had uncovered a cache of buried rice, some warm ashes, and the empty rucksack of a Vietminh Regular. Bigeard carried on a long dialogue with a spotter plane while we ate cheese and biscuits washed down with warm water from our canteens. My feet were radiating heat and I could visualize the blisters swelling under my socks.

We headed back to Dien Bien Phu taking a different route to forestall an easy ambush. As the pace quickened, I abandoned the headquarters group to drop back on the following company and concentrated on keeping the dust out of my eyes and mouth. Slogging over the crest of a hill at dusk, we could see the smoke rising from the cooking fires of Dien Bien Phu. By this time I had fallen back to the third company and my right foot was a swollen furnace. It took us an inordinately long time to reach the perimeter. I'd now joined the rear guard. The column bunched up and halted as it fed through the narrow, unmined gap in the wire. Some Legion paras chided us about our uneventful *promenade*. The thoughtful padre had borrowed a walking stick from a young officer and insisted that I use it.

It was dark when I limped up to the CP. Bigeard had already made his report and returned to his bivouac. General Gilles had been watching my laborious approach. He waved me inside, asked his orderly to serve me a pastis, and fixed me with his good eye while the shadow of a smile played on his lips.

"So, *l'Amerloque*," he said, nodding his head slowly, "you have made the entire march with Bigeard. Would you like to accompany him again soon?" My emphatic "No!" filled the CP with laughter. General Gilles, in his own way, had avenged the incident at Ninh Binh.

The next day, while I was having my burst blisters treated at the aid station, a noncom from the 6th Paras tracked me down and delivered an invitation. I was asked to lunch with Bigeard in his headquarters hut at noon "sharp." I limped to the rendezvous and found the major busy with his maps. A field radio hummed and spat static in a corner of the hut. The rough wooden table was covered with small arms and binoculars. I thought I'd misunderstood the invitation. I hadn't. Bigeard greeted me and shouted to his orderly that we were ready to eat. One of his officers cleared the table and we sat down.

My host was already a legend in the French Army. A former enlisted man, he had been parachuted into France in 1944 at the age of twenty-eight with the temporary rank of battalion commander to head the *Maquis* in the Département of the Ariège. He had served in Indochina since 1945, spending much of this time in the T'ai country, where he perfected small-unit tactics against the Vietminh, studying and adapting their methods to his own use. His insistence on physical conditioning, offensive spirit, and comradeship had made his battalion a crack unit on call for difficult "special" operations. He was one of the few French officers the Vietminh feared and respected. Often a headache to his superiors and always idolized by his men, Bigeard was the epitome of the *esprit para.*

He was also a man who found eating while in the field an irritating necessity. His orderly slid mess kits in front of us. Each contained a thin slice of ham and one small, isolated boiled potato. Hot canteen cups of steaming tea accompanied this main course. Bigeard opened a penknife and meticulously peeled his potato while we talked about the Vietminh. Although he despised their Marxist philosophy, he respected the Vietminh as soldiers. Bigeard spoke of the enemy's political indoctrination and dogged determination in battle. In the course of our discussion it became clear that Bigeard believed the retraining and revitalization of the Expeditionary Corps was essential to success in Indochina. Wizened apples from Normandy were served as dessert and our lunch was finished. Bigeard presented me with one of the distinctive soft jungle caps worn by the 6th Battalion. It resembled Japanese Army headgear of World War II, complete with a sun-protector neck flap. He pinned the metal insignia of his battalion on my jacket and said I'd be welcome to join him on operation at any time. He then went back to his maps and radio as if to recoup lost time. The next day I joined some of the battalion's noncoms for lunch. The culinary contrast was striking. We ate beef, onions, and potatoes stewed with red wine and drank enough pastis, Mâcon, and brandy to send me reeling back to the hut. How I negotiated the notched-pole ladder and found my bedroll remains a profound mystery.

General Gilles's replacement arrived in early December. Col. Christian Marie Ferdinand de la Croix de Castries was the complete opposite of Père Gilles. A tall, aloof, and aristocratic cavalryman, de Castries arrived at Dien Bien Phu sporting a shooting stick, a foulard, and the red *calot*, or peaked overseas cap, of the cavalry. Gilles, relieved at the thought of leaving the "chamber pot" valley of Dien Bien Phu, took the new arrival on a tour of the strongpoints. De Castries had served under General Navarre during the campaign in Germany and had a reputation as a dashing tank commander. Word soon spread among the departing paras that de Castries planned to crush the enemy with armor. This only confirmed their general negative opinion of the colonel and spawned a number of bitter comments about his command abilities.

Some of this prejudice rubbed off on me. Admittedly, the cold-fish handshake and blank look I'd received from the colonel when Gilles had introduced us had colored my thinking. Navarre and de Castries seemed to have come from the same cool and supercilious mold. My disinvitation to the CP mess following the departure of General Gilles and Colonel Fourcade reinforced my bias. In fairness to the "cavalier," the presence of an "official" U.S. correspondent in his new fief might have been disconcerting. On the other hand, what I took for a calculated cold shoulder could have been a simple manifestation of complete indifference.

I was visiting strongpoint "Isabelle" when the news came through that Lai Chau had been evacuated prior to the imminent arrival of the 316th Vietminh Division. No amount of verbiage from the Army press officers could cover the fact that the loss of Lai Chau was a serious military reverse. This capital of the T'ai tribes had been a symbol of French support and presence in northwestern Vietnam. It had figured in General Salan's recommendations as one of the three bastions, along with Nasan and Dien Bien Phu, that would allow the French to block an invasion of Laos and mount offensive action against the Vietminh. With Nasan abandoned and Lai Chau gone, Dien Bien Phu now stood alone.

CHAPTER 9

Writing
on the Wall

It was like a scene from an old World War II film—until you realized the wounded were stained with real blood. Most of the Regulars from the Lai Chau garrison had been evacuated by air, but the T'ai partisans had been ordered to travel by foot over seventy kilometers of jungle trails to seek haven at Dien Bien Phu. Despite supporting air strikes and some help from the GCMA, the T'ais had been attacked and harassed all the way. Their casualties had been high. Some partisans, deeply affected by the evacuation of their traditional capital, had chosen to make their own separate peace, slipping out of their uniforms and heading back to their villages.

I'd been driven out early in the cool morning by some officers from the CP to meet the first arrivals. The T'ais had come shuffling through the dust in a long column, arms slung, leading small, heavily laden mountain ponies. Their gaunt faces were blank with exhaustion. Some were carrying their wounded on makeshift bamboo litters, others supported a limping comrade. The slow-moving cavalcade exuded an aura of defeat. The members of the Dien Bien Phu garrison watching the column's arrival were grim-faced and thoughtful. One sensed a certain resentment on their part, as if the partisans had brought with them some unwanted, threatening virus.

A battered jeep appeared in the distance and sped toward us, throwing a cloud of dust in its wake. The driver braked to an abrupt halt and a short, stocky T'ai, dressed in khaki with a holstered .45 on his hip, jumped to the ground. He was one of the lieutenants of Deo Van Long, the French-supported *seigneur* of the T'ai tribes, governor of the region, and descendant of the Black

Flag pirates. The T'ai officer began to shout and curse, berating the French officers, his voice rising as he stamped back and forth, gesticulating. A flustered staff officer took me by the arm and led me away, asking if I'd like to speak with some of the partisans. But the shrill voice of the T'ai could not be stilled. As I was politely but firmly hustled from the scene, I heard him repeat the word *trahison*—betrayal.

I had inadvertently witnessed the airing of some dirty linen between the French and their Black T'ai allies. If an officer of the T'ai partisans was accusing the French of betrayal to their faces, what must the feeling be among the men? They had been forced to leave their capital, abandoning their villages and families to the Vietminh despite all the previous guarantees. Now, bloodied and exhausted, they were to bolster the defenses of Dien Bien Phu and participate in a form of warfare for which they were totally unsuited.

A few days after the partisans arrived, some of de Castries's staff were openly questioning the dependability of the T'ais in the event of a Vietminh attack. I learned later that a monumental snafu had taken place during the evacuation. A large amount of arms, ammunition, and explosives had been left behind at a schoolhouse in Lai Chau. Luckily, the error had been discovered in time. A team of engineers had been choppered in to blow the cache before the Vietminh arrived.

By mid-December 1953, Giap's band of steel had already begun to tighten around Dien Bien Phu. A three-batallion patrol of paras had made a hard contact only seven kilometers outside the perimeter defenses. One battalion had been surrounded. The all-day battle to relieve it had resulted in heavy French casualties. The tanks promised to Colonel de Castries for the application of his classic armored cavalry tactics had begun to arrive. The ten M-24, U.S.-supplied Chaffees were delivered by air in two pieces—chassis and turret—to be assembled with a primitive rig of logs, chains, and pulleys. The para officers remaining at Dien Bien Phu welcomed the tanks as mobile gun platforms but expressed grave doubts about their ability to operate over terrain even the paras found difficult.

There was a strange atmosphere in the camp. Like all static positions it had taken on the aspect of a military city with its own character, rules, and procedures. At the same time the strain of waiting for the unknown was palpable. The officers remained cocky and determined, but the men, particularly the North Africans, T'ai, and some of the Vietnamese seemed to have been affected by the boredom, the lack of movement, and the threat of what was "out there." A troubled silence fell over the dark valley after sundown. Nervous gunners occasionally loosed a stream of seemingly slow-moving tracers into the night, jeeps with hooded headlights bumped over the rough roads, and the odiferous open latrines glowed with the phosphorescence of seething maggots.

Not privy to the intelligence reports indicating the speed and severity of the Vietminh buildup, and advised by de Castries's staff that a long period of waiting lay ahead, I decided to leave Dien Bien Phu and return to Saigon for Christmas.

For the first few days after my return I was busy preparing follow-up articles on Dien Bien Phu and captioning the photos that went with them. George Hellyer asked me to draft a field message for Washington detailing my observations, and I briefed a number of embassy and MAAG officers on what I had seen. My informal presentations were exceedingly pessimistic and in some cases unpopular. Certain American officials preferred to accept the information fed them by the French military authorities. My comments on the vulnerability of Dien Bien Phu, the questionable optimism of the artillery commander, the evacuation of Lai Chau, the proximity of the enemy, and the general mood of the strongpoint did not fit the official pattern of support for the Navarre Plan. I soon learned that the French had done a good job of selling Dien Bien Phu to many in the American Mission as a favorable turning point in the war. Whatever a lower-ranking American civilian might have to say about the military situation in the field was to be taken with a grain of salt and a certain bemused tolerance. Understandably, my report was feather-light on the scale of acceptability in comparison to the optimistic picture being painted by General Navarre and his staff. What one wants to hear is always more acceptable than the citing of potential problems.

Christmas in the tropics is always a hybrid occasion for Westerners. There is something incongruous about decorating a spindly tree with perspiration dripping off your chin, sipping a traditional egg nog under a ceiling fan, or listening to Christmas music while the street noise of a busy Asian city provides a background. I plunged into the round of drinks, parties, and official receptions marking the Christmas season. Colored lights gleamed from sagging cables near the cathedral, there were small trees swathed with silver garlands in the bars along Rue Catinat, and the food shops had mounted displays of fine wines, foie gras, and truffles flown in from Paris.

It was a different world from the one I'd left at Dien Bien Phu. I was troubled by the contrast. Most of my American colleagues had no idea what was going on outside Saigon. My gloomy tales of the T'ai partisans' fate and the crude burials of dead paras threw a momentary pall over the holiday celebrations. At the same time, I was trying to decipher the various insights I'd collected on the state of the war. It seemed that two wars were going on at the same time: the traditionally military contest led by General Navarre and his staff with field commanders such as Colonel de Castries; and the real conflict of lightning attacks, ambushes, and surprise practiced by General Gilles, Major Bigeard, and other advocates of unconventional tactics. The first group planned major operations in comfortable headquarters buildings, drawing bold arrows and sweeping lines on their maps, preparing elaborate actions as if they were still involved in a European campaign. The debilitating realities of the Indochina landscape counted for little in their deliberations, and an ingrained contempt for Giap's "peasant" army led them all the more easily toward disaster.

The second group never underestimated the Vietminh. They had lived through deadly ambushes, marched long distances over tortuous terrain with the enemy at their heels, and watched the stoic, almost sacrificial performance of the Vietminh *Bo Doi* in battle. Through studying the enemy's tactics and motivation, they had decided that success in the field would not come with more artillery, armor, aircraft, or fortifications, but from matching and bettering the Vietminh at their own game of guerrilla warfare. Unfortunately, Group One was destined to make the major decisions and Group Two was to suffer the physical consequences. Although no one saw it at the time, both groups were playing out an unscripted tragedy dictated by the historical and political realities of postwar Asia in the twilight of colonial rule.

My ponderings on the state of the war were leavened by an increased interest in Mary Alice Turner, the AID Mission secretary I'd met a few months previously. I had introduced her to Yvonne at Le Papillon and we often met there for lunch. We were regulars at the upstairs bar of the Majestic Hotel, dined at l'Amiral, and danced in the seedy ambiance of the Tour d'Ivoire. We were both free agents with no commitments, but something was happening. M.A.'s green eyes, her personality, and her laugh had become an obsession. Although she was also going out with someone else, I had to see her each day. This was indeed a new experience. I wasn't sure just where it would lead.

A few days before Christmas, Dixie Reese asked me if he could visit Dien Bien Phu on his own to gather more photo coverage. I knew of his continued desire to try his professional hand at combat photography and approved his request *if* he could get clearance from the French. He did, and ended up joining a column marching through the Laotian jungle to link up with a liaison group from Dien Bien Phu. The exercise was designed to prove that Dien Bien Phu could still be relieved by land. It was another example of the High Command's disregard of jungle warfare realities. The column arrived at the rendezvous exhausted, racked by typhoid and dysentery, and assailed by leeches and mosquitoes. Brigitte Friang, a tanned and petite French government war correspondent and former Resistance member, had parachuted to join the column. She found that the emaciated Legionnaires reminded her of her fellow inmates in the wartime Nazi death camps.

Reese, wearing slacks, a tie, and polished Oxfords, had been lifted to the column by helicopter. Loaded down with two cameras, a heavy sack of film, and a bottle of bourbon, he joined the Legionnaires for the remainder of their exhausting trek. The ordeal was made more difficult by the necessity of playing hide-and-seek with Vietminh patrols and avoiding large tracks and roads in favor of ridgeline footpaths and jungle fords. To his credit, Reese stuck with the column. Tales of his exploit and sangfroid went the rounds of French Army messes for months to come. It also temporarily dampened his enthusiasm for combat photography until 1955, when a totally different, personal approach was to prove fatal.

In late December 1953, General Giap sent seven battalions from his 304th and 325th divisions slicing into central Laos. It appeared to be a major effort to cut Laos in half at its narrowest point. The Vietminh move had caught the French by surprise, and the town of Thakhek had been evacuated. Word of

the new offensive spread quickly among the correspondents at the Hotel Continental. There was speculation that it might be Giap's answer to the Navarre
Plan, a masterly stroke at a weak point in French defenses while the bulk of
the Expeditionary Corps' combat units were contained and isolated at Dien
Bien Phu. Not wanting to miss what might be a turning point in the war, I
obtained an *ordre de mission* from Gardes's office and prepared to leave for
Savannakhet early in the morning of January 1, 1954. I had learned that a
grouping of para units, including Bigeard's 6th Battalion, had been sent to the
Laotian base of Seno. I hoped to join them there.

A New Year's Eve party at the Majestic Hotel had kept Mary Alice and me
up till all hours. I arrived at Tan Son Nhut in a semicomatose condition, with
a delicate stomach. My state did not improve when I saw the waiting, light
army monoplane with the spindly features of an oversized mosquito. The chain-
smoking pilot lounging against the fuselage said we'd take off as soon as the
other passenger arrived. When he did, I took some comfort in seeing I was not
alone in suffering from a hangover. Graham Greene and I exchanged a cool
acknowledgment. It took no great perceptivity to sense Green's displeasure at
being paired with an "official" American. We climbed aboard and buckled ourselves in. The flight was a continual, jolting, roller-coaster ride. There was nothing to do but attempt to sleep.

A jeep was waiting for us at the Savannakhet strip and we were soon heading
north toward Seno. A white-hot sun sledgehammered down. The dry, yellowed
palms threw brief patches of shade over the dusty road, and the jeep's overheated engine sounded like a dentist's drill. Our vehicle appeared to be the
only one on the road. The driver's bolt-action rifle seemed meager insurance
against marauding Vietminh patrols. But security wasn't our prime concern.
Mutual adversity often brings people together for brief periods, and we both
agreed without reservation that we were suffering from a monumental, throat-
scorching thirst. We searched each new bend in the road for the welcome sight
of a village or the tents of a French camp. Nothing. Just more flat, dry land
and desiccated foliage.

I'd inured myself to the situation and turned my thoughts to the cold glasses
we'd soon be clutching at Seno when the driver pointed to a small canvas-
covered installation by the side of the road. It was almost a miracle. In the
middle of nowhere an aged Laotian woman crouched beside a vendor's stand
stocked with sun-dried cigarettes, fly-covered sweets, coconut quarters, *and* bottles of Tiger beer. The bottles were warm to the touch, but the beer had the
effect of a restorative elixir. Even Greene managed a shadow of a smile and we
continued on our way different men. On our arrival at Seno, Greene and I
were briefed, shared a mess lunch, and went our separate ways.

General Gilles was at Seno with his airborne group under the command of
General Franqui, who was then the titular head of operations in central Laos.
For the first time Gilles greeted me with some warmth, using the personal *tu*,
and asked if I'd brought my pistol. But he didn't have time to waste and rushed
off on some important business. There was a definite sense of urgency at Seno.

Bigeard and Maj. Jean Brechignac had taken their battalions into the dry bush to make contact with the enemy, feel out his strength, and determine his intentions. After a long discussion with Colonel Bastiani it became obvious the paras were involved in the type of operation during which a correspondent would be decidedly unwelcome. They were moving cautiously but speedily through the jungle, pushing themselves to the limit to head off the Vietminh probes.

From the first hard contacts on January 5 at Ban Som Hong to the paras' withdrawal from the combat zone on January 7, the Vietminh were to lose over 400 men. Their direct orders to encircle and wipe out Bigeard's 6th Battalion would prompt an assault on Ban Som Hong only to find that "Bruno" had already guessed their intentions, pulled his men out of the village, and arranged a deadly welcoming committee of Bearcat fighter-bombers. Shortly thereafter Giap would abandon his effort in central Laos. Much later, when Bigeard was captured by the Vietminh, enemy commanders congratulated him on his tactics in avoiding their encirclement and the 6th's fighting withdrawal.

Colonel Bastiani saw to it that I visited a para support unit near Seno, and I was able to interview some Laotian troops who had taken the brunt of the first Vietminh attacks. But I had learned not to waste unproductive time in the field. When I said goodbye to Bastiani, he expressed concern over the enemy buildup around Dien Bien Phu and suggested we might well meet there again in the near future. I left some photos I'd taken at Dien Bien Phu for Bigeard and was driven to Savannakhet to catch a liaison flight back to Saigon.

Word had reached Saigon that my stories and photos from Dien Bien Phu had been well received at USIA. The detailed field message had also made an impression in Washington, having been distributed to a number of civilian agencies and military recipients. Lt. Gen. "Iron Mike" O'Daniel and some of his staff had visited Dien Bien Phu, been given the standard jeep tour of the strongpoints by Colonel de Castries, and been briefed on how the defenders would decimate the enemy as they tried to breach the wire. O'Daniel made polite public noises about the French installation at Dien Bien Phu, but he remained concerned over the "fish-in-a-barrel" aspect of the valley positions if the enemy ever dominated the high ground.

It had now been two years since my arrival in Vietnam, and Washington duly telegrammed my home leave orders. I was under no obligation to return to Saigon. It was rated a "hardship post" by the Department of State and the assignments were set at two years. But George Hellyer was a firm believer in continuity. Black Jack Pickering, who had returned to Washington, had been replaced by Ed Stansbury, a former *Time* correspondent, and Hellyer hoped to keep as many of his experienced staff as possible in Saigon. He lobbied me over a period of time until I agreed to return for an additional year. A promotion and the promise of an American assistant were part of our agreement.

In the 1950s many American Foreign Service officers still traveled to and from their posts by sea. The government would pay the minimum first-class passage available on an American line, and the travel would not be deducted from your home leave time. If there was no urgency in returning to Washington, the sea voyage was an ideal prelude to a homecoming. I arranged for an April passage from Hong Kong to San Francisco on the *President Wilson* and prepared for departure. I also found myself in a considerable personal quandary. Mary Alice's tour of duty would end during my absence and she'd be gone when I returned. For the first time in my life I recognized that I'd fallen in love and was seriously considering the possibility of marriage. It was decision time in Saigon and I was waffling.

We were both invited to lunch with General Gilles at his residence and dined with the Hellyers and the O'Daniels at the general's villa. I said my temporary goodbyes to the staff, the press contingent at the Continental, and Yvonne and the regulars at Le Papillon. Mary Alice flew up to Hong Kong to see me off and we spent a wonderful week together. Our farewell dinner at Gaddi's in the Peninsula Hotel was difficult for both of us. I was still tongue-tied, uttering platitudes about the "seriousness" of my feelings and tap-dancing around the question of marriage. Weeks later, after the long voyage home and some hard thinking under the redwoods of the Santa Cruz Mountains, I finally sent a telegram to Saigon.

"Will you marry me?" it read. "Reply care of Johnnie's Cash Store, Boulder Creek, California." The reply was positive and I settled down to await Mary Alice's arrival while following the news from Vietnam.

By April 1954, the situation at Dien Bien Phu had worsened. The Vietminh *had* transported their guns over many miles of jungle trails and manhandled them into position on the heights above the valley. Secure and well camouflaged, the enemy 105mm howitzers, 75mm mountain guns, and 120mm and 81mm mortars had soon made the airstrip untenable. The first heavy barrage had targeted the CP of the Legion, killing Colonel Gaucher. Colonel Piroth, crushed by the inability of his guns to counter the Vietminh fire, had committed suicide, using a hand grenade. Supplies and reinforcements were being dropped by parachute at night to avoid accurate fire from the Soviet-made 37mm antiaircraft guns the Vietminh had placed on the ridges above the strongpoint. Earthquake McGovern of the Flying Tigers had died on a resupply mission when his C-119 was hit by groundfire. Bigeard, despite a sprained ankle, had returned for the final act, jumping with his battalion. Sergeants Schoendoerffer and Peraud had gone back in. Some of the air-dropped reinforcements were volunteers: cooks, mechanics, and service troops who had never used a parachute before.

As the siege intensified, tireless Vietminh sappers, working in relays under heavy fire, pushed their trenches closer and closer to the French positions. The parachute battalions and the Foreign Legion formed the backbone of the defense, fighting off the assaults and counterattacking when enough valid men were available. Colonel de Castries's remaining tanks, which had never been able to fill their dashing role in sweeping the countryside clean of the enemy, were knocked out one by one as they supported the counterattacks. Hundreds of dead and wounded fell around the strongpoints and in the trenches. With no evacuation possible, the French wounded lay on litters in the busy surgical dugout. Those beyond help were piled in abandoned trenches or left where they had fallen. As the perimeter narrowed, the drop zone became smaller, and men and supplies dropped too soon or too late fell directly onto enemy positions.

Colonel de Castries had by now withdrawn into himself, and the effective command of the garrison had passed to the para commanders, Lt. Col. Pierre Langlais and Bigeard. The bloody fighting had turned the valley of Dien Bien Phu into a nightmare landscape torn by heavy explosives and littered with the debris of smashed equipment and fallen aircraft. Some units had ceased to exist as fighting entities. Their shell-shocked survivors, including many North Africans and T'ais, had sought shelter from the bombardments by burrowing into the raised banks of the Nam Youm to earn the scathing label "Rats of the Nam Youm" from those still engaged in the fighting.

The first assault against the strongpoint Beatrice on March 13 had cost the Vietminh 500 casualties. Although General Giap was determined to end the campaign as quickly as possible, his tactics now called for rolling up the strong-points one by one, avoiding a costly general assault. While his troops died and were wounded under the French guns, they also faced a barrage of proclamations and orders of the day produced by Vietminh political officers and signed by their general. In the Vietminh view, political mottoes ranked close to ammunition in importance, and they were addressed to the fighting soldiers and *Dan Cong*, or road laborers, alike. Victory was the key word: "Opening the road for the artillery is to work actively for victory." "Building solid positions is to guarantee success." "Assuring the continuity of communications is to snatch victory," "One more man working on the road means one more chance of victory," "One more centimeter of thickness in a (fortified) position is an added arm to contend for victory."

General Giap was facing not only heavy losses, but also illnesses, coupled with a shortage of drugs and medicines, and the constant problem of supply. Remembering his previous defeats, he was wary of French capabilities. The fear that his troops might underestimate the enemy was constant. As recounted in his book *Dien Bien Phu*, his message to the army on the Dien Bien Phu front two days after the assault on Beatrice warned, "His [enemy] morale is affected, his difficulties are numerous, but don't underestimate him. If we underestimate him we'll lose the battle. . . . " Another message to "Cadres and Combatants Prior to Attack on the East Sector of the Fortified Camp of Dien Bien Phu" dated March 29 hinted at internal problems among the assault forces. "The first difficulty," Giap warned, "comes because certain comrades, unaware of the actual situation and the forces involved, show subjectivity and underestimate our adversaries, from which comes a weakening of our combat organization, that can lead easily to defeat."

While the officers and men I'd shared rations with were fighting and dying, the French were desperately and unsuccessfully seeking massive American air intervention at Dien Bien Phu. In Geneva the preparations for an international conference to settle the Indochina "problem" were being completed. I was sleep-walking through my home leave in the shadow of these events. Family and friends listened politely to my explanations and tales of Vietnam, but it was a distant, unreal world to them. I wrote special articles on Dien Bien Phu for the San Francisco *Chronicle* and the *Call Bulletin* and briefed some newsmen informally, but the American public had just put the Korean War behind them. France's problems in some obscure colony were of little interest. Most of my contacts were surprised to hear the extent of U.S. involvement in Vietnam and many expressed the view that the sooner we got out of Southeast Asia the better.

Dien Bien Phu fell to Vietminh assault forces the night of May 7, 1954. General Giap's red battle flag, bearing the gold-lettered slogan *Fight and Win*, flew from the captured command post, and exultant *Bo Doi* began rounding up prisoners, many of whom would not survive the long marches and privations of captivity. Two days later I received a welcome, unexpected phone call from Brigitte Friang. She had been on a French-government-sponsored tour of the United States, speaking on the war and her experiences. She was now in San Francisco for a brief stopover before returning to Saigon. We arranged to meet in her room at the Clift Hotel that evening.

It was an awkward encounter, a sort of wake, in the midst of unrelated opulence. She had put on some needed weight during her absence from the battle zone and looked particularly attractive, but nothing could hide the sadness in her eyes. If those undergoing the hardships and humiliation of Dien Bien Phu were acquaintances of mine, they were her longtime comrades. We sat together, scotch in hand, sharing the bits of information available to us. She confirmed that Schoendoerffer and Peraud had been there till the end and that both were undoubtedly among the captured, that Bigeard's battalion had exacted a high price from the Vietminh with its counterattacks, and that losses among the paras had been heavy. What galled us was that no one around us seemed to care. I don't think we grasped the true significance of the defeat that evening. She was returning to Indochina and I would soon take the same route. In my mind the war was still not lost. When the brooding silences became obvious, I embraced her and took my leave.

The next day, using a borrowed typewriter, I put some of my frustration into a bit of doggerel. I was obviously seeking a scapegoat and I targeted the type of French officer I'd grown to detest.

INDOCHINA EPITAPH

Camembert for the Colonel's table,
Wine in abundance when we're able.
Indochina may be lost,
Our Colonel eats well despite the cost.

Pernod iced and cognac sec,
To get it here we risk our neck.
Foie gras sours . . . so serve it first,

Timed between each mortar burst.
Air-drop lamb for the Colonel too,
A Spahi eats only Cordon Bleu.

Parachute the escargot!
Follow them with old Bordeaux,
And on our graves near Dien Bien Phu
Inscribe these words, these very few,
"They died for France, but more . . .
Their Colonel ate well throughout the war."

The verses were unfair to many serving French officers but they echoed my feelings at the time. It was hardly the proper state of mind with which to approach the most difficult period of Franco-American relations in Indochina.

CHAPTER 10

Our Man in Saigon

By the time I was due to return to Vietnam in mid-June of 1954, the entire political-military situation had changed. The defeat at Dien Bien Phu had sounded the death knell for the French in Indochina. Although the Expeditionary Corps still held the strategic deltas, the population centers, and continued to repulse Vietminh attacks, the will for offensive action was gone. An international conference in Geneva, begun on May 8, was thrashing out a settlement to the Indochina problem.

Prime Minister Mendès-France had gone to Geneva determined to end the war that was sapping France's strength and tearing the nation apart. Other negotiators included Zhou Enlai of China; Anthony Eden of Britain; Pham Van Dong of the Vietminh; Vyacheslave Molotov of the Soviet Union; U.S. Secretary of State John Foster Dulles; Georges Bidault of France; and representatives of Laos, Cambodia, and the Vietnamese emperor, Bao Dai. Meanwhile, Emperor Bao Dai, ensconced safely in his chateau in southern France, ruling through his surrogates and more of a distant figurehead than ever, had named Ngo Dinh Diem prime minister. In January of 1953, when Diem had requested a meeting with John Foster Dulles in Washington, an internal State Department background memorandum had described him as "a Vietnamese politician. He is a Catholic, a nationalist, tends to be anti-French and is also anti-Bao Dai. He was a Minister some years ago and his name is occasionally mentioned as a candidate for Prime Minister. He appears to be a man of integrity although not particularly practical. . . . " Diem, at fifty-two, was a short, portly man with the detached air of a scholarly mandarin. He had left Vietnam in

1950 under a Vietminh death threat and spent two years with the Maryknoll fathers in New Jersey. During this period he had made a number of important contacts among American congressmen interested in Indochina and become a protégé of the influential Francis Cardinal Spellman of New York. Later Diem argued for Vietnamese independence in Paris. His position as a noncommunist, anti-French nationalist assured an audience among some Vietnamese exiles, but his Catholicism and habit of lecturing his interlocutors alienated others. Diem was now destined to play a leading role in a period of deepening U.S. involvement in Indochina.

I had tried to keep up with developments in Vietnam during my home leave but other, more personal events had taken priority. Mary Alice and I had been married on June 1. After a week's honeymoon in California we'd spent some time in Washington, D.C., where I shuttled between USIA and the State Department, preparing for my return to Saigon and contributing what I could to the woefully meager supply of official knowledge on Indochina. Some unknown benefactor in the agency had added a week's consultation in Paris to my travel orders. But there wasn't much the European-oriented embassy officers in Paris who had never been to Asia could tell me about Vietnam. Since France's defeat at Dien Bien Phu, Indochina was no longer one of their priorities. My "consultation" thus became more of a honeymoon extension. A week and a half later, after an overnight stay at the old Oriental Hotel in Bangkok—where a huge water jar and scoop served as a shower—we arrived back in Saigon.

George Hellyer and his wife, Meg, met us at Tan Son Nhut airport. He briefed me on the latest local developments as we drove into the city. Granville "Red" Austin, a young, energetic New Englander, had arrived to act as my assistant and allow me more leeway for special assignments. Saigon appeared the same on the surface, and the conclusion of the Geneva Conference was still to come, but the atmosphere was electric. The French, smarting from their military debacle and suspicious of what might come out of Geneva, were searching for a scapegoat. The Americans in Saigon were an easy target. Had we not let them down at Dien Bien Phu, refusing to provide the requested air support? Weren't we now poised to replace them in Indochina, courting Vietnamese officials and expanding our local contacts? This growing resentment was most noticeable in the French business community and among the longtime colonial residents, who stood to lose everything in the event of a French withdrawal. I even sensed a certain coolness among the small-time entrepreneurs and shady Corsican regulars on returning to Le Papillon.

Col. Ed Lansdale had arrived in Saigon on June 1 with the cover title of assistant air attaché to set up his CIA operation in South Vietnam. This small group of operatives was to be known as the Saigon Military Mission. The embassy, the CIA's Saigon station chief, some of the military attachés, and certain MAAG officers were wary of these newcomers. Lansdale & Co. had a well-earned reputation for freewheeling, out-of-channel procedures in the Philippines. Nevertheless, with the help and support of General O'Daniel and George

Hellyer, the cautious tolerance of Ambassador Heath, and his own disarming but effective methods, Lansdale was soon "in place" and functioning.

Even while the negotiations in Geneva continued, the United States had decided to do what it could to forestall Communist domination of the whole Indochina Peninsula. The Eisenhower administration had no intention of becoming involved in another costly ground war in Asia following the Korea experience, but the domino theory was still very much alive in Washington. Something had to be done to fill the power vacuum that would follow any French withdrawal and leave South Vietnam open to the Vietminh. What better man for the job than Lansdale, the "kingmaker" who had masterminded the rise of President Magsaysay and assisted the Philippines in crushing the Communist Hukbalahap revolt?

Lansdale had come to Vietnam with the blessings of John Foster Dulles and his brother Allen Dulles, the director of CIA. Although no one could be sure how the Geneva Conference would end, the prime task of the Saigon Military Mission was to save what was left of Vietnam by helping the Vietnamese establish a viable, united, national government. The men Lansdale had selected for the SMM were a mixed bag: hard-bitten, experienced operatives; quiet intellectuals; young, naïve world-changers; and a few inveterate hell-raisers. All of them appeared to have two things in common: a devotion to Lansdale and a commitment to hard, sometimes dangerous, work. In addition to its task of countering Vietminh activities and organizing paramilitary forces for special operations, the SMM inaugurated its own psychological warfare program. Lansdale and Hellyer worked together on this initiative, sharing know-how, personnel, and funds. SMM officers often visited our offices in the Galerie Eden to coordinate projects and arrange for the design and printing of propaganda material. As this cooperation continued, one of Lansdale's team, Rufus Phillips, a young Army officer assigned to work on psychological warfare projects with the Vietnamese National Army, was given a desk in USIS.

My wife and I moved into an apartment in the building I'd occupied on my first arrival in Saigon. I went to work reorganizing the press office to handle the increased work load. The war was still going on, and General Giap continued to order his units to attack. These actions underlined Vietminh determination and increased political pressure on France for a speedy, positive conclusion to the Geneva Conference. Shortly after my return, Hellyer and Stansbury asked me to fly to Hanoi. USIA had requested press coverage of the post–Dien Bien Phu Vietnamese National Army to prove that it still existed and continued to fight. At the same time, I was to confer with the USIS officers in Hanoi on the eventual evacuation of our Vietnamese staff, depending on the outcome in Geneva.

Hanoi was a city marking time, waiting for its fate to be decided. The press camp was semideserted, with most of the familiar faces gone. The few correspondents and Army press officers remaining on the premises were drinking enough to make up for the absentees. There were wild rumors about the fate of the officers and men captured at Dien Bien Phu: Bigeard had escaped and had organized a *maquis* in the mountains; some Legion prisoners had gone over to the Vietminh, formed a company, and were now fighting with the Communists; Schoendoerffer and Peraud had been sighted in the jungle by friendly mountain tribesmen. None of these reports proved true. They were the product of overactive imaginations subliminally augmenting the dull fare of official communiqués.

The possibility of covering one of the last battles of the Indochina War sent me to a sun-bleached, shell-scarred headquarters near Hung Yen. A Vietnamese infantry battalion was on an operation against some Vietminh Regional troops, and the French officers in the headquarters, explaining that they couldn't spare a jeep, pointed me in the right direction. They suggested I follow in the footsteps of a Vietnamese demining team that was on its way to join the battalion. Obviously, the days of Franco-American cooperation in the field—none too good at the best of times—were over. I had the feeling no one in that headquarters would shed a tear if the sunburned *Amerloque* suddenly disappeared in a puff of smoke from an unnoticed mine.

Two hours later, after carefully walking in the dusty footprints of a slow-moving Vietnamese soldier wielding a mine detector, I arrived at the site of what had been an early-morning battle. It was a depressing sight. The Vietminh Regionals, thinking they were attacking an understrength Vietnamese battalion, had blundered onto an entrenched French armored squadron. The heavy weapons and automatic fire from the tanks had cut the attackers down in windrows, chopping their bodies in jagged patterns, voiding them of entrails, separating heads from bodies and limbs from trunks. The dry paddy field filled with fly-covered dead smelled like an exploded sewer. The French officer who walked beside me shook his head.

"It was an idiotic attack," he murmured, eyeing the carnage. "They ran right into it."

The small, stinking battlefield at Hung Yen seemed a perfect illustration of war's waste. Thousands of miles away the well-dressed, well-fed diplomatic delegations in Geneva were approaching a cease-fire agreement. At Hung Yen a band of Regionals in peasant garb, wearing sun helmets and sandals made from rubber tires, had made a reckless frontal assault on a strongly held position in the waning days of a long conflict. One French trooper had died in the assault and several had been wounded. By the time I'd arrived, the momentary excitement of the clash had faded and been replaced by a postaction slump. It had been a kill-or-be-killed situation, but it took no skill at mind-reading to see that the "victors" fervently wished the attack had never occurred.

When I finally located the CP of the Vietnamese battalion, I noted the obvious change in attitude among both the Vietnamese officers and their French advisers. In the face of an uncertain future, those in command had decided that self-preservation was the better part of valor. Supposedly on an offensive sweep, the battalion was hunkered down in defensive positions. A French officer told me that desertions were on the rise. He also said that echoes of the events in Geneva—distorted by the word-of-mouth bamboo telegraph—had reached the rank and file, spreading doubt and uneasiness about French intentions. Paradoxically, some of the Vietnamese officers seemed to have retained a firm faith in their French mentors. Perhaps it was a case of wishful thinking, a psychological need to believe that France would never pull out of North Vietnam.

I returned to Saigon with a detailed list of the Vietnamese employees in our Hanoi office and their immediate families. We were pledged to get them out in the event of a Communist takeover, but I'd noticed the list was inordinately long. I recall speculating that our male staffers must be particularly virile to produce such large families. When I turned the list over to George Hellyer, I didn't give it much more thought, unaware that I'd soon be called on to make the decisions as to who would qualify to be flown south.

Events in Saigon were suddenly accelerated as if someone had speeded up the presentation of a film. Ngo Dinh Diem arrived at Tan Son Nhut on June 26. The new prime minister was greeted by a meager crowd drummed up by his Catholic supporters, augmented by some unenthusiastic French officials, sympathetic American Mission representatives, and a scattering of curious foreign diplomats. His sedan sped through the streets of an indifferent capital directly to Norodom Palace, the prime ministerial seat of government and residence. I had not seen all the high-level, classified cable traffic between the embassy and Washington relative to Diem's return, but within twenty-four hours it became apparent many of us would soon be working full time to support his government.

The morning after Diem's arrival George Hellyer rushed out of the office in the company of Ed Lansdale. When he returned, he called me in to say he had just met the prime minister. He told me Lansdale hoped to work closely with Diem in the future. For his part, Hellyer had offered Diem all the help our office could provide. Although he had not yet cleared it with the ambassador, he had proposed my services to Diem as an unofficial press adviser. He painted a melancholy picture of the new prime minister in an empty, understaffed palace with a minimum of guards. Hellyer had been shocked by Diem's apparent inability to grasp the importance and subtle dangers of media relations in the current situation. He speculated that any hasty exposure to the international press would find the journalists—particularly the French—eating Diem alive.

"He's going to need all the help he can get," Hellyer told me.

The new Vietnamese leader was in a difficult position. Although the phrase "nation-building" had not yet entered the official lexicon, he was attempting just that, working with the equivalent of string and baling wire. The chronically diverse body politic of Vietnam had been jarred from its moorings. The majority of Vietnamese politicians had operated with the watchful approval of their French masters. With all indications pointing to a French withdrawal, they now scrambled for new alliances and personal safeguards to retain their influence and place in society. The Vietnamese National Army had suddenly become crucial to the preservation of a noncommunist Vietnam and essential to Diem's survival. Unfortunately for the new prime minister, his inherited chief of staff, General Nguyen Van Hinh, was already plotting his downfall.

The religious-military sects and the Binh Xuyen, with their own armies, hamlets, and large tracts of valuable land, were mustering to defend their interests and extend their own power. The French administration in Indochina was monitoring developments in Geneva and preparing for the contingencies of evacuation. The Expeditionary Corps was busy containing the aggressive Vietminh with a minimum of losses. Meanwhile, the operatives of French Intelligence were moving stage center to foil the new, American-supported prime minister and salvage something from the French defeat. The Action operatives of the 2ème Bureau, whose tough Corsican commander, Major Savani, had maneuvered the Binh Xuyen into a position of strength as the shock police of Saigon, were preparing to match "dirty tricks" with Lansdale's SMM, using the Binh Xuyen, the Cao Dai, and the Hoa Hao as French surrogates.

It was against this backdrop that I first met Ngo Dinh Diem. Both Hellyer and Lansdale had now agreed that Diem needed media exposure both at home and abroad, despite the hazards involved. As things stood, he was the little man who wasn't there, the lonely, threatened occupant of a pretentious palace. My visit was intended to lay the foundation of a working relationship. I was to contribute advice and suggestions that would help the prime minister emerge from his cocoon of anonymity. This would mean putting his case and planned policies to his nation and the world through the media. I also wanted to observe Diem as an individual, to better understand how his strengths and weaknesses might affect his public performance.

When I drove my jeep through the high iron gates of Norodom Palace, the afternoon sun blazed down on the grounds. My suit coat was already damp with perspiration and I could feel the prickly heat spreading under my knotted tie. I prepared to talk my way past the guard post but the lethargic Army sentries waved me through without question. Swinging up the approach circle, I parked near a side entrance and climbed the wide staircase. The sentries at the portico were more businesslike—loyal Catholic bodyguards in civilian clothes. I identified myself, and a member of the prime minister's staff appeared to lead me into the palace's cool interior.

I waited in the same high-ceilinged room where I had met previously with Prime Minister Tam, who had faded from view following the defeat of his French benefactors. Sitting before a low inlaid table on which multiple brands of cigarettes were arrayed, I luxuriated in the air currents from the ceiling fans. A servant glided over the tiles to serve me a fizzy orange drink. I was tempted to light a cigar but decided against it. The prime minister then appeared, alone and unannounced. I'd witnessed his arrival at the airport, but he'd been swallowed up by the reception committee before I'd had a good look at him. Now he came toward me almost shyly, extended his hand in a limp handshake, and sat down, indicating I should join him. He made a great show of offering me a cigarette. When I declined, he lit one for himself. He was dressed in a shiny, white sharkskin suit with large lapels and baggy pants. Thick black hair framed his oval face; intense dark eyes blinked under black eyebrows. An uneasy silence ensued until I introduced myself.

Diem nodded, indicating he already knew who I was, and waited for me to continue. I cleared my throat and, following Hellyer's lead, referred to my readiness to be of what help I could in his press relations. I also referred to the great international interest in his new government and the current problems it faced. He drew deeply on his cigarette and continued to nod. I wasn't sure he was signaling that he understood my French or that he agreed with me. When I'd finished, he exhaled a cloud of smoke and began to talk. He talked slowly but the pace increased as he continued. It was as if a dam had suddenly collapsed under intense verbal pressure.

He spoke of his hopes for a free, prosperous Vietnam, of the inherent qualities of the Vietnamese people, of Communist perfidy and cruelty. He touched on the negative aspects of colonialism, including the exploitation of Vietnam's resources, and underlined the Vietnamese peasant's devotion to his land. At one point he paused to ask if I had ever been to North Vietnam. When I told him I had and began to enumerate the extent of my travels in Tonkin, he cut in immediately to continue his calm, insistent diatribe. The ashtray filled with cigarette butts. I sat transfixed but increasingly restless, the prime minister's sole audience. The half hour set for our meeting had long passed when one of Diem's staff mustered enough courage to inform him that other business awaited. The prime minister directed that I be introduced to his press office staff, thanked me for my "help," and walked, slouch-shouldered, out of the room trailing a wisp of smoke.

I met with the nervous, white-suited young men of the palace press office, offered my cooperation, and exchanged office and home telephone numbers. I also noted that their ground-floor offices were woefully underequipped for the task ahead. A clerk was two-finger-typing a document on an ancient machine, and an equally aged mimeograph was under uncertain repair.

I reflected on the meeting with Diem as I drove through the traffic crush on Rue Catinat. Only weeks before, Norodom Palace had been filled with French civilian and military advisers supervising the French-supported Vietnamese government. Now, although Diem had been appointed by Bao Dai and the French still controlled Indochina, there hadn't been a Frenchman to be seen in the palace grounds. Had the French thrown in the towel to that extent? Or were they so sure that Diem would fail that they were just biding their time before replacing him with another one of "their" Vietnamese? If the French were truly out, did this mean we now had to replace them? Somehow, the idea of Norodom Palace crawling with American advisers seemed ludicrous. But to me, as a young, comparatively inexperienced officer, the situation had a certain heady appeal. I had just come from a long tête-à-tête with the head of state of a war-torn country and *he* had thanked me for my visit! It was as if I'd been given a role in an oriental version of *Alice in Wonderland*.

My report to Hellyer was less sanguine. I'd had the feeling that Diem still didn't fully understand the reason for my visit. His monologue, I suggested, indicated he may have thought I was one of the foreign journalists he was supposed to impress. Hellyer puffed on his pipe and frowned. It was my job to clarify the situation, remain in contact with Diem's press office, and be available to the prime minister on a twenty-four-hour basis. We both admitted that Diem was an enigma, a definite unknown quantity, and we had our doubts about his political longevity, but he was now Washington's "man in Saigon" and our work was cut out for us.

I was soon a regular visitor to the palace, using the front entrance when escorting an American journalist or the side door when I wanted to confer with the prime minister's press office. The palace was not yet crawling with Americans, but the trend was there. Colonel Lansdale and members of his team were in and out regularly, Ambassador Heath's car was often parked in the drive, Hellyer was an occasional visitor, and other Americans, including General O'Daniel and senior AID officials, came and went. Ngo Dinh Nhu, the prime minister's younger brother, was a constant presence, appearing unexpectedly at Diem's side during the most mundane official business, his constant smile belied by cold, calculating eyes. His wife, Madame Nhu, was petite and shapely with long, lacquered fingernails. She glided among the guests at one of Diem's first official receptions in a form-fitting *ao dai*, trailing the fragrance of perfume and chatting flirtatiously with young officers, be they Vietnamese, French, or American. Few if any of her male admirers at the time could guess that by the summer of 1963 she would have metamorphosed into the influential and dangerous "Dragon Lady," belittling the self-immolation of a Buddhist monk (*bonze*) by commenting that all the Buddhists had done was "barbecue a bonze."

The results of the Geneva Conference hit Saigon like a bombshell in late July of 1954. The final agreement provided for a military truce, the "temporary" division of Vietnam at the seventeenth parallel, the withdrawal of French forces from the North and Vietminh forces from the South, and the scheduling of free elections in two years' time, in July of 1956. Any civilian wishing to move north or south would be allowed to do so prior to May 18, 1955, without threat of reprisal. An International Control Commission including India, Poland, and Canada would oversee the implementation of the Geneva Accords. The United States had given an unenthusiastic promise to abide by the agreement but warned that any "renewal of aggression" would be viewed with grave concern. Vietnamese Foreign Minister Tran Van Do called the transaction "catastrophic and immoral." He insisted on the "sacred right of the Vietnamese people to territorial unity, independence, and freedom" and had asked to have his government's reservations noted in the final declaration of the conference. This was refused and the embittered Vietnamese delegation returned to Saigon with heavy hearts.

The Geneva timetable calling for the Vietminh occupation of Hanoi on October 9, 1954, left us precious little time to close down the USIS office in Hanoi and evacuate our Vietnamese employees. The U.S. consulate there had the same problem, although it was to remain as a reduced operation with a skeleton staff. The weeks of August seemed to flash by in a rapidly increasing aura of crisis. Reports from the field emphasized the chaos in the countryside. The Vietminh victory had impressed many South Vietnamese. There was a certain secret pleasure to be found in the French defeat at the hands of their country-men, who might hopefully be more nationalist than Communist. Vietminh political cadres were putting the time left before traveling north to good use, proselytizing the peasantry, concealing arms caches for future use, and identify-ing dependable sympathizers for more active roles in Communist "popular fronts" seeded throughout the South.

Meanwhile my liaison trips to the palace, coupled with conversations with knowledgeable newsmen and official embassy reports, confirmed Diem's politi-cal fragility. Opposed by his army, distrusted by the sects, disobeyed by the Binh Xuyen–dominated police, and facing the active hostility of influential French and Chinese business leaders, the prime minister seemed more and more a hapless pawn in a ruthless power game. As if this wasn't enough, the Geneva Conference's provision for free movement between North and South for a limited period promised to flood a war-racked South Vietnam with home-less refugees.

My advisory contributions had been modest. I screened interview requests from the international press, made contributions to the drafting of statements and speeches, assisted the press office in its day-to-day work, and diplomatically tried to convince Diem he could make his points with less verbiage. I was begin-ning to enjoy the freedom of this unusual assignment, but it was short-lived. I was asked to return to Hanoi, see to the evacuation of our Vietnamese employ-ees there, and close down the USIS office. I tried to wriggle out of the task, pointing out that it was a purely administrative job and that I was needed at the palace. My argument was rejected. All had been decided. Hellyer would take up the slack at the palace and "Red" Austin would act as embassy press officer. Martin Ackerman, a cultural affairs officer whose talents were being wasted in the tense climate of Hanoi, was to return to Saigon. I "knew" North Vietnam, I was told, and someone was needed to make "hard" decisions on the evacuation. Besides, IPS and VOA were interested in firsthand reports from the North during the transitional period.

If the goings-on in Saigon's Norodom Palace had seemed like a version of *Alice in Wonderland*, Hanoi in September of 1954 could be compared with a downmarket production of *Don Quixote*, directed by Salvador Dali. In the heavy *Götterdämmerung* atmosphere of defeat the French Expeditionary Corps chose to mark their impending departure with a number of impressive military ceremonies and parades. I was told these martial displays were designed to re-store morale and bid a fitting farewell to Tonkin. Whatever the purpose, the ceremonies only underlined the defeat of a modern, once-proud Western mili-tary force by an Asian "people's army." They also added a strange, surrealistic counterpoint to the more sobering realities of the end of an empire.

General Cogny took the salute in one of the last parades in Hanoi before the bulk of his command withdrew to the port of Haiphong. His tall figure could be seen saluting the flags of various famous regiments as Paras, Legionnaires, Senegalese, North Africans, naval detachments, and troops of *La Coloniale* marched by, followed by tanks and armored vehicles. It was a dull, rainy day. The treads of the heavy tanks chewed up the asphalt of the broad avenue near Hanoi's *Petit Lac*, and the martial beat of the music echoed through the empty, damp streets.

Hanoi's Hôtel Métropole was filling with journalists sent to cover the last days of France's presence in Tonkin and the arrival of Giap's divisions. American, French, and British correspondents filled the tables of the bar, from where they could watch the reception desk for new, interesting arrivals. Members of the International Control Commission, who would oversee the transfer of power, were easily identifiable by their uniforms: Indian Army officers with swagger sticks and bristling Guard's mustaches, pale-faced Poles in their odd triangular caps, and beer-drinking Canadians speaking their own puzzling version of French. There was already a run on air transport as French, Vietnamese, and Chinese businessmen and their families began to fly south.

I worked for several days closing down the office, burning files, and preparing office equipment and vehicles for shipment. Around the corner the consulate was going through much the same process. Thomas J. Corcoran, an unflappable Foreign Service officer, had been designated to remain at the consulate following the transition period with a minimum of staff and facilities. Once the nuts and bolts were out of the way, I had to face the painful task of approving or disapproving the staff's applications for evacuation. My guidelines were basically simple. Each Vietnamese employee and his or her immediate family were eligible. It sounded easy enough. But the Vietnamese view of what constitutes an immediate family is far different from ours. To complicate matters further I'd been authorized to decide when "special circumstances" could be applied.

Playing God in such a situation was a humbling experience. We didn't have a large staff, but each case presented problems and varying degrees of heartache. A senior employee, well dressed and sure of himself, arrived with a lengthy "family" list. A detailed discussion, taking each nominee one by one, eventually revealed that two women listed as "sisters" were the man's mistresses. A minor employee with a large family, who had spent most of his time cleaning the office, appeared in a newly laundered and patched white shirt and worn, carefully pressed trousers. He bowed his head, hesitated, and put a wrapped parcel on my desk. It contained a lacquered box that had obviously taken a large bite out of his meager wages.

In Western terms he was attempting to "buy" his way south, but in his culture he was only following the age-old system of paying tribute to someone in power with the hope of reciprocation. I refused free passage for the two mistresses with some misgivings. I needn't have worried. Their protector drew on his own resources to send them to Saigon in style on Air Vietnam. I returned the lacquered box to the cleaner, assuring the confused donor that he and his family would be on the evacuation list.

The interviews continued for three days, filling my office with extended families: Tonkinese grandmothers with betel-stained teeth; silent, big-eyed children; voluble husbands with wives whose giggles showed their nervousness. Halfway through the process I learned that the U.S. AID Mission was being particularly liberal in their evacuation policy. I decided to follow suit. We knew that our people, in the eyes of the Vietminh, were guilty of working for a U.S. "propaganda agency" and could expect to be treated accordingly. One elderly employee informed me he had decided to remain in Hanoi. I tried to dissuade him, but his mind was made up. I didn't probe for his reasons. I dug a bottle of scotch out of an otherwise empty filing cabinet and we had a last drink together in the gathering dusk. I found myself speculating that he may have been a Vietminh sympathizer all along. It was more likely he was simply tired of the war and convinced that the Vietminh, as fellow countrymen, would be no better or no worse than the previous authorities. In the end, with the exception of a few employees who were sent to open a temporary office in Haiphong, all our staff and their families were evacuated in good time.

After completing the evacuation arrangements I returned to Saigon for a brief period. I was scheduled to cover the Vietminh takeover in Hanoi, but there was no reason to cool my heels in the North during the interim. I found the embassy staff deep in deliberations on the refugee problem. Early estimates of the number of Northerners wishing to come south had been woefully low. The Vietnamese government was expecting no more than 10,000 or 12,000 refugees. The French were planning on approximately 30,000, but refugee registration was skyrocketing. Reports from Tonkin were now speaking of the possibility of hundreds of thousands seeking refuge in the South. Fearing Communist oppression and urged on by their priests, entire Catholic population centers in the Tonkin Delta were opting to leave their ancestral homes. The French, who had promised to provide air and sea transport for the refugees, were already finding their capabilities inadequate and had come to us for help.

Both Colonel Lansdale and George Hellyer saw this flight from a Communist regime as a major propaganda asset. If the fate of Vietnam was to be decided by a plebiscite, it made sense to encourage as many people as possible to leave the North, to "vote with their feet" against the Communist regime before voting again as residents of South Vietnam in the formal balloting. The spectacle of hundreds of thousands of Tonkinese fleeing before the Vietminh was bound to have a worldwide impact. Lansdale was convinced the exodus could reach well over the million mark.

I accompanied Hellyer to a special meeting called by Ambassador Heath to discuss the refugee situation. The ambassador and some of his staff were cool to the prospect of saddling the already shaky Diem regime with the logistic and political problems inherent in a major influx from the North. They were particularly chary about Lansdale's avowed purpose of encouraging such emigration on a large scale.

Lansdale argued with persistence, backed by Hellyer and Rob McClintock, but the debate became entangled in technical detail. A great deal of time was spent debating the U.S. Navy's willingness or capability to play a major part in the ferrying of refugees from Haiphong to Saigon. At one point the ambassador turned to me—as someone just back from Hanoi—and asked my opinion. I replied to the effect that it would be inconceivable if the leader of the "Free World," a nation that had put Marines ashore throughout the Pacific in World War II, couldn't now assist the fleeing noncommunist refugees of North Vietnam. It was a spontaneous comment prompted by exasperation at the officious bickering. Later, when the embassy's telegram urging full support for the refugee operation was sent to Washington, my impromptu contribution was included as part of the successful argument. It was a small, passing victory in a game of increasingly large stakes.

CHAPTER 11

Gray Dawn, Red Flags

October 9, 1954, dawned cold and damp in Hanoi. Gusts of wind rippled the surface of street puddles, and intermittent downpours filled the gutters with rushing water. An unaccustomed silence hung over the city center. The streets were empty except for a few stationary French armored cars posted at main intersections and the occasional passage of the white sedans from the International Control Commission. Offices, private villas, apartment buildings, cafés, and restaurants were closed and shuttered. The city seemed to have been emptied by some sudden plague.

By 9:00 A.M. there was a marked increase in street activity. French Army jeeps filled with officers wearing armbands rolled along the avenues on their way to the outskirts. Hired sedans crowded with journalists weren't far behind. An hour later a distant hum rose on the edge of the city and increased in volume as if a wasp's nest had been disturbed. Then the identifiable sounds of clapping and bursts of song carried toward us on the shifting wind.

The first elements of General Giap's army appeared in the distance. They came forward in two files, one on each side of the street, small men in drab uniforms wearing leaf-woven, cloth-covered helmets fitted with camouflage nets. Loaded down with weapons and equipment, the *Bo Doi* of the 308th Division were entering an environment totally unknown to most of them. Their approach was heralded by the soft shuffling of hundreds of feet in cheap tennis shoes. The Vietminh entry into Hanoi was destined to be one of the most silent victory marches in the history of the world's conquering armies.

Seeing the Vietminh face to face was a revelation. Although the United

123

States had not been technically at war in Indochina, we had always considered the Vietminh our ideological "enemy." I had seen the remains of Vietminh dead in the field. I'd watched them file past as bedraggled prisoners, I'd targeted their weak spots in psywar campaigns, and I'd been on the receiving end of their incoming rounds. Now the "invincible People's Army" appeared both impressive and vulnerable. The discipline was there, exemplified by the tight-lipped officers and political cadres who made sure their men had no personal contact with the ICC representatives or the Western press. But the naïveté of the peasant soldiers was evident in their gawking wonder at the multi-storied buildings and broad avenues of Hanoi and the shy smiles that passed over their faces as the international photographers cajoled and wheedled them to pose.

A sudden, isolated flash of red at the far end of the drab street soon became a general blossoming of color. As the Communist vanguard passed an apartment building or a row of shops, the shutters were raised, the windows flung open, and yellow-starred red flags appeared. For weeks the neighborhood "liberation committees" formed by the Vietminh cell leaders in Hanoi had been secretly producing the flags. Now they were displayed on balconies and waved by Vietnamese residents as they appeared hesitantly on the sidewalks to greet Giap's troops. Although many of the country-bred Vietminh soldiers appeared reserved, as if not quite trusting their urban countrymen, Army propaganda sections worked hard to raise the level of popular enthusiasm. Wherever a large group of civilians had congregated, the Communist psychological warriors dropped out of the line of march to sing a song, shake their victory bouquets, and lead their audience in shouts of "Free Vietnam!" and "Ho Chi Minh—one thousand years!"

Small detachments of French military police, tasked with ensuring an orderly turnover, retreated block by block, the engines of their armored cars growling in low gear, the rain hissing on the hot engine grilles. The Vietminh veterans of the assault on Dien Bien Phu eyed the French troops with curiosity. The grim-faced Frenchmen stared back, noting the Czech automatic rifles, the canvas slings of Chinese stick grenades, the captured French weapons, and the cheap white enamel mess cups stamped with the Vietminh, Chinese, and Soviet flags. Some of the Vietminh were pushing bicycles. A passing propaganda section was made up primarily of young women. Their black, shoulder-length hair hung straight under their helmets, and the shortest of them carried a guitar slung over her shoulder.

I had been in Hanoi for a week prior to the Vietminh entry. I had slept in the empty USIS residence and closed out the office for good, making sure that nothing remained behind and that all our employees had left on schedule. I'd also participated in a memorable luncheon of caviar and champagne at the restaurant Le Chalet cohosted by Dwight Martin, Don Wilson, John Mecklin, and Howard Sochurek of *Time-Life*. The unconventional Martin had decided it would be heresy to abandon the restaurant's stores of gourmet delicacies to the Communists. During a long, bibulous afternoon our small band of correspondents and government officials did its best to apply a culinary scorched-earth policy, courtesy of Henry Luce. How Martin ever justified this heavy expenditure to the accountants of *Time-Life* remains a mystery.

On my way to Hanoi I'd stopped over in Haiphong, where a U.S. Navy task force under Adm. Lorenzo S. Sabin, Jr., was soon to join the refugee evacuation effort. A number of official Americans from the embassy, AID, and MAAG were temporarily based in Haiphong. "Red" Austin had been assigned as the USIS representative to handle press liaison with the Navy and work on psywar projects designed to highlight the refugee's flight from North Vietnam. A team from Colonel Lansdale's Saigon Military Mission under the command of Maj. Lucien Conein was also present in Hanoi and Haiphong to instigate a number of shadowy "special warfare" projects.

Now, as the endless columns of the Vietminh 308th Division padded by in the cold *crachin* rain of Hanoi, I was sharing a jeep with Conein and one of his staff. I'd left my rucksack in a correspondent's room at the Hôtel Métropole, should I have to depart Hanoi in haste, and linked up with Conein to "cover" the Vietminh arrival. We were an outlandish, khaki-clad threesome wearing French Army bush hats and nothing that would identify us as Americans. I was making good use of the Rolleiflex I'd finally mastered. In a nonsensical version of official cover, I was to tell any Vietminh officer who questioned my identity that I was a Polish press officer. The only thing that came close to that description was my closely cropped hair. The fact that I didn't speak a word of Polish was troubling but not serious—as long as I stayed clear of the Poles of the ICC.

Major Conein, on the other hand, was running a considerable risk. But risk was an essential part of his life, and he thrived on it. Lucien "Lou" Conein, a.k.a. "Black Luigi," "Three-Finger Lou," or "Lou-Lou," was one of CIA's top action operatives in the Far East and already a legend in his own right. An American born in France, he had left the United States to join the French Army at the beginning of World War II. Following the fall of France, he returned to America and enlisted in the Army. Assigned to the Office of Strategic Services (OSS), Conein was dropped into occupied France to work with the Resistance. In 1945 he jumped into south China to join a Franco-Vietnamese commando group in an attack on a Japanese garrison in North Vietnam. Shortly after the war, Conein was sent to Hanoi to assist in the liberation of French prisoners detained by the Japanese. For his part in the mission he was awarded the Legion of Honor. Now, as the leader of Lansdale's team in North Vietnam, his operational brief included organizing a paramilitary "stay-behind" group of anticommunist North Vietnamese and preparing for the sabotage of industrial assets in North Vietnam in addition to overseeing a psywar campaign.

A tough, hard-drinking, and outspoken officer, the muscular, shorthaired Conein was straight from the pages of an adventure novel. His unorthodox methods, no-holds-barred reports, and frequent disregard of official hierarchy were often the bane of his superiors, both military and civilian. His experience and the depth of his contacts in Indochina were to cast him as a leading actor during America's Vietnam period. He was the type of man ambassadors and generals would turn to when things got rough—despite their personal reservations about his style and flamboyant character.

It was a strange experience to drive through the streets of Hanoi that day—two CIA officers and a USIA man—completely surrounded by Vietminh troops. At times the flow of Giap's columns was so thick we were engulfed, motionless in their midst. Once, impatient to move on but blocked by a Vietminh supply unit leading loaded mountain ponies, Conein instigated a series of cheers from the troops by shouting, "Long Live Ho Chi Minh!" in Vietnamese and punching his fist into the air. The surprised Communists responded in kind and parted before us as Conein gunned the engine and I wielded the Rolleiflex.

We witnessed the Vietminh takeover of the Lanessan Hospital, the central government buildings, and the main police headquarters. At one point I was able to photograph the legendary Soviet cameraman Karmen, who had made an international reputation for his coverage of the battle of Stalingrad. Later we turned a corner to come face to face with a group of ICC officers: Poles, Canadians, and Indians. In a brief but bizarre encounter we photographed them while they photographed us.

We returned to the Hôtel Métropole in the early afternoon. John Mecklin of *Time* magazine left a group of working journalists and took me aside. A French officer had told him the Vietminh military police were looking for a U.S. government "agent" posing as a correspondent. Mecklin suggested it might be wise for me to leave. I was never able to verify his tip. All things considered, it seemed wise to bid Hanoi adieu. I retrieved my rucksack, and Conein dropped me off near the Doumer Bridge, the exit point for the last French troops leaving the Northern capital. Conein headed back into the city on unspecified business and I tried to flag down a half-empty command car. It sped by, dousing me with muddy water. A covered Dodge truck finally rolled to a stop and I climbed over the tailgate. A disconsolate group of blanket-swathed Senegalese soldiers eyed me with indifference. One of them finally pulled an open bottle of rum from under his blanket and offered me a shot. I took a stiff swig as we rolled onto the bridge. Hanoi gradually faded from sight as another downpour drummed on the truck's canvas cover.

Haiphong was the spigot on the evacuation funnel. It had the aura of a boom town facing imminent closure. The old port city was seething with refugees, French troops waiting for sea transport, and carousing crews from French naval and merchant ships. Some official Americans working in Haiphong were quartered in the Hôtel Regina, a small establishment noted for the cracks in its walls and recurrent water shortages. It became my home for a few days as I waited for the arrival of Admiral Sabin's flagship. My plan was to cover the U.S. Navy refugee lift from Haiphong to Saigon. Meanwhile, I visited temporary refugee camps, interviewing village officials and Catholic priests who had convinced their parishioners to flee south.

Many of these priests were the modern equivalent of warrior-monks, having led their own militia forces against the Vietminh. They had been fighting a religious war in which little quarter was asked or given. One Belgian priest in a ramshackle Haiphong seminary told me of his fighting withdrawal from a small hamlet in the Tonkin Delta following the signature of the Geneva Agreements. He kept a loaded Luger on his desk, and two armed militiamen stood guard outside the door to his drafty, bare room. His men had inflicted heavy losses on the local Vietminh in that last battle. The Communists had sworn he would not leave North Vietnam alive. The priest's brown eyes burned with the fanaticism of a latter-day Torquemada. His parting comment that the Vietminh intended to dominate South Vietnam had the somber weight of prophecy.

Lansdale's SMM worked hard during the evacuation period to ensure a maximum exodus of refugees. The fine art of "gray" and "black" propaganda was used to convince wavering Tonkinese that their salvation lay in the South. Rumors spread by Vietnamese agents working for the SMM exploited the Northerner's dislike of the Vietminh's Chinese "allies." Leaflets purporting to have come from the Vietminh, hinting at tough Communist controls on commerce and extreme financial rigor, convinced local merchants to pack their bags. Close to 680,000 Catholics took the road to Haiphong, some convinced by the catchphrase that "the Virgin Mary is moving south" and promises of a good life under Diem, a devout Catholic leader.

Tales of Vietminh atrocities added to the impetus. After fighting the Vietminh for many years, the Catholics of Bui Chu and Phat Diem knew what might be in store for them if they remained behind. Many non-Catholic villagers remained unconvinced. Horrific accounts of Vietminh exactions and torture often tipped the scale of decision. Some of the stories were true, some were not. While Giap's triumphant divisions were entering Hanoi, Vietminh secret police had been busy combing the back streets of the city, well away from the ICC observers, rounding up "collaborators" and other targets on their long-established list of "people's enemies." Their ultimate interrogation and fate could only be imagined. At one point I recall arguing with Lansdale over a propaganda story about village children whose eardrums had been ruptured by the insertion of chopsticks during a Vietminh torture session. There was something about the account that didn't ring true. I had seen and heard enough of torture by both sides during my time in the field. Chopsticks had never featured as a preferred instrument. There were many more direct, simple, and horrifying methods. Lansdale only flashed his all-knowing smile and changed the subject. The chopstick story soon spread through Haiphong and was picked up by the Saigon press and some Western correspondents. The veteran psywarrior obviously knew his business.

The streets of Haiphong had become home for thousands of refugees. They lived, cooked, ate, slept, washed, and defecated on the sidewalks and in the gutters. Kerosene lamps and candles turned night into day, children cried, women argued, and men gathered on the pavement in small groups to gamble. Some villagers remained together, maintaining their hierarchical structure and discipline, ensuring that the meager relief supplies were shared. Others drifted throughout the city, following the trail of vain rumors that promised better accommodation and more plentiful food. There was already a black market in food and medicine. Some refugees parted with family gold and jewelry to procure nourishment and drugs for their sick children and elders.

Only when I joined a group of refugees to be lifted to Saigon by the U.S. Navy did I understand the human dimensions of the evacuation. I'd left the Hôtel Regina at 6:00 A.M. and arrived at the loading area an hour later. The gray skies had parted and a fiery sun was already turning mud to dust. A small U.S. Navy Higgins boat was pulled up on the beach. A beach party of two Marine Corps noncoms and some sailors sat a short distance away, smoking and talking. They were waiting for the refugee-laden trucks to arrive from the staging camp. The beach party was there to assist in the clearance and loading of the refugees onto a French LSM for the trip out to the Baie d'Along, where Admiral Sabin's flagship, a Navy transport, was waiting. Two squads of scruffy Vietnamese militia had been assigned to search the belongings of the refugees for weapons, grenades, animals, or combustibles before they boarded the LSM.

The trucks arrived in a din of squeaking brakes, banging tailgates, and authoritative shouting. The pall of dust settled slowly and the first truckload of refugees was allowed to climb down. Old men and women, their high cheekbones straining at wrinkled flesh, had to be lifted out of the truck by the more able. Bare-bottomed children tottered around the base of the truck, grasping their parents, who were loaded down with household effects, sleeping mats, and fire-blackened pots. Small girls, hardly able to walk themselves, carried their infant brothers and sisters slung papoose-style in dirty linen. These were Roman Catholics, and many wore small, heavy-cut wooden crucifixes around their necks. Three framed portraits of the Virgin Mary were among the household effects on the first truck. Two were cheap color lithographs, but one was painted directly on glass, in the Chinese style, with heavy reds and blues, the halo and edges of the portrait rich with gilt.

Little dramas erupted as the nervous refugees settled onto the rocky beach to await the landing craft. One woman had unsuccessfully tried to hide her small kitten in a wicker basket. A militiaman spotted the pet and pushed his way through the huddled peasants to snatch the animal. The woman's husband protested and at least twelve people were soon involved in an ear-piercing, if futile argument. An old man with a Ho Chi Minh beard refused to give up a kerosene bottle until a priest convinced him there would be no need to cook at sea. A Catholic militiaman among the refugees reluctantly gave up his old Mauser when he was given the choice of staying behind with the rifle or boarding without it.

The LSM finally appeared pushing a flicker of white froth in front of its bow, the tricolor snapping from a halyard. Fighting the current, it nosed into the beach and dropped its ramp with a mighty clang. French sailors in grease-stained shorts ran mooring lines ashore and made them fast. A desultory stream of refugees climbed up the metal ramp into the hot, cramped vehicle deck. Tarpaulins had been stretched over the deck to keep off the sun, but they in turn had transformed the center of the ship into a fetid furnace. I went up the ramp when the last of the 180 refugees were aboard. The ramp was lifted, the reversing engines kicked up a muddy froth, and we backed off the beach. As the bow swung seaward, another LSM was running toward the shore for the next load.

We ran into a heavy, oily swell in the Baie d'Along and the flat-bottomed landing craft began to roll. Within minutes the majority of refugees were seasick, retching and groaning on the now slippery deck. The ship's commander, a stocky, red-haired Breton, had asked me to join him on the towerlike, swaying bridge. As the stench from the hellhole below reached us, he ordered a hose detail to keep the deck clean and the canvas dampened. He then invited me below for a midmorning snack. I accepted without enthusiasm. With the bridge swaying like a pendulum, I was beginning to doubt my sealegs. The snack of coarse liver pâté on heavily buttered bread and lukewarm vin rosé served in a cramped, hot galley redolent of stewing pork and beans quickly sent me back to the open bridge.

We eventually sailed into smooth, sheltered water and past churchlike granite islands rising abruptly from the sea, capped by green brush and distorted, wind-twisted trees. The task force flagship lay off one of these islands, surrounded by squawking seabirds, its generators and cooling systems thrumming. The LSM swung alongside the loading platform at the foot of the gangway and American sailors helped the French crew tie up. The rails of the Navy transport were lined with curious gobs staring down at our untidy, odiferous cargo of refugees. A thin young naval officer appeared at the top of the gangway with a bullhorn and began to relay his captain's messages to the LSM's commander in hesitant but correct French. Navy doctor Tom Dooley was getting his first look at the suffering he would soon be working to alleviate. The time he was to spend ashore in the refugee camps would also propagate a fierce personal anticommunism later reflected in his book *Deliver Us From Evil* and numerous personal appearances on the lecture circuit in the United States.

The refugees were brought aboard and deloused. They were served generous portions of rice from huge stainless-steel vats and settled in their new quarters. I was shown to an empty cabin and told I'd be eating in the wardroom during the trip south. Late that evening, while I was taking a saltwater shower, the ship's engines began to vibrate, the transport's anchor was raised, and we headed for Saigon with our cargo of 1,800 refugees.

The trip took three days. The long, impressive coast of Vietnam passed on our starboard side. Abrupt, palm-tipped cliffs towered over deserted white sand beaches. Waterfalls spouted from rocky promontories. The mouths of roiling rivers were masked by thick forests of green bamboo, and thatched fishing villages clustered in reef-protected bays. Examining some coastal hamlets south of the seventeeth parallel through the powerful fixed binoculars on the bridge, we could see Vietminh flags flying over the huts. One morning the sea around us looked like a butterfly convention, dotted with the white sails of small fishing vessels. I filed some stories on the refugees to USIA and interviewed crusty Admiral Sabin on the Navy's role in the evacuation.

The refugees adapted quickly to their temporary floating home, staking out their family territory on the open decks. The children, now wearing sailor hats and baseball caps, had discovered chewing gum and Hershey bars. Solicitous sailors attempted to teach them English. "Okay" and "Number one" were the mainstays of their vocabulary. The sick bay was always full. Tuberculosis and malnutrition were endemic, particularly among the aged. Doctors and corpsmen worked round the clock treating everything from burns to worms. A screen was rigged for film projections under the stars, and the mesmerized refugees watched the glittering productions of Hollywood, murmuring, clucking their tongues, and laughing at the international language of slapstick.

By the time we nosed into the Saigon docks I was more than eager to debark. It was a stifling, humid day. The muddy Saigon River was unruffled by any breeze. I was anxious to see my wife and dying for a cold bottle of Tiger beer on the terrace of the Continental. I had survived the Navy's blue-stocking rule on alcohol, but Navy coffee and Coke were not my idea of tropical coolants. The refugees were being mustered on deck with all their belongings, and a reception committee had gathered ashore. I scanned the dock until I located my wife. She was standing well away from the main group. It soon became apparent why she was keeping her distance. The American Women's Club of Saigon had gathered in the full bloom of their well-meaning, do-gooder philosophy to welcome the refugees. The AWC members were mostly embassy and MAAG wives, bolstered by the spouses of some expatriate Americans in the oil or export business. Now, as lines were thrown ashore, the gangway was made ready, and ambulances backed closer to the dockside, the American women edged forward.

It was an unbelievable sight. Most of them were dressed in light, colorful frocks and some—in the interest of protocol—were actually wearing hats and gloves! They positioned themselves on each side of the gangway and prepared to hand out welcoming gifts to the refugees. I gritted my teeth when I recognized one of Dixie Reese's Vietnamese photographers standing by to record the immortal moment. As the first refugee family stepped onto the dock, confused and fearful in their new environment, the president of the AWC stepped forward to present them with several bananas and a large, cellophane-wrapped block of American cheese. The presentations continued, the camera clicked, and the refugees climbed aboard the waiting trucks that would take them to their tent camps. The Tonkinese, not being cheese-eaters, were thoroughly confused by the thick yellow slabs. Twenty-four hours later the first complaints were received from the camps. The American "soap" was *pas bon*. It didn't produce suds or clean properly. When the refugees finally discovered they were dealing with cheese, they sold it to middlemen, who in turn sold it to Saigon's street merchants, who sold it back to Americans at an inflated price. For months toasted cheese hors d'oeuvres were a feature at official American receptions in Saigon.

My resentment at the publicity-seeking charade at dockside was quickly forgotten when I was reunited with my wife. The tensions and sadness of the last days in Hanoi were shelved for an intimate celebration. At four the next morning I was awakened by the sound of noisy engines and singing. I walked out onto the balcony. For a moment I thought I was back in Hanoi. Uncovered military trucks filled with Vietminh troops were driving through the center of Saigon on their way to the docks. Fully uniformed and waving red flags, the Vietminh were chanting and shouting slogans, doing their best to wake up the city. These were Communist units that had been fighting in South Vietnam but were now being sent north under the Geneva Accords. The French had planned to sneak them to their ships in the early-morning hours, but they hadn't counted on the political cadre's determination to milk the situation for the utmost propaganda. Only Saigon's deep sleepers remained unaware of the boisterous Vietminh departure.

When I flopped back into bed exhausted, my wife said she had something to tell me. I suggested it could wait till daylight, but she insisted it was important. I dozed off as she spoke, but some of the message must have lodged in my subconscious. I awoke with a start at 7:00 A.M. and shook her awake. Was I imagining things, I asked, or had she told me . . . ? Yes, it was true. She was pregnant. A celebratory breakfast was definitely in order.

Political storm clouds were gathering over Saigon by mid-October 1954. The Vietnamese chief of staff, General Nguyen Van Hinh, was openly plotting against Prime Minister Diem, refusing direct commands and making his lack of respect for Diem known to the media. The Army's psychological section had shifted their effort from the Vietminh to the Diem regime and some bright young officers were using their press contacts to spread stories about the prime minister's inability to rule.

I had known General Hinh since 1952, having brought American journalists to his headquarters for interviews and talked with him informally at George Hellyer's pool parties. He was an intelligent and personable officer, but he was also a French citizen with close links to the colonial past. He maintained direct contact with the fickle Emperor Bao Dai, who had never been overly fond of Ngo Dinh Diem. My first visit to General Staff Headquarters on routine business following my return from Haiphong took place in an unusually cool atmosphere. Although some of Hinh's staff were willing to discuss the reports of Vietminh arms caches near the seventeenth parallel and the need to publicize them, they were obviously occupied with planning Hinh's move on Diem. Under the circumstances, official American visitors had a low popularity rating among his staff.

While Hinh was plotting to unseat Diem, General Bay Vien of the Binh Xuyen was flaunting his own close association with Bao Dai in a way that was certain to offend the moral scruples of the prime minister. He had built The Hall of Mirrors, a gigantic new bordello complex near Cholon. This walled, landscaped sex emporium was more upmarket than the Parc aux Buffles. Well-constructed small villas separated by paths, ponds, trees, and plants housed from six to twelve prostitutes under the direction of a "house mother." Mirrors were the salient feature of these love nests. There were mirrors on the walls and ceilings of the small rooms, mirrors in the reception area and behind the bars. Exhausted customers could regain their strength in a luxurious restaurant or dawdle at the tables of a gambling casino. The entire project, an ostentatious display of Bay Vien's position as both warlord and vice king, was an abomination to Diem and his advisers as they tried to cope with the influx of destitute refugees and the post-Geneva chaos.

General Hinh, confident that the Army—the only real power in South Vietnam—would remain loyal to him, and counting on help from his longtime French supporters, had refused Diem's order to give up his command. Even after a warning from Lansdale that any move against Diem would mean the cutoff of U.S. funding, Hinh continued on a collision course. At one point his psywar experts took over the Radio Vietnam studios in Saigon and ridiculed Diem in their output.

In the ensuing "battle of the press conferences" Hinh put on a virtuoso performance at his villa during a morning meeting with Vietnamese and foreign journalists. He appeared sure of himself and forceful, underlining his role as a military leader in the war against the Communists, stressing his loyalty to Bao Dai and the nation, and expressing concern that the Diem regime was not up to its task.

Later the same day I received a call from Diem's office asking my assistance in preparing for a press conference the prime minister intended to give that evening. I hurried to the palace, now renamed *Doc Lap*, or "Freedom" Palace, where I was asked to update the press office's list of foreign correspondents in Saigon. Diem's staff was frantically telephoning the media to make sure no one went uninvited. In the end, it would have been better if they had. The press conference was a disaster. The prime minister appeared visibly tired and shaken. He answered the journalists' questions in monosyllables, his head down. It was as if he had already accepted his fate. I sat on the edge of a delicate gilded chair, mentally framing the obvious responses that never came. Most of the newsmen left that night with the obituary of the Diem government in mind. Some of them put it into print. My report on the conference to Hellyer was equally gloomy. I didn't believe Diem would be around much longer.

But the press, and many of us at the embassy, had underestimated the effectiveness of Lansdale's fine Machiavellian hand. The quiet colonel, advised that Hinh was planning a definitive coup in late October, invited the general and two of his top aides and fellow plotters to visit the Philippines over the same period of time. Hinh declined, but as the purpose of the junket was to profit from counterinsurgency lessons learned in the Philippines, he agreed to let his aides travel. The general could hardly have used the planned coup as an excuse to keep them in Saigon. While Hinh's aides were kept busy and entertained royally in Manila, Lansdale carried out a crash program of shoring up support for Diem, improving the palace's defenses, and restoring the prime minister's confidence. Although General Hinh's plotting continued, the right moment for a successful coup had passed. But Diem was now faced by a new threat. Encouraged by the diehards of the 2ème Bureau and SDECE, the Binh Xuyen and the religious-military sects were moving toward an armed alliance designed to topple the Diem government.

CHAPTER 12

Politics
& Payoffs

It was an unusual party. Preoccupied by the refugee evacuation and the threat of a possible coup led by General Hinh, many of us had not been monitoring the return of prisoners released by the Vietminh. Not so Dixie Reese. In late October he'd methodically traced the movements of our friends captured at Dien Bien Phu and organized a small drinks party for them at his apartment. The men we hadn't expected to see again were suddenly there in the flesh.

After the first greetings a pall settled over the celebration. There was the usual abundance of liquor and food and the gangling, smiling Reese outdid himself as a host. But all the attention and sympathy in the world would never bridge the gap between those who had experienced Vietminh captivity and those who had not. These were men who had survived death marches, starvation, illness, and constant psychological pressure in compulsory "reeducation" sessions. They were gaunt and thin. They seemed to float in their newly issued uniforms. No army quartermaster could have imagined fitting such scarecrows, and yet the returnees had been under special care and feeding for weeks since their release.

Bigeard, the para commander, was there, chin high but unusually quiet. He was now a lieutenant colonel, thanks to his battlefield promotion at Dien Bien Phu. Combat cameraman Schoendoerffer stood by the bar sipping a bourbon, his face still puffy from the rice diet of the camps. For an hour or more, until the alcohol had taken effect, the conversation was light and meaningless, skirting the defeat, the significance of Geneva, and the coming French withdrawal.

133

In the awkward, forced gaiety of the moment only a very brash American would have questioned the French guests on their personal experiences in captivity. We sensed an invisible wall between us. We could see ourselves in their eyes as well-fed, secure dilettantes whose horizons were limited to the outskirts of Saigon and the next diplomatic reception. To make things more awkward, political reality had rewritten the scenario. We were no longer "allies" in Indochina. To a certain extent we had now become rivals.

As the evening progressed and the whiskey flowed, it became obvious that some of our friends *did* want to talk of their experiences. They wanted us to understand what they had endured in the camps and the threat others might face in the future. I believe they also wanted to shed some of their clinging, sleep-troubling memories by bringing them out in the open.

Bigeard and I stood alone on the balcony as he told me of the bravery and fate of his *gars*, the men of the 6th Battalion whom I had met and patrolled with during my stay at Dien Bien Phu. He spoke of the psychological techniques practiced in the camps by the Vietminh, the constant lectures on the evils of "imperialism," and the reward and punishment tactics used to divide and subdue the prisoners. A slight addition to the 800 grams of rice a day for those who cooperated, and a cut in the ration for those who didn't, a matter of survival or death to those suffering from beriberi, dysentery, and other diseases. Bigeard was seriously concerned about the future of the French Army following Indochina. He had seen the effects of the moral gangrene of defeat and the effectiveness of Communist indoctrination, particularly among the colonial troops. This troubled him deeply, as echoes of unrest in Algeria were filtering through to Saigon. Algeria was soon to be part of Bigeard's future, along with more combat, wounds, decorations, and fame as one of the few French commanders who could match the guerrilla warfare skills of the Algerian rebels.

Schoendoerffer described the escape attempt he and Peraud had made from a nighttime convoy on the way to a prison camp. They had carefully noted that their Molotova truck was in darkness for a few seconds when the truck behind them rounded a curve. They'd made a quick decision. At the next temporary blackout they'd leaped to the ground and sprinted for the jungle. They'd become separated. Schoendoerffer told of hiding himself in a swampy depression among fallen tree branches, hearing the shouts of the searching guards and seeing their flashing lights. When a *Bo Doi* approached he'd ducked under water. Luck had not been with him. The guard stepped on his submerged head, and his reflex reaction had given him away. Beaten and threatened with death, he was thrown back on the truck. Later Schoendoerffer and Bigeard—who had also made an escape attempt—had been bound together back to back for several days as an example. Peraud had not returned. Schoendoerffer was profoundly upset by the disappearance of his close friend, but hoped for some miracle, a technical delay or administrative error that might still find his colleague appearing in a late release. This was not to be. The carefree Peraud was never seen again.

Shortly after Reese's party I learned of another tragedy that had been muted in the aftermath of the armistice. A captain of commandos with whom I shared early-morning coffee at La Pagode told me that many tribal partisans of the GCMA had been abandoned to the tender mercy of the Vietminh in the rush toward evacuation. Messages had been sent instructing these loyal guerrilla fighters to trek southward to join the main French forces. Compliance in almost all cases had been impossible. They were isolated in their mountains and jungles, tracked by specially trained Vietminh units, and their supply drops had been discontinued. Another instruction recommended surrender as an option. Those who knew the no-quarter character of the GCMA's war in the shadows considered such a suggestion a humorless joke in very poor taste.

The brutal abandonment of the tribal guerrillas following the Geneva Agreements provided the Vietminh with a propaganda theme for future use among the tribal minorities. The treatment of the GCMA was cited as an example of the white man's exploitation of what Europeans considered inferior races. It also had a profound effect on French officers who had been forced to abandon the small partisan units with which they had lived and fought. A few French officers and noncoms opted to remain with their commands, fighting to the end. As long as two years after the cease-fire, desperate radio messages pleading for ammunition and supplies were to be picked up by monitoring facilities. The stigma of guilt attached to this episode was to surface again in the early 1960s, when elements of the French Army, faced with the abandonment of Algeria, revolted against the authority of the Paris government. The same pattern appeared in Vietnam later when American Special Forces officers working with tribal groups actually sided with the Montagnards in their opposition to Vietnamese government control. At the time of the U.S. departure, some CIA operatives and Green Beret officers had deep personal misgivings about leaving these tribal fighters in the lurch.

November of 1954 saw another changing of the guard in Saigon. Ambassador Heath packed his bags and prepared to hand over the American residence to special presidential envoy Gen. J. Lawton "Lightning Joe" Collins. The calm, low-key Heath, whom many of us had criticized as too conservative and hesitant, had performed an intricate diplomatic balancing act during a particularly difficult period. He had managed to follow Washington's directives to keep the French fighting and relatively happy. At the same time he'd reassured Vietnamese nationalists that U.S. policy supported a free and independent Vietnam. Perhaps his most difficult task had been to ride herd on a constantly growing American Mission including elements of the military and many separate civilian agencies that often quarreled among themselves over responsibilities and precedence. The diminutive Heath, with his flat-brimmed fedora, hid a fiery temper under his benign exterior, but he always had time to cope with the personal problems of his staff. Shortly before his departure he and his wife calmly presided over the wedding of a young officer and a local Frenchwoman at the ambassadorial residence. The bride was hugely pregnant but the Heaths carried it off with grace and aplomb.

George Hellyer had also completed his tour in Vietnam and left for an assignment in Washington as USIA's deputy director in charge of the Far East section. His second, Ed Stansbury, took over in Saigon. Hellyer's wartime service in Burma, his experience as a tea planter in the Far East, and his knowledge of the French and the French language had combined to make him the right man at the right time in Saigon.

General Collins, the former army chief of staff, had made a name for himself in Europe during World War II under Eisenhower's overall command. He, like General O'Daniel, was the type of officer President Eisenhower trusted and felt comfortable with. Collins was also a friend of Gen. Paul Ely, the former French chief of staff, who had replaced General Navarre. The author of the famous Navarre Plan had left Saigon with the utmost discretion. The pencil-thin Ely, reputed to be a diplomat as well as a soldier, had been sent to oversee France's last days in Indochina. It was thought that Ely and Collins could work well together, minimizing Franco-American tensions. But the gray-haired, steely-eyed Collins, like many high-ranking American military men who were to follow him to Vietnam, was entering a new, totally different world. Saigon was a confused, chaotic political environment where yes often meant no and the best staff work in the world could become meaningless overnight.

General Collins and Colonel Lansdale were poles apart in their backgrounds and methods. Collins was accustomed to the orderly course of planning, the framework of military hierarchy, and the movement and progression of divisions, corps, and armies.

Lansdale's world was that of special operations, counterinsurgency, subterfuge, and political maneuvering. In the months following Collins's arrival, the two of them were to differ repeatedly on methods and goals. By early December Collins was already expressing doubt about Diem's ability to hold the country together. But, after a detailed briefing on General Hinh's plotting activities, Collins did agree with Lansdale that the recalcitrant general should leave Vietnam. Once again the specter of an American aid cutoff was waved at Bao Dai. Although the emperor had been suggesting that Diem include Hinh in his cabinet, he finally ordered the general to France and dismissed him for "ill-advised statements." Hinh effortlessly changed uniforms, becoming a French Air Force general and later deputy chief of staff of the French Air Force.

The press section of USIS was now shorthanded and overworked. "Red" Austin was still in Haiphong and I was finding it hard to keep up with the demands on our services. Luckily Dinh Le Ngoan and Jimmy Hao, the chiefs of our Vietnamese and Chinese sections, were professional staffers able to keep the day-to-day operations running smoothly. I remained the embassy press officer, responsible for the new ambassador's media relations. The U.S. AID Mission, MAAG, the Saigon Military Mission, and visiting American officials called on us for help. There had also been an increase in the flow of American and foreign correspondents seeking briefings and appointments with U.S. and Vietnamese officials. My absence in Haiphong had diminished my role at the palace, where Lansdale had become a full-time adviser and confidant to Diem. In addition, an American friend and supporter of Diem, Professor Wesley Fischel of Michigan State University, had put together a contract team to advise the new government on everything from land reform to "public safety," or police procedures. But I could still count on two or three calls a week from Diem's press staff asking for practical assistance and advice. Bob Gildea, a newly married ex-newsman from Pennsylvania, arrived in Saigon in December and was assigned to my section as an assistant press officer. Gildea's sense of humor in the most difficult of times was to prove a welcome asset.

Our active participation in Franco-Vietnamese psywar projects had ended with Geneva, but the publication and press sections of USIS had increased their collaboration with the SMM. One of Lansdale's objectives was to build support for Diem in Saigon's Vietnamese-language newspapers. All newspapers in Vietnam had traditionally depended on the government for their survival, and there was a long-established censorship mechanism. Under the French any newspaper that didn't toe the line was automatically deprived of newsprint.

The immediate post-Geneva period had thrown the local press into turmoil. Pro-French papers and those supported by the sects had joined the anti-Diem camp, walking a difficult tightrope between so-called constructive criticism and outright denigration. Fence-sitting editors were testing the turgid waters of a shaky press freedom with criticisms of the former French administration and Bao Dai. With help from our office Lansdale made contact with a number of publishers and editors, including Anna Cang, a seductive newspaper proprietor known as the Dragon Lady. At one point he stepped in to keep her paper from being closed by the government. He was to write in a SMM team report later published in *The Pentagon Papers* that she "found it profitable to heed our advice on the editorial content of her paper." Following other such visits, certain editors became more supportive of the Diem government and receptive to USIS-supplied material. The pro-government newspapers *Tu Do* and *Hoa Binh* began a propaganda campaign, supported by vitriolic cartoons, attacking Ho Chi Minh and his Chinese "masters." They also sniped at the French and their Vietnamese "puppets," an indirect reference to the religious-military sects.

By late December 1954, a joint French-American command had been hammered together to train the Vietnamese National Army. The operation of the Training Relations Instruction Mission (TRIM) was far from smooth. Many French officers assigned to TRIM were now short-timers who resented the growth of U.S. influence. Their American counterparts were eager to take over full training responsibilities. But TRIM did function, thanks in part to the Ely-Collins friendship. If nothing else it provided a measure of cohesion and purpose to an army that had been badly shaken by the Vietminh victory and faced an uncertain future. The training responsibility would eventually pass to the United States. The Vietnamese destined to become the cadre for the Army of the Republic of Vietnam (ARVN) had already suffered from a split personality under French command. They would now have to absorb the imported military methods of a Western army with little if any knowledge of Vietnam, its history, military traditions, language, or terrain.

The threat to the Diem government from the sects increased during the first weeks of 1955. Cao Dai and Hoa Hao troops had rushed to take over territory formerly controlled by the Vietminh before government forces could assert their authority. Diem's attempts to control the police and security forces in Saigon had met with blatant opposition from Bao Dai's protégé, General Bay Vien of the Binh Xuyen. By early January it had become apparent that the government would have to act or lose what little authority it had. Diem decided to hit the Binh Xuyen where it hurt. He refused to renew the gambling license of Bay Vien's Grand Monde. At 6:00 A.M. on January 16, the small wooden balls ceased to click around the brightly painted roulette wheels and the sing-song voices of the Chinese girls behind the busy dice tables were stilled. The largest and most profitable gambling hall in Vietnam had taken in its last piaster.

To Bay Vien, the tough vice lord and former river pirate, Diem's move was the equivalent of a declaration of war aimed both at him and Emperor Bao Dai. Encouraged by his French "advisers," Vien began to flex his military muscle while planning coordinated action with the Cao Dai and Hoa Hao. Binh Xuyen troops set up arbitrary checkpoints and road barriers in the Saigon-Cholon area. Hoa Hao units began to block food supplies headed for Saigon. Cao Dai soldiers harassed Vietnamese Army outposts near Tay Ninh. Tension built as green-bereted Binh Xuyen troops installed sandbag and barbed wire defenses around their police and security headquarters on Rue Catinat within rifle range of Diem's palace.

In the middle of this turmoil my wife and I moved to a small house in Saigon's western residential area. She was expecting our first child in a short time, and the downtown apartment would have been too small for us. The house was low and well ventilated. Bougainvillea and frangipani blossoms perfumed a small open patio fitted with a bamboo bar, and geckos clicked and scurried on the walls and ceilings. The security situation left much to be desired. We were far from any other American residences and the nearest police post was at a considerable distance. There was a Catholic church around the corner protected by some resident militiamen, and a French noncom and his wife lived a few doors away. A French Army camp housing Senegalese and North African troops was two minutes distant by jeep, but its presence provided cold comfort. The state of Franco-American relations being what they were, only a dreamer could envisage help from that quarter. We hired an excellent Vietnamese cook and his daughter as live-in servants. Gildea presented us with a twist-tailed, randy black cat. A cross section of the Saigon press corps and colleagues from the Vietnamese government and American Mission dropped by for an impromptu housewarming and we settled into our first home in Saigon.

It was a strange experience driving to work each day past the barricaded police headquarters in the center of Saigon. Binh Xuyen machine gun positions covered the Rue Catinat, the wide square in front of Saigon's cathedral, and the post office. Several hundred yards away, Diem's praetorian guard of Catholic militiamen and loyal Army troops had set up defensive positions in the palace grounds. A great deal of crucial bargaining was going on behind the

scenes of this bellicose standoff. Diem, with the help of his brother Ngo Dinh
Nhu, had launched an intensive campaign of intrigue against his opponents.
Colonel Lansdale and his SSM concentrated their efforts on breaking up the
alliance of the sects and fragmenting their military unity. Bountiful CIA funds,
including pay for their troops and promises of high rank in the National Army,
were used to convince "dissident" sect leaders to rally to the government.

Two days before the January 16 gambling crackdown, Col. Nguyen Van Hue
of the Hoa Hao had brought his 3,500 men into Diem's camp. Two weeks later
another Hoa Hao contingent of 1,500 fighters under Maj. Nguyen Day joined
them. For several months Lansdale and his staff had been working to bring
Cao Dai general Trinh Minh Thé into the fold. Thé was a thin, intense guerrilla leader with long experience in the hard school of survival. A hefty sum,
to be used as "back pay" for his troops, put Thé and his 5,000 men on the
government's side. This influx of new allies brought strange visitors to the palace. Some of the black-clad Hoa Hao and Cao Dai officers looked more piratical than the Binh Xuyen. Loud, scarred, and heavily armed, they resembled a
gathering of Asian Rambos spoiling for a fight.

Le Quang Vinh was one of these Hoa Hao military leaders. He was better
known as *Ba-Cut* ("cut finger") since the day he'd chopped off one of his digits
with a hatchet, swearing to drive all Frenchmen from Vietnam. Now, with
funding and an adviser supplied by Major Savani of the 2ème Bureau, Ba Cut
threw in his lot with the anti-Diem forces. It was a decision that would cost
him his head.

While more sect leaders, including another Cao Dai general, Nguyen Thanh
Phoung, and Hoa Hao general Tran Van Soai, were courted by the Diem regime, the Binh Xuyen pushed for the formation of a "Unified Front of Nationalist Forces." Pro-sect Vietnamese politicians carried out an active campaign
attempting to convince Americans that Diem was destroying national unity
and thus delivering the nation to the Vietminh. I was on the receiving end of
this effort after accepting an invitation from a Saigon editor to dine at a Vietnamese restaurant in Cholon. One of Gen. Bay Vien's "advisers," a chubby
politician in a spotless white suit, sat opposite me at the table. As we worked
our way through the house specialty of seven beef courses and three bottles of
Bordeaux, the politician tried to convince me that Bay Vien was a fervent
anticommunist and supporter of the "Free World." He charitably described
Diem as naïve and inexperienced, a well-meaning man who was no match for
the Vietminh. By the time we reached our coffee and cognac he had brushed
a broad picture of Binh Xuyen military prowess and suggested I meet some of
these "truly nationalist" fighters. I declined that invitation, as well as one to
accompany our host to a nearby bordello noted for its young girls. Driving
back to Saigon, I decided the Binh Xuyen were making an effort to reach the
middle-grade officers of the American Mission because their top-level contacts
were practically nonexistent. Either that or they had an exaggerated idea of my
official status.

The political situation continued to deteriorate. On March 22 the sects issued an ultimatum demanding that Diem restructure his government to include a cabinet of "National Union" in which they would be well represented. He was given five days to comply. Tension in the city became bowstring tight, and it wasn't confined to the armed opponents. A distinct division was now apparent within the American Mission. On the surface it was pro-Diem and anti-Diem. On a more profound level the conflict reflected the differences between Ambassador Collins and Colonel Lansdale, between those who believed the French could still play a stabilizing role and took General Ely at his word and those who saw the French as spoilers and wanted them out of Vietnam as soon as possible. The former group included many State Department officers. The latter group was made up largely of officers from USIA, AID, MAAG, and the SMM. I was firmly in the latter category as one of the embassy's so-called "Young Turks."

I was also on the verge of becoming a father for the first time. Mary Alice had borne the burden of an uncomfortable pregnancy in a steamy tropical climate without complaining about my long, uncertain hours, the sudden appearances of newsmen and government colleagues in search of food and drink, and the ever-present danger of the volatile situation. She was under the care of Dr. Dé, a U.S.-trained Vietnamese obstetrician, and tentative arrangements had been made for a bed in Saigon's Clinique Saint-Paul.

I had kept some other concerns to myself. Working so closely with the Diem regime in liaison with Lansdale had marked me—along with certain other USIA officers—as pro-Diem and anti–Binh Xuyen. My role as embassy spokesman and the fact that I had been in Indochina since 1952 and had developed a wide spread of Vietnamese and French contacts meant I was comparatively well known in Saigon. Rumors had reached me that my name figured on a Binh Xuyen death list. The rumors had been supported by a number of hints from Vietnamese newspapermen that I should pay more attention to my personal security. As the most pointed of these comments came from pro-sect sources, I took them to be a mild form of psychological warfare. Nevertheless, my wife's vulnerability in an isolated, unguarded villa was a constant worry.

On March 28 Diem, rather than responding to the sects' ultimatum, issued one of his own. The Binh Xuyen were to vacate immediately the installations they'd occupied in Saigon. He also ordered National Army parachutists to reclaim the police station held by the Binh Xuyen on the Boulevard Galliéni, between Saigon and Cholon. Diem's precipitate action set the telephone lines humming as General Ely moved to intercede and the sects prepared for a showdown.

The afternoon of March 29, as mobile Army and Binh Xuyen patrols began shadowing each other through the streets of Saigon, my wife's labor pains began. Dr. Dé had left for a short visit to Paris and his replacement was unreachable. We decided it best to go directly to the hospital. Driving cautiously along the deserted streets, and straining our ears for the sound of approaching vehicles, we passed the French camp. It was on full alert, all positions manned, gleaming cartridge belts fed into the machine guns. A grim, no-nonsense nun at the Clinique-Saint Paul signed my wife in and guided us to a fourth-floor room. It opened onto a long, wide balcony that circled the old colonial building, providing a good view over Saigon. The nun assured me that the birth was still hours away. Once my wife was settled, I drove to the office to check the latest developments and warn Gildea that I'd be spending the night at the hospital.

It was dusk when I returned. The contractions were more frequent and the nun was trying to contact the doctor. I was holding my wife's hand, nervously uttering platitudes, when an explosion made us both jump. The unmistakable *crump-spang* of exploding mortar rounds was followed by the deep *tock-tock-tock* of a heavy machine gun. Then there was the sudden popping of small-arms fire and the wail of a distant siren. I reached the balcony in time to see a jeepload of Binh Xuyen troopers speed through a cross street below. Seconds later a half-track filled with National Army infantry sped by in the opposite direction. If they'd met at the intersection we'd have had a firefight within fifty yards of the hospital.

The main action was taking place in the direction of Cholon. Deceptively slow-moving tracers were skimming horizontally over the rooftops. Ricochets bounced skyward to disappear in the low clouds. Dr. Dé's French replacement joined me on the balcony. He had left his wife in town and was worried about her safety. Extremely agitated, he told me that during all the time he'd worked in Afghanistan he'd never experienced open warfare. A cry from my wife sent us back to her room. The doctor finished his examination and briefed me on the use of a portable anesthetic mask. He asked me to help by sharing the mask between my wife and an Indian woman whose room was farther along the balcony.

I spent the rest of the night sprinting from one room to the other as the expectant mothers called for the soothing mask. The sound of battle made it possible to follow the ebb and flow of the fighting. A diminution meant the government troops were pushing toward Cholon; an increase signaled a Binh Xuyen counterattack in the direction of Saigon. Ambulances had begun to arrive in the hospital's courtyard. The nuns performed a quick triage, and litter bearers carried the wounded inside. By dawn all firing had stopped, the Indian woman had given birth to a chubby, raven-haired daughter, and my wife had fallen into an exhausted sleep. I called Gildea, who told me a truce had been arranged by the French after the government troops had taken the police headquarters on Boulevard Galliéni. The authoritative nun, who'd been busy with the wounded all night, suggested I get some rest and promised to call me if the birth appeared imminent. I drove home, uneasily aware that my jeep was painted the same dark green as those of the Binh Xuyen.

I awoke with a start. I'd taken a quick shower and lain down for a short nap. The short nap had gone on for over two hours. I hurried back to the hospital to find that our first daughter, Shawn, had been born in the interim. Later, while sending telegrams to the new grandparents from the central post office, I encountered an Agence France Presse correspondent. He had been covering the fighting and had just filed his story to Paris. I proudly told him I was a father for the first time. He ignored my euphoria completely.

"You Americans had better drop Diem," he warned, "before he tears this country apart." At that particular moment I came dangerously close to committing voluntary homicide.

CHAPTER 13

Blood in the Streets

An uneasy peace had descended on Saigon. It was marked by a loosely enforced nighttime curfew in Cholon and surreptitious preparations for a renewal of hostilities by both sides. The French-imposed cease-fire was a one-sided affair. French tanks blocked the movement of Vietnamese government troops while ignoring the resupply of Binh Xuyen forces arranged by their 2ème Bureau advisers. Ambassador Collins's approval of General Ely's action in stopping Diem's move against the sects was interpreted by the beleaguered prime minister as the possible first step toward repudiation of his government by the Americans. In addition, Diem's request for assistance in transferring some badly needed Army battalions from central Vietnam to Saigon had been turned down by the French.

Through it all the "Pearl of the Orient" still glowed. Despite the untouched, sandbagged stronghold of the Binh Xuyen at the top of Rue Catinat, the street remained brightly lit, its bars and restaurants full. But violence simmered just under the surface. Bloated, unidentified Vietnamese corpses were fished from the *Arroyo Chinois*, hands bound, bullet holes behind the ears.

We were leading a highly charged, nerve-jangling existence: adjusting to an infant's nocturnal demands, boiling water for the formula, and keeping an eye out for mammoth cockroaches near the crib. At the same time we remained alert to any change in the pattern of street noises or signs of a prowler and slept with a loaded .38 within reach. I would rush to the office early and hurry to the palace, to Vietnam Presse, to the embassy, or to some doubtful rendezvous with a Vietnamese contact who had something "important" to pass on.

One moment I'd be filing a story on the Saigon situation to Washington, the next I'd be arguing on the phone with a sympathetic but unreactive administrative officer about the need for a twenty-four-hour guard at our villa. Bomb threats directed at Americans prompted an embassy security officer to give an uninspired demonstration on how to carry a suspected bomb out of range on the blade of a shovel. It was not a confidence-building performance.

The crisis atmosphere at Diem's palace was palpable. The normally spotless floors were scruffy with bootprints from the coming and going of soldiers and Catholic militiamen. Troops were improving their positions in the palace grounds, wielding entrenching tools, and filling sandbags. The brief clash with the Binh Xuyen had encouraged some young Vietnamese parachute officers who now felt the Binh Xuyen could be defeated. They resented General Ely's intervention, accusing the French of stepping in to save their unsavory protégés. Other elements in the Army were fence-sitting, hoping the confused situation would clarify itself before they were forced to make a choice.

If the political advisers of the Binh Xuyen–led "Unified Front of Nationalist Forces" had been busy before the fighting on Boulevard Galliéni, they were now downright frantic. The politician and adviser to the Binh Xuyen I had dined with in Cholon sent one of his emissaries to my office with word that he would like to see me at Binh Xuyen headquarters. His messengers gave me a signed pass. I discussed the invitation with Ed Stansbury. After consultation with the embassy's political section, it was decided I should go. Considering the situation, every scrap of information we could get on the Binh Xuyen, their intentions, or willingness to compromise could be important. Because of the risk involved, the final decision was left to me and I was warned not to go alone.

The next morning, with Bob Gildea beside me, I drove our press jeep out along Boulevard Galliéni, through the National Army lines, and into the silent no-man's land leading to the first Binh Xuyen roadblock. We'd been joking about which one of us would remain behind if the Binh Xuyen demanded a hostage, but our levity faded at our first encounter with Bay Vien's men. The long-haired officer who waved us down was wearing a red sport shirt and camouflage trousers. His gold-capped teeth were clamped on an ivory cigarette holder. He held a cocked British revolver in his hand, and a holstered Colt automatic hung from his hip. The .50 caliber machine gun in a sandbagged position was pointed directly at our windshield. The officer approached slowly, examining the lettering BAO CHI-HOA KY (American Press) on the jeep's front panel. His eyes had the same dull, expressionless quality I'd noted among the black-clad professional assassins who worked for French Intelligence in North Vietnam. I held out my pass and he examined it at great length before calling two of his companions over for a brief consultation. He finally returned the paper and waved us through.

Three roadblocks later we drove onto the Y bridge leading to Binh Xuyen headquarters, inched through the oil drums and wire of a last barrier, and rolled up in front of Bay Vien's fortified stronghold. The nerve center of the

Binh Xuyen's military effort was a busy place. A tall radio mast rose above the roof of the headquarters building, and groups of officers in a mix of military and civilian garb were scattered over the wide entrance stairway. As agreed, Gildea remained in the jeep while an armed sentry led me inside. The adviser was waiting, impeccable in the same ice cream suit. We sat down in a wide central room, where I happened to be facing a closed door. From the position of the mast I'd seen outside, I guessed the door led to the radio room.

I was greeted with the usual *politesse*, served a lukewarm orange soda, and listened to a justification and defense of Binh Xuyen actions. The principal theme was that we Americans just did not understand the seriousness of the situation. By supporting Diem we would break the spirit and resolve of true nationalists and hand Vietnam over to the Communists. If the armies of the sects were crushed, large areas of the countryside would fall to the Vietminh. As my host warmed to his theme, I was surprised to see a French soldier wearing the crash helmet of a motorcycle dispatch rider stride across the room and disappear behind the closed door.

It was difficult to listen to the adviser and keep an eye on the mysterious door, but I was soon rewarded when a French captain emerged from the radio room. His shirtsleeves were rolled up and he held a clipboard full of papers. He paused to look around and began to walk toward us. Seeing me, he stopped dead in his tracks, turned, and disappeared behind the door. I felt a surge of anger followed by a certain elation at having caught the French red-handed. My contact continued his proselytizing. When he'd finished, I asked him if the Binh Xuyen planned to continue fighting. He informed me my question was "indiscreet" and asked if I would relay what he had told me to the embassy. I assured him I would and we said goodbye. As I walked down the entry stairs, another French Army dispatch rider roared up, skidded his motorcycle to a halt, and rushed into the headquarters with a leather folder under his arm.

"The French are running the goddamn show," I told Gildea as we headed back toward Saigon. He had come to the same conclusion watching the arrival and departure of the couriers.

There had been much heated discussion and argument within the American Mission about the extent of French support to the Binh Xuyen. Now that I had seen their contribution at first hand I was anxious to make my report. Back at the Galerie Eden I burst into Stansbury's office to give him a blow-by-blow account of what we had seen and heard. In minutes I was on my way to the embassy to repeat the story to the chief political officer. He was as shocked by my news as Stansbury had been and immediately telephoned General Ely. It soon became obvious that Ely was doing most of the talking. I sensed something was wrong when the political officer began nodding in apparent agreement. He eventually put down the phone and turned toward me with a sigh of relief. General Ely had clarified the situation. The French officer and the couriers I had seen at Binh Xuyen headquarters were members of Ely's "Good Offices Mission" working with the Binh Xuyen in order to end the hostilities.

I argued that the French were obviously directly involved in Binh Xuyen operations and possibly filling a command function. I insisted the French officer's reaction on seeing me was hardly that of a legitimate peace-seeker. I pointed out that the constant courier traffic was too heavy for messages involving a cease-fire that was already functioning. It was all to no avail. General Ely had spoken from his lofty position, and our political section was buying his story. I left the embassy both frustrated and furious. Later, when I shared the information with Ed Lansdale, he indicated with a sage nod of his head that what I had seen was no great surprise to him.

The following week Stansbury asked me to work on a draft speech being prepared for delivery by Diem. It was to be a call for national unity coupled with a stern warning to the sects that the time for dissidence had passed. Others, including Lansdale, Ngo Dinh Nhu, and the palace press office, were involved in the same project, so there was little pride of authorship involved. Channeling the frustration left over from my devalued report on the Binh Xuyen into my draft, I banged out a tough commentary on the fragility of democracy. I emphasized the government's duty to protect it by force of arms. The pugnacious paragraph, along with an order for the Binh Xuyen to withdraw from Saigon's streets, was included when the speech was broadcast by Radio Vietnam. We later heard that these words, considered a direct threat of action by the government, convinced the Binh Xuyen the time for talk had ended. True or not, it was a sobering lesson in the use of words during a crisis situation and their direct contribution to bloodshed—the type of lesson one doesn't forget.

Thanks to continued French pressure and Ambassador Collins's negative reports, Washington was on the brink of withdrawing support from Diem. In late April of 1955, Ambassador Collins decided to fly to Washington to convince President Eisenhower that the obstinate Diem had to go. A few days after his departure all hell broke loose in Saigon.

It was one of those quiet midday periods in the tropics when the streets suddenly empty of noisy traffic and both the European and Asian residents prepare for lunch and siesta time. I was at home on April 28, 1955, relaxing under a ceiling fan with a cool gimlet in my hand, when the shelling began. Diem had ordered his army to move against the sects. This time the Binh Xuyen riposte was no exercise in intimidation or hesitant probing of government targets. It was a well-aimed, wholly professional mortar barrage directed at Diem's palace and designed to kill. The confusion, urgency, fear, courage, tragedy, and occasional low comedy of the following weeks can best be described in a series of remembered vignettes:

• Once again the prime battlefield is the broad Boulevard Galliéni. The Binh Xuyen, pushing in from Cholon, have been stopped on the approaches to Saigon by the paras of the National Army. Now there is a stalemate while the vicious whiplash of automatic weapons makes the empty boulevard untenable. A heavy exchange of mortar fire has set the tinderbox huts blazing in the huge slum near Cholon. As the paras take cover, the first frightened refugees hurry by, carrying whatever belongings they can salvage. Gildea is taking 35mm shots from across the road while I use the Rollei. During a lull in the firing I join him to inspect a small, bullet-riddled panel truck that has smashed into a tree. Vietnamese troops are removing the body of a stout French civilian killed in the first burst of crossfire. His blood has darkened the shattered windshield. Why he risked running the gauntlet is a mystery. After the body is dragged to a litter, two soldiers return to the truck and begin to search the cab. Curious, I peer over their shoulders. They seem to have found what they're looking for, but they hesitate. I see why. The dead man's brain is lying on the floorboards near the brake pedal, miraculously intact as if removed by a surgeon. Finally, with expressions of disgust, the soldiers push the gray mass onto an old newspaper with a stone and carry it off to join the corpse.

• Ollie Russell of UPI is sitting on a sand-filled oil drum in the middle of Boulevard Galliéni when the fighting resumes. Everyone sprints for cover, but Ollie remains where he is, seemingly inured to the danger. We yell and shout but he doesn't move. A Vietnamese officer runs out to herd him to shelter. When we accuse him of utter insanity, he informs us he'd turned off his hearing aid and had been oblivious to the storm of fire around him.

• A Binh Xuyen heavy machine gun located inside the shattered roof of a house some 500 yards distant is dominating the boulevard. The para officers are shouting into their radios demanding support. Three American-made armored cars appear and begin firing their cannon at the Binh Xuyen position. A sudden deep clang signals a hit on one of the armored cars and it goes into reverse, careening backwards toward us on three flat tires. It brakes to an abrupt stop, the turret opens, and two crew members manhandle the body of a comrade out of the turret and onto the ground where some paras take over, carrying the limp corpse out of the line of fire. The crewmen climb into the turret. With a grinding of gears, the armored car limps back to battle, its wheel rims throwing sparks from the pavement.

• On the third morning of the fighting I'm alone, driving my jeep on a road parallel with Boulevard Galliéni in search of the indistinct "front line." The photos we've shot have turned out well and carry an undeniable message. The National Army, without French cadre or direct American help, is fighting on its own with courage and determination. The calm professionalism of the paras, exemplified by one photo of a young company commander directing his men in full view of the enemy, has already impressed the skeptics who were predicting Diem's downfall and the Army's collapse. Now, as I turn a corner, a colonel of parachutists passes me in a jeep heading in the opposite direction. We exchange waves and I drive on. There is shouting off to my right from some paras dug in around the ruins of a building. They, too, are waving and I return the greeting. Firing erupts without warning, the rounds cracking dangerously close. I swing the wheel to the left, bounce over some rubble, and brake to a stop behind a wall. A nearby para motions me toward his hole. All is suddenly clear. The waves and the shouts were not greetings. They were warnings. Crouched beside the grinning para, I wince as another burst of fire sends a cascade of plaster and stone chips onto the hood of my jeep.

• Late on the night of April 30 I receive a frantic call from one of Diem's press officers. He insists I come to the palace immediately to witness "grave events." Jumping into my jeep, I speed into the city and enter the palace grounds. The press officer meets me on the steps, signals the need for silence, and leads me toward a wide reception room where angry words are being spoken in Vietnamese. I stop, half concealed by a heavy curtain, to watch the incongruous melodrama. General Nguyen Van Vy, the pro-French, Bao Dai loyalist and chief of staff of the Vietnamese Army, is standing near the center of the room with a sheet of paper in his hands. The insignia of rank has been torn from his uniform. A microphone and recorder sit on a nearby table. The general is sweating profusely. Cao Dai general Trinh Minh Thé, in civilian clothes, is lecturing Vy while armed members of Thé's newly formed pro-Diem "Revolutionary Committee" have taken up positions by the doors and windows.

The press officer speaks in a whisper, informing me of what is happening. General Vy is being asked to read a prepared statement calling for an end to French interference in Vietnamese affairs, repudiating Bao Dai, and pledging his loyalty to Ngo Dinh Diem. Vy is responding to Thé's harangue in a low voice, trying to argue his case. The veins on Thé's forehead are standing out and it's obvious he is fast losing his temper. Suddenly Thé pulls a Colt .45 from his belt, strides forward, and puts its muzzle to Vy's temple. Thé pushes Vy to the microphone, the heavy automatic pressed tight against the general's short-cropped gray hair. I wince, waiting for the Colt's hammer to fall. The repetitive clicking of a camera is the only sound in the tense silence. Howard Sochurek of *Life* is recording the scene from the half-cover of a curtain on the far side of the room. Vy begins to read the text into the mike, the paper shaking in his hands. His face is ashen, and perspiration stains his collar. Thé complains he can't hear and demands that Vy speak louder. When Vy finishes, Thé puts his automatic away.

General relief sweeps the room. A number of journalists have been quietly ushered in the palace since my arrival. General Vy is now sitting down under guard, looking straight ahead. Trinh Minh Thé and his men are conferring while members of Diem's staff rush in and out. The press officer tells the foreign journalists that Vy has been guilty of plotting against the government, but thanks to the vigilance of patriotic nationalists supporting Diem, he has recanted. All journalists are then asked to leave. I linger behind, thinking my adviser status will entitle me to more detailed information. But the embarrassed press officer indicates it is time for me to leave also and hurries me to the door.

I sense a crisis in the offing and there is one. The commander of the Army's parachutists, informed of the trap set for General Vy and told of Trinh Minh

Thé's highhanded humiliation of the chief of staff, has telephoned Diem to demand Vy's immediate release. He is threatening to shell the palace. The government and Trinh Minh Thé have misread the Army's attitude toward General Vy. Pro-French or not, he is still one of their own. The thought of Vy being held at gunpoint by a Cao Dai "general" cannot be tolerated.

General Vy is released, the powder keg situation defused, and Diem's violent new allies are cautioned to treat the Army with more respect. Shortly after pledging "loyalty" to Diem, Vy will take the exile's road to Paris, where he will trade his stars for the *galons* of a colonel in the French Army. The deposed general will then return to Vietnam following Diem's assassination and serve as defense minister in 1968 in the cabinet of President Nguyen Van Thieu.

• The battle zone is an eerie nocturnal landscape. An old air raid siren, shorted by gunfire, wails continually. Burning buildings throw an amber light over the darkened streets, and the sudden collapse of a charred roof throws a fireworks display of crackling sparks into the air. Driving homeward through the Cathedral Square, I see a number of white-uniformed policemen armed with rifles grouped under the tall tamarind trees. As I pull to the curb one of them fires up into the overhead foliage. In the midst of a revolt they are hunting fruit bats. One policeman proudly exhibits his bag of two plump, foxlike creatures and makes the finger-kissing gesture of anticipatory gourmandise.

• Arnold Ehrlich, our former publications officer in Saigon, has come down from his post in Hong Kong to lend a hand. On his first night I take him for a quick look around. As we drive home, the gunners in the French camp open fire on our jeep. I push down on the accelerator, hunch over the wheel and shout, "Get Down!"

"My God!" Ehrlich says, sliding effortlessly from his seat to the floorboards, "they're shooting at *us!*" Rounding the corner on two wheels, we find my wife waiting at the door to inform us there's been some firing in the neighborhood.

• The Binh Xuyen are putting up a desperate fight on the approaches to the Y bridge. Dickie Chappel, a veteran American female combat photographer, has died, gunned down while accompanying a National Army advance. Some of the Army's fence-sitters have come over to Diem, providing the government with a few more battalions, a sorely needed edge that could mean victory. I am now using a rented black Peugeot rather than the easily identifiable green jeep. I drive carefully, keeping Chinese warehouses and loading docks between the Peugeot and the *Arroyo Chinois* and well out of sight of Binh Xuyen gunners. Pulling to a stop not far from the Y bridge, I grab the Rollei and leave the sedan. I haven't taken three steps when machine gun fire echoes through the street and two rounds sledgehammer into the Peugeot's bumper and trunk. A stringer for AP, drawn by the firing, arrives to examine the damage and question me on my narrow escape. I am shaken but ludicrously more concerned with the damage to the rented sedan than about what might have happened. Within hours my aged parents in California will be reading an AP story headed SHOTS PERIL S.F. ARTIST IN SAIGON, and a USIA spokesman in Washington will announce that, "His car was riddled with bullets shortly after he left it but so far as we know he's not hurt."

• The resilience and sangfroid of Saigon's population are unbelievable. They have lived so long with war and the threat of death that they seem to have reached a certain modus vivendi. On the pavement, a few blocks from the actual fighting, children are playing a Vietnamese version of jacks, and a fortune teller has unrolled a colorful oilcloth full of astrological signs and omens. An ambulant vendor has wheeled his soup cart close enough to serve the lounging machine gun crew of a National Army roadblock, and an old man squats on the curbing, calmly rolling a cigarette of dark tobacco and squinting up at the dark, cinder-laden smoke that hangs over the city. Downtown, the terrace bar of the Hotel Continental is full of thirsty newsmen in dirt-smudged clothing just back from the Cholon fighting. I stay only long enough to gulp a Tuborg and flee to escape the constant questioning on whether or not the United States has decided to stick with Diem.

• Dixie Reese's lab has been working twenty-four hours a day to process our photos of the fighting, but a sudden lag in print production is puzzling. I telephone several times but the lab foreman gives evasive answers and Reese is not at his apartment. Arriving at the lab, I hear the sound of weeping and find Reese's Vietnamese secretary slumped, red-eyed, behind her desk. Gradually, between sobs, the story unfolds. Reese, in his obsessive quest for recognition as a combat photographer, has rented a small private aircraft to shoot aerial photos of the fighting. He and the French pilot are now long overdue. The mystery turns to tragedy when the Binh Xuyen announce the downing of an aircraft and the death of an "American spy." The bodies of Reese and the pilot will not be recovered from the wreckage until the National Army drives the Binh Xuyen from the capital.

• In early May General Bay Vien and the remnants of his forces have fled their headquarters to seek refuge in the swamps and reed-bordered canals east of Saigon. I join a force of Vietnamese troops in a landing craft to cross the narrow *Arroyo Chinois* to Bay Vien's deserted villa. It is a hot day. The stench of putrefaction hangs in the still air as we land and climb the bank to the once luxurious villa now torn and shattered by shellfire. The rotting, fly-covered inmates of Bay Vien's zoo account for the smell. His tiger looks like an outsize, deflated child's toy; and the python, its coils ripped and torn by shrapnel, resembles a thick, discarded electrical conduit. In one cage a black monkey, stiff with rigor mortis, lies on its back, its two long arms extended. An unfamiliar, sweetish odor engulfs us as we approach the rear of the villa. Here we find the Binh Xuyen's opium-packaging equipment, a racheted capping apparatus, hundreds of small tins, and what look like large paint buckets full of sticky, dark opium. One room contains an open, empty safe. A treasure trove of Binh

Xuyen identity cards is scattered over the floor, each with a photo and information on its former bearer. The Vietnamese troops are grinding the cards into the broken tiles with their heavy boots. I convince a young officer to keep his men out of the room and rush back to the landing. Thirty minutes later I interrupt an official Sunday luncheon at Ed Stansbury's villa, where I know General O'Daniel is among the guests. O'Daniel, Stansbury, and I retire to another room while I describe the intelligence bonanza abandoned in Bay Vien's villa. With the Binh Xuyen pledged to carry on a clandestine struggle against the government, the cards have a particular importance. Without hesitation O'Daniel calls Ed Lansdale to suggest that someone retrieve the cards.

The Diem government's successful fight against the Binh Xuyen tipped the scales in Washington in favor of continued support. Some of the tipping was due to Colonel Lansdale's telegrams shared by the Dulles brothers as secretary of state and CIA director. One of Lansdale's advantages during this period was the fact that his cables were vibrant accounts of what he had witnessed himself during the Saigon fighting. The events and conversations he reported backing Diem's actions had an impressive "I was there" quality. The more traditional embassy reporting based largely on conversations with officials and politicians, much of it taking a dim view of Diem's chances, could not compete.

While the National Army continued to mop up the sect armies, Bao Dai sent Diem a message accusing him of causing unnecessary bloodshed and ordering him to France. Buoyed by his success and with the United States and his army now behind him, Diem defied the emperor. With Lansdale's urging, Diem would soon begin planning for a referendum that would strip Bao Dai of his chief of state title. The election, held in late October and pitting Diem against Bao Dai, was to be marked by questionable psywar techniques and strong-arm tactics. Despite Lansdale's warnings on the negative political effect of stuffed ballot boxes, Diem's brother Ngo Dinh Nhu and his security forces were determined to ensure a Diem landslide. Militant members of Nhu's Can Lao party haunted the polling places, to lean on the voters and threaten those who might be loyal to Bao Dai. Diem was destined to garner a totally unbelievable 98.2 percent of the vote, a figure that would have made a Tammany Hall boss blush. In Saigon alone the final tally would outnumber the registered voters list by many thousands. Unrepentant, elated and beaming, the little man in the palace would then declare himself president of the new Republic of Vietnam.

The last days of the fighting and the collapse of the sects produced a number of changes in South Vietnam. General Trinh Minh Thé, the Cao Dai dissident who'd joined forces with Diem, was killed by a shot to the head while he watched his troops attacking Binh Xuyen forces near Binh Dai. Who fired the fatal round remains a mystery. Reports that the entry wound was in the back of the skull lent credence to the thesis that Thé's death was a political assassination and not the result of a stray bullet from the fighting. The extravagantly mustachioed Gen. Tran Van Soai of the Hoa Hao surrendered. A carefully choreographed press conference in which he pledged his allegiance to Diem seemed more of a return to the fold than a surrender. Although the Cao Dai general Nguyen Than Phuong had come over to Diem, Pham Cong Tac, the Cao Dai pope, fled to Cambodia. "Ba-Cut," the wild-eyed, long-haired Hoa Hao leader was lured from his swamp redoubt and publicly guillotined. Bay Vien, the vice lord of Saigon-Cholon, fled to a well-provided retirement in Paris.

The political adviser's warnings during my visit to Binh Xuyen headquarters had contained elements of truth. The collapse of the sects' control over important areas of South Vietnam was to leave them open to Communist infiltration and eventual domination. Thousands of armed sect soldiers, abandoned by their leaders, would link up with clandestine Vietminh stay-behinds and join them later as Vietcong in their attacks on the Diem regime. But, in the euphoria following Diem's victory, such developments were far in the future. We had worked hard for Diem's success. Although it had often been touch-and-go, he'd made it. It would take some time for objective reality to set in.

With the fighting ended, Saigon returned to a condition approaching normal, but Franco-American antagonism grew. Even the sometimes prickly professional relationships between American and French journalists worsened. The revolt of the sects had been seen by die-hard French colonists and certain French officers as a last chance to maintain some influence in Vietnam. That hope was now extinct, replaced by resentment and bitterness. French military trucks sped through the city's streets, forcing Vietnamese civilians to run for their lives. Some French officers I had known and worked with passed me on Rue Catinat without a sign of recognition. If the murderous looks of the old French *colons* on the Continental's terrace had been knife blades, I would have died a hundred times over.

It was at this particular period that I began to consider leaving the government. Up to this point I had been too busy to contemplate such a move. Now I found myself thinking about the possibility. Perhaps, without realizing it, I was burned out. We may have salvaged South Vietnam with Diem's installation, but the Franco-American effort against the Vietminh had been a failure. I had seen too many defeats, too many blunders, and too much death. I wanted to write about what I had witnessed in a novel and, with the optimism of my thirty years, I had little doubt that it could be done. On a more personal level I had become disenchanted with government service. The promotion I'd been promised when I'd returned to Saigon had never materialized. This was particularly irritating as I'd turned down an offer to join *Time* magazine as their regular Saigon stringer on the strength of that promise. Also, working with what Dennis Bloodworth, the Far East correspondent of the London *Observer*, has labeled America's "tightly furled" diplomats had me yearning to return to the easy, open camaraderie of a newspaper's city desk.

Fate, in the form of infectious hepatitis, stepped in to speed up the process. After a few days of very high fever I was evacuated for treatment to the Air Force hospital at Clark Field in the Philippines. Mary Alice and Shawn remained behind in the uncertain political climate of Saigon. Jack Andrew, another officer from USIS Saigon, had preceded me to Clark Field with the same complaint and we shared the same ward. Andrew was to die of complications a week after my arrival. The same strain of hepatitis then struck Ed Stansbury and he too was evacuated and appeared in our ward.

I arrived back in Saigon much thinner and under doctor's orders to reduce my normal work schedule for at least a month. Paul Garvey, a portly, wisecracking correspondent for USIA's International Press Service and an old friend, met me at planeside. Garvey, an unflappable newsman, had covered the Korean conflict, and listed Toots Shor's bar in New York as his home leave address. Now, with a sarcastic "Welcome back to Saigon" he handed me a mimeographed sheet. In tortured English the Binh Xuyen, or what was left of them, were claiming to have poisoned Jack Andrew, Ed Stansbury, and myself. They were also warning other Americans working with the "tyrant" Diem that they could expect a similar fate. When I'd finished reading the flyer, Garvey suggested that, as the only member of the "poisoned" trio back in Saigon, I might want to keep a low profile. We laughed off the Binh Xuyen warning as a propaganda ploy, but years later I recalled that some of us—including Andrew and Stansbury—had eaten couscous two or three times at a small restaurant run by North African troops in the French camp near our villa. It was the same camp whose gunners had used Ehrlich and me as moving targets. Infecting someone with hepatitis does not require a paramedic. All that's needed is a cooperative cook. If the 2ème Bureau or their Binh Xuyen allies had wanted to even some scores, it would have been a foolproof method of incapacitation. Balancing retroactive paranoia against the realities of the time, I would say there was a fifty-fifty chance the Binh Xuyen claim contained a seed of truth.

While I had been lolling in the hospital, my wife had been living alone with the baby in our isolated Saigon villa. The guard promised by the embassy had never appeared. During my absence our neighbors, the French noncom and his Vietnamese wife, had been found sprawled in their entry hall, chopped down by an automatic weapon. To make matters worse, Father O'Conner, an American correspondent-priest for a Catholic news service, had been visiting my wife to urge a quick baptism for our daughter as "anything could happen" in Saigon. Shawn was eventually baptized in the Saigon cathedral. The officiating Vietnamese priest had to interrupt the ceremony midway to chase a street urchin and retrieve my wife's snatched purse.

I had now made up my mind about resigning. I filled out the required forms and wrote a formal letter of resignation to the director of USIA. Some hurried calculations convinced us we had enough money to cover a year's residence in Mallorca, at the time an inexpensive haven for writers, while I wrote my Indochina novel. We booked passage on the old French liner La Marseillaise for its last voyage from Saigon to Marseille via the Suez Canal. I phased out of the press officer job and "Red" Austin took over. My remaining months in Saigon were spent monitoring developments in North Vietnam through FBIS radio reports and interviews with newly arrived Northerners. I took one final trip to the seventeenth parallel to slog through the mud with Vietnamese soldiers as they searched for Vietminh arms caches. But my heart wasn't in it. Mentally I was already under a parasol on a quiet Mallorcan beach tapping out the great American novel.

CHAPTER 14

Interlude

Watching Saigon slide out of sight behind the tall palms as the *Marseillaise* moved slowly down the river was a moment of mixed emotions. It was mid-September 1955 and I felt relief at leaving the heat, frustrations, and threats behind. At the same time, I knew that Saigon had been so much a part of our lives that it could never be forgotten. I was also sure that we would never see Vietnam again.

The seventeen-day sea voyage was the perfect antidote for tension. Short port calls at Singapore, Colombo, Djibouti, and Port Said broke the monotony of shipboard life. After docking in Marseille we flew to Palma, Mallorca, and began house-hunting. We eventually rented a seaside villa in the small fishing village of Puerto Andraitx for thirty-five dollars a month, rowboat included. I settled down to write while my wife coped with the wood-fueled stove, the daily marketing, and the new world of Mallorcan culture and procedures. The first mail delivery brought a letter from Theodore Streibert, the director of USIA. He had "reluctantly" accepted my resignation. A handwritten note at the bottom of the page expressed the hope I would return to the agency after I had gotten the year in Mallorca "out of my system." He concluded by stating "we will be glad to have you back at any time." A few days later I received word from George Hellyer that I was to receive USIA's highest honor, the Award (medal) for Distinguished Service. Jack Andrew, who had died in the hospital ward at Clark Field, was to receive the same honor posthumously.

The next few months passed pleasantly as I roughed out six chapters of the novel. One day, while in Palma, I bought a *Newsweek* at a kiosk and read a review of Graham Greene's *Quiet American*. I was not aspiring to Greene's literary eminence, but I was shocked to see that his setting and characters were much the same as my own. This jolt was followed by a real body blow. The

Internal Revenue Service informed me that I owed a substantial amount of tax on the 25 percent hardship allowance earned while serving in Vietnam. Our planned one-year stay in Mallorca was suddenly shortened by six months.

We returned to California in the spring of 1956 and found a small apartment perched high above Sausalito's "Hurricane Gulch." After a month of freelancing I went to work on "This World," the Sunday news roundup of the San Francisco *Chronicle*. It was an ideal newspaper job, turning out a weekly review of national and international news during a forty-hour work week in a four-day period. I spoke on Indochina before the Northern California World Affairs Council and at the San Francisco Press Club, but my novel was shelved. I was in no mood to face a typewriter after pounding one all day at the office.

Echoes of events in Vietnam reached me during this period like messages from a distant planet. One letter spoke of the bogdown in refugee resettlement and of the Vietnamese government's decision to move some refugees to the remote mountain areas of the Central Highlands, populated by Vietnamese-hating mountain peoples. My correspondent pointed out that Vietnamese security forces had offered the tribesmen bags of salt as bounty for Vietminh heads and posed the question, how do you tell a Vietminh head from that of a Vietnamese refugee? The obvious, chilling response was that you couldn't.

After a short three months as a working newsman in San Francisco I was afflicted with an incurable case of wanderlust. Riding the daily commuter bus across the Golden Gate Bridge offered stupendous vistas, but the daily grind held less and less attraction. It all came to a head one night as we sat over coffee and brandy after dinner.

"What would you think—" I finally ventured. Without losing a beat my wife completed the sentence.

"—if you went back into the agency?" We had both been harboring the same thought for weeks.

I placed a call to George Hellyer in Washington. He was pleased at my change of heart but hardly surprised. He warned that slipping back into the fold would not be easy, but promised to do what he could. It wasn't easy but he succeeded. The personnel office, as expected, had taken a dim view of the whole procedure. To make their point I was offered the choice of two hardship posts: Lagos, Nigeria; or Kathmandu, Nepal. The post report for Kathmandu suggested a newcomer bring Coleman lanterns and rat traps along with household effects. All things considered, we opted for Nigeria.

Nigeria was moving toward independence and it was an interesting period. I traveled throughout the country and the neighboring Cameroons and made a number of friends among the ebullient journalists of Lagos. I wrote and directed short documentaries on the Queen's Own Nigeria Regiment and the National Police Academy for USIA's African Newsreel; argued the intricacies of U.S. policy with Nigerian lawyers, businessmen, and politicians at the bar of the Island Club, where Caucasians opting for membership risked being "white-balled"; and learned to eat ground-nut stew and palm-oil curry. Housing was tight in Lagos and we moved five times during our two-year stay. Our second daughter, Lisa, was born on February 19, 1958, in a nursing home run by a British obstetrician who operated in a bloodstained gown and offered new mothers their choice of tea or Guinness while they were still on the table. Toward the end of our tour in Nigeria I was informed of my next posting. I had finally broken into the exclusive "European Club" and was to direct USIA's Marseille office.

Marseille was warm, colorful, vibrant, and gutsy. Its well-deserved reputation as a gangland city tended to obscure its rich legacy of history and culture. We occupied a government-owned, nineteenth-century town house filled with period furniture within walking distance of the consulate general. A piquant touch was added to my workday by the *belles de nuit* working our street who habitually greeted me in the evening with a friendly "*Bonsoir, monsieur le consul.*"

In addition to establishing contacts with the media and government officials, I constructed a tenuous friendship with Marseille's crusty mayor, Gaston Defferre, an influential socialist and former Resistance leader who was also a deputy in the National Assembly. Thanks to a State Department Leader Grant, I was able to send Defferre to the United States in time to join John F. Kennedy's presidential campaign as an observer. It was an experience the longtime mayor never forgot. I acted as a public affairs adviser to the U.S. Sixth Fleet—at one point blocking the admiral's plan to land Marines on the beach at Nice during the height of the tourist season as a demonstration of "readiness." Once a year I attended the Cannes Film Festival as a member of the U.S. delegation. During my second assignment at Cannes, a telegram from the agency arrived at the consulate ordering me to Laos. I had no desire to return to another hardship post so quickly. Luckily the prompt intervention of the consul general and the ambassador kept me in France.

Vietnam was ever present, whether in the columns of local newspapers, reports from the Algerian War mentioning those officers I had known in Indochina, or through unexpected encounters with old Indochina hands or former Vietnamese officials transiting Marseille.

I began to work in earnest on the long-delayed novel in Marseille, using every free moment I could put aside. The six chapters I'd produced in Mallorca had been amateurish and were abandoned. Over a year later I was able to send the first draft off to a New York agent. *To a Silent Valley*, a fictional amalgam of Nasan, Dien Bien Phu, Saigon, and Hanoi, was published by Alfred A. Knopf in 1961. Like all first novelists I soon learned the fragility of most fiction. Despite good reviews, *TASV* slid quickly into oblivion. As one candid friend put it, "Who cares about Vietnam?"

After two years in Marseille I was reassigned to the press attaché's office in the Paris embassy. It was a hectic workplace, involving everything from preparing for presidential visits to supporting European unity, from drafting ambassadorial statements to courting influential Paris pundits over heavy bistro lunches awash with Beaujolais. The Algerian War had swept General de Gaulle to power and much of our time was spent countering his government's negative attitude to U.S. policy and France's anti-NATO stance. Although we were living in a beautiful old apartment overlooking the Jardin du Luxembourg, I longed to return to Marseille. When my successor there was unexpectedly reassigned, I volunteered to replace him. My wife was pregnant when we returned to Marseille, and Kate, our third daughter, was born there on March 11, 1963.

In Vietnam, Diem's authoritarian government and the political abuses of Ngo Dinh Nhu and his power-hungry wife had sown the seeds of rebellion among some of the same Army officers who had rallied to Diem's support in 1955. In early November of 1960 an abortive but bloody attack on the presidential palace by Vietnamese parachute units had shaken the Eisenhower administration and raised doubts about Diem's staying power. Ed Lansdale, who had left Vietnam in 1956 and was working as a brigadier general in the Special Operations Office of the Pentagon, had been sent back to Vietnam to prepare a report on the situation. The report, bluntly direct about Vietcong proliferation and highly critical of embassy attitudes toward Diem and his government, had a quality of urgency that caught the attention of the new president, John F. Kennedy.

Kennedy's inaugural pledge to "pay any price" in support of freedom and his fascination with counterinsurgency as an answer to Communist aggression would result in a steadily increased flow of U.S. military advisers to Vietnam. In a comparatively short time their number would climb to over 15,000. Inevitably, the advisers would inch closer and closer to participation in actual combat. John Mecklin, the *Time* correspondent who had warned me that it was time to leave Hanoi in November of 1954, was now USIA chief in Saigon. I didn't envy him his job. Saigon's bamboo telegraph, reaching as far as Marseille, had informed me that some of Mecklin's Vietnamese employees had been discovered printing anti-Diem tracts on a mimeograph machine hidden in his residence.

By 1963 the situation in Vietnam had worsened. Diem's inability to share power, brook criticism, or accept an opposition party, and his brother's secret police procedures, had alienated noncommunist Vietnamese both at home and abroad. The Buddhists were in open revolt, and the newsphoto of a monk's self-immolation in protest over government policies had made front pages around the world. Madame Nhu's brutal comments on the barbecued bonze had shocked even Diem's staunchest international supporters. The Vietcong, profiting from government stagnation, corruption, and the disaffection of the population, were making dangerous gains in the vital Mekong Delta. The Army generals Diem had depended on in the past were now planning a coup, and Washington was seriously considering ways and means of removing Diem from power.

During this period I had more immediate concerns. The Algerian War had ended and the political and human flotsam of that colonial defeat was coming ashore in Marseille. Thousands of *pied noir* French settlers whose families had lived and worked in Algeria for generations, *Harki* irregulars, and other Algerians who had sided with the French, and a disillusioned Army were returning to France in a desperate and bitter state of mind. Marseille and Paris soon echoed to the sound of plastic explosives as the OAS (*Organisation armée secrète*) carried out a terrorist campaign against the de Gaulle government. Although the American consulate general, including my office, was not directly involved, many *ex-colons*, the OAS, and the French Right blamed U.S. policy in North Africa for contributing to the loss of Algeria. Where before we had been dealing only with the standard Communist media attacks and the continued hostility of de Gaulle's government, we were now on the receiving end of anti-American propaganda originating from the Algerian debacle. While I crossed swords with right-wing editors, reported government obstructionism, and wondered if our office would be the target of an OAS bomb, I still kept one eye on developments in Vietnam.

The successful anti-Diem coup in early November of 1963 seemed a logical, almost inevitable extension of Vietnamese politics, but the assassination of Diem and his brother came as an unpleasant surprise. Word that the CIA's Lou Conein, with whom I'd shared a jeep in Hanoi, had acted as the embassy's liaison with the coup leaders only emphasized the continuity of intrigue in Saigon. Despite the OAS bombing campaign I considered myself lucky to be in Marseille.

Later the same month I received an unexpected evening telephone call at home. There was much loud conversation in the background and I had trouble hearing the caller until he shouted for silence. It was a Marseille docker calling from a waterfront bar. He wanted to know if "it was true." I had no idea what he was talking about and asked for clarification. He had just heard that President Kennedy had been assassinated in Dallas and wanted me to tell him it was an error. Numb with shock, I took his number, dialed the Paris embassy, and switched on the TV and radio. Fifteen minutes later, with a positive reply from the embassy supported by continual media updates, I called the docker back. There was a long pause when I confirmed his fears followed only by sobs and the sound of the receiver being hung up.

In the succeeding months President Lyndon B. Johnson would take his first steps into the quagmire of Vietnam. I didn't know it at the time, but I would also be involved in the escalating U.S. effort to seek some light at the end of Vietnam's steadily darkening tunnel.

CHAPTER 15

The "First Team"

In the early 1960s the International Film Festival at Cannes was not all fluff and bikinis. The Cold War cast its cool shadow on the proceedings. Western and Eastern Bloc delegates watched each other carefully and maneuvered for propaganda points. It was a surrealist atmosphere, with Soviet security heavies protecting their female stars from "decadent" Western influences; the French government providing free room, meals, and wine for the delegates and their spouses at the luxurious Carlton Hotel; and each delegation combing the official attendance list for the presence of known "spooks."

The festival opening in May of 1964 marked my fourth year as a U.S. delegate. I was now a seasoned veteran. I had learned the hard way that sitting through all screenings was neither required nor advisable, that the Sixth Fleet flagship had an uncanny knack for appearing off Cannes at festival time, and that one of my prime duties was to keep the White House–appointed chief delegate happy at all times. I was expected to write an official report on the festival, detailing the U.S. delegation's work and providing a résumé of foreign film entries. Part of the report always dealt with the activities of other delegations, particularly those from the Iron Curtain nations.

A few days into the festival I was on the Carlton beach one late morning with George Stevens, Jr., our chief delegate and director of USIA's film section; Arthur Schlesinger, Jr.; and Gore Vidal. We were carrying out a postmortem on the films that had been shown the previous evening when the manager of the Carlton's beach restaurant approached to summon me to the telephone.

My wife was calling from our room and asked me to return to the hotel—quickly.

She had received a strange message from a duty officer at the consulate general in Marseille, suggesting I telephone someone at the Paris embassy immediately. Luckily that someone was a friend. He told me a priority telegram had arrived from Washington that promised to change my life considerably. It was classified but he hinted at the contents. I helped him by posing some questions.

"Was it a reassignment?"

It was.

"Where?"

He cleared his throat and said nothing.

"Was it a post I had known previously?"

It was.

It did not take a genius to decipher the location. Washington would hardly use a classified message to send me back to Lagos.

We left Cannes and drove to Marseille, where I read the telegram. It was simple and direct: I was being assigned to Saigon as an adviser to the new prime minister of Vietnam, Maj. Gen. Nguyen Khanh. I had two weeks—including a short period of consultation in Washington—to get there. My shock at the unexpected orders was soon replaced by doubts and questions. I didn't know anything about General Khanh and wondered why he should suddenly need my advice. Didn't USIA recall that I had already been labeled a "spy" by the official Communist Party newspaper in Hanoi and that the Binh Xuyen had claimed to have poisoned me in 1955? Did they realize that, in addition to my wife, I'd be taking along three young daughters and that a fourth child would be due soon? Why would they want to send a retread from the French period and the Diem installation back to Vietnam? My trepidation took on extra weight when I recalled a recent *Time* magazine cover story on the U.S. ambassador in Vietnam, Henry Cabot Lodge. According to the text, Lodge thought it necessary to keep two handguns, one of them a Magnum revolver, in his desk drawer. If the ambassador felt that insecure within the semifortress of his embassy, what were things like on the street?

Answers to these questions would have to wait while we packed and prepared to leave Marseille. I didn't know that a decision had been made to seed American specialists into the Vietnamese government at high administrative levels to assist the Vietnamese in the fields of foreign relations, economics and finance, public affairs, and psychological warfare. As Vietnam expert Robert Shaplen explained in his book *The Lost Revolution*, these Americans were to create a "shadow government of nonmilitary advisers" who would permit Washington to formulate and implement "a national campaign plan that is beyond the competence of the Vietnamese government."

Faced with the frustrations and uncertainties of Vietnam and the petty political feuding of high-ranking ARVN officers, the Johnson administration had decided to take a more active role in "nation-building." In sum, we were going to save the Vietnamese from themselves. The Vietnamese were understandably cool to the idea from its inception, but were still paying lip service to the project when I received my orders. As it turned out, I would be the only member of this supposed "brain trust" to arrive in Saigon.

My return to Washington was a hurried round of consultations and briefings punctuated by a litany of catchphrases. Yes, there were certain risks involved in my return: but this time "it is different." It was our "last chance in Vietnam." I would be a member of the "first team." My expertise was needed to advise the prime minister on information and press matters and the ARVN on psychological warfare. The briefing officials were sincere and enthusiastic, even if most of them had never seen a Saigon sunset. One thing was certain. Carl Rowan, the director of USIA, had promised the White House quick action and I was going whether I liked it or not and the sooner the better. At that point it was much easier to accept the "first team" syndrome. With a little practice I might even begin to believe it myself.

In the midst of this Washington whirl I found a note waiting for me at USIA. Ed Lansdale had called and wanted me to call back. He had retired as a major general and was now in a stopgap position with the Food for Peace organization.

I returned Lansdale's call and we agreed to meet for lunch at a small Chinese restaurant near the agency. He arrived with some members of his old Vietnam team, including Charles T. R. "Bo" Bohannan, a gruff former Army officer who had been with Lansdale in the Philippines and Vietnam. We were hardly into our first beer when it became apparent that Lansdale & Co. were still deeply interested and involved in what was going on in Vietnam. To my surprise I learned that Lou Conein, continuing his liaison role with the coup generals, was still in Saigon acting as an adviser to Nguyen Khanh. Lansdale said he had told Conein of my imminent arrival and "Luigi" was ready to help if I needed any assistance.

Lansdale also suggested I arrange to meet with Bui Diem, a Vietnamese official I'd known in Saigon who was later to become South Vietnam's ambassador to Washington. Bui Diem was on his way back to Vietnam after some time in the United States. Unfortunately our travel schedules clashed. When I explained this, Bohannan informed me I'd have to change my plans. It was more an order than a suggestion. I flatly refused to change my departure date. I was to arrive in Honolulu in time for a high-level conference on Vietnam at CINC-PAC (Commander in Chief, Pacific) and the meeting with Bui Diem would have to wait. Lansdale accepted my refusal with a smile and a shrug, but Bohannan, unused to anyone countermanding his boss, glared at me throughout our five courses.

I said goodbye to my wife and family—they were to join me later in Saigon—and arrived in Honolulu on June 1, 1964, the night before the conference was to begin. A Navy sedan took me to Pearl Harbor, where Barry Zorthian, the USIA chief in Saigon, was waiting. He was now the director of JUSPAO (Joint U.S. Public Affairs Office), a small empire of civilian and military officers that had spread out from the original USIS operation to incorporate all American press, information, and psywar programs in Vietnam both military and civilian.

Zorthian, a former Voice of America program manager, was a hard-driving professional who worked long hours and expected his officers to do the same. The short, stocky Zorthian had served in the Pacific as a Marine during World War II and was a colonel in the Marine Corps Reserve. He had only been in Vietnam a short time, and admitted he had a lot to learn. His carefully gauged candor and fast mental footwork in daily contacts with the aggressive, Saigon-based American media representatives had already earned him the nickname "Zorro."

For me, the conference in Honolulu was the equivalent of entering a time tunnel. The Cannes Film Festival seemed like a distant dream. Aside from the young majors slapping at briefing maps with their collapsible stainless-steel pointers, I must have been the lowest-ranking official in the CINCPAC briefing room. There were more stars in the front row of seats than you could find on a clear night in the South China Sea. Secretary of Defense Robert S. McNamara, with his strange bartender's haircut, listened attentively to the presentations, surrounded by his Pentagon "whiz kids." Secretary of State Dean Rusk pondered the proceedings, his sphinx-like countenance indecipherable. Gen. Maxwell D. Taylor, the silver-haired chairman of the Joint Chiefs of Staff, who would shortly replace Lodge in Saigon, posed regular, pertinent questions with the air of a Roman senator. CIA Director John A. McCone, surrounded by his own team from the Agency's Langley, Virginia, headquarters, relaxed in his seat, his florid face and white hair giving him the appearance of an out-of-season Santa Claus. Gen. William C. Westmoreland, the commander of MACV (U.S. Military Assistance Command Vietnam) sat erect, eager to reply to questions or supplement the briefings of the officers he'd brought with him from Saigon.

Search as I might, I didn't see a single old Saigon hand from the French period. I soon learned that the lessons of recent history were not on the agenda. The French had lost. We were going to win. Sifting through the errors of the past was obviously considered a waste of time. Listening to the positive tone of the briefings, the constant flow of figures, and the optimistic predictions was a weird experience. I could have shut my eyes and imagined myself sitting through a briefing at the French High Command in 1953. Without stretching the imagination, and with a change of uniforms, Maxwell Taylor could have filled the role of General Navarre and Westmoreland would have made a credible General Cogny. General Nguyen Khanh was being described in some of the same glowing terms we had applied to Ngo Dinh Diem. He had now become "our man" in Saigon and we were determined that his regime would survive.

I found the continual barrage of statistics, readiness estimates, enemy strength appraisals, plans for clandestine operations, emphasis on air power, and "nation-building" projects depressing. I sensed a great, possibly dangerous, gap between what was going on in the air-conditioned conference room and what I had known as the on-the-ground reality of Vietnam. Perhaps things had changed in the nine years I'd been away, but I doubted it. I have often pondered what might have happened if I had found the courage to claim the floor, even for a short period, and told that constellation of high-ranking planners my version of the difficulties and dangers that lay ahead. No Vietnamese government could possibly be so acquiescent and agreeable to the initiatives and recommendations being discussed. Didn't these people realize that when a Vietnamese civilian official or army officer agrees readily with outside advice you're likely to be in trouble? Hadn't we yet learned that the Vietnamese willing to argue his case with his American counterpart had a potential greater than that of the eager yes-men we found easier to deal with? Even worse, the Vietnamese were being cast as the little men who weren't there. To all intents and purposes they appeared to have become outsiders in the struggle for their own country.

While these thoughts ran through my mind, I remained in my comfortable seat and kept my mouth shut. Retrospectively, I suppose any unplanned, unprepared intervention on my part would only have produced raised eyebrows and whispered queries of "*Who* is he?" At the best I would have given USIA a black eye and created doubts as to the agency's bona fides as a member of "the team." At the worst, I could have found myself on the first flight back to Washington with a lot of explaining to do. Nevertheless, it was a moment of inaction I shall always regret.

My brooding was interrupted by the mention of my name over the well-modulated PA system. Barry Zorthian was on stage behind the mike concluding his briefing on JUSPAO operations in Vietnam. Referring to the "brain trust" plan, he was proudly informing the assembled brass that the agency had produced an experienced press adviser for Vietnam's prime minister, that I was present in the briefing room, and would shortly be on my way to Saigon. Later that night I had a long conversation with one of Dean Rusk's aides at the officer's club bar. He was interested in my Vietnam experience. In the course of these "war stories," my misgivings about returning to Vietnam surfaced. A family man himself, he found it odd that the agency couldn't have found a bachelor for the adviser slot. Although we saw each other on the closing day of the conference, we didn't speak further and I thought that was the end of it. How little I knew Washington. By the time I arrived in Saigon, Zorthian had received a rocket from Carl Rowan, USIA's director. State had questioned him about the logic of my assignment. Rowan wanted to know what the hell I was up to. After a brief wrist-slapping session, Zothian was able to reassure the director that I was on deck, ready to work, and that my grousing period was over.

If the Honolulu conference had been troubling, my return to Saigon came as a shock. The heat and the smells were the same but the whole city seemed to have changed. The tall plane trees that had shaded the Rue Catinat—now Rue Tu Do—had been decimated. The sidewalks were cracked, and the rattling, fuming flow of traffic had doubled. The sleepy colonial capital had become a crowded, dirty wartime metropolis. For old time's sake, I declined a room in the air-conditioned Caravelle Hotel and moved into the Continental Palace

across the street. Minutes after my arrival, the gray-haired Taiwanese head barman recognized me as an old and steady customer. Later, trying to treat my jet
lag in one of the Continental's lumpy beds, I heard the thump of distant artillery. Things had not changed completely.

I was granted a free day to get my feet on the ground before meeting the
prime minister. I used it to refamiliarize myself with Saigon and seek out some
old contacts. My initial impression of a changed city faded rapidly. If you
scratched the surface, the old Saigon was still there. "Père" Franchini was no
longer holding court among his acolytes on the Continental's terrace, but a
quick noontime sweep of some familiar bars and restaurants off the Rue Tu Do
confirmed my suspicion that some of the Corsicans had remained in place and
were apparently thriving. Attractive and graceful Vietnamese women were still
wearing the traditional *ao dai*, but a new generation of street prostitutes had
chosen skin-tight jeans and see-through blouses as a uniform.

Robert Shaplen, *The New Yorker*'s veteran correspondent in the Far East, was
occupying a large room in the Continental. He brought me up to date on the
coup that had put Nguyen Khanh in the prime minister's palace and ticked off
the current status and whereabouts of Vietnamese friends I had known as
young officers. Some of them were now wearing general's stars, others were in
exile, and a few were dead. The Continental was also home for a floating contingent of French correspondents and Vietnam experts who arrived periodically to observe the Vietnamese-American effort in Indochina. Many of them,
including Max Clos, Jean Larteguy, Jean Lacouture, and Lucien Bodard, were
old acquaintances. They were now the outsiders, reporting with inherent pessi-
mism and considerable irony on what was rapidly becoming "our war."

I ended my first full day back in Saigon over a Chinese dinner at "Cheap
Charlie's" with Paul Garvey. He had been in and out of Saigon a number of
times since my departure, reporting for IPS and the VOA. He had watched the
Diem regime collapse and observed the waltz of American officials and generals
who had come to Vietnam with high hopes of doing better than their predeces-
sors and had left disillusioned and puzzled.

Garvey filled me in on the rumors and scandal concerning the Khanh government. Street gossip credited the ubiquitous Vietcong with incredible feats
and efficiency while the ARVN was described as a questionable force ridden
by internal squabbling. Garvey also revealed snippets of the insiders' disrespect-
ful code descriptions for some of Saigon's principal players. Ambassador Henry
Cabot Lodge was known as "cabbage" and Gen. Nguyen Khanh had been
labeled "the beard."

The next day, Barry Zorthian introduced me to Ambassador Lodge at the
embassy and the ambassador took me to meet the prime minister. Henry Cabot
Lodge had been in Saigon since August of 1963. He had ridden out the rough
weather of the generals' coup and the Diem assassination, and was now about
to return to the United States to put in his bid for the Republican presidential
nomination. The former U.S. senator from Massachusetts and U.S. representative at the UN had, as a colonel in World War II, acted as a liaison officer in

Europe with General de Lattre de Tassigny's French First Army. We drove to the prime minister's palace in the ambassador's black Checker cab, a spacious, armored vehicle that allowed the tall Lodge adequate head and leg room.

We were ushered into an air-conditioned waiting room hung with lacquer paintings and decorated with vases from Bien Hoa. The prime minister arrived, smiling broadly, and the introductions were made. General Khanh was a chunky man with a small, dark goatee and slightly protuberant eyes. He was wearing a sharply creased field uniform and his boots shone like mirrors. A graduate of the French-run military school at Dalat, he'd had a number of field commands during the Indochina War, and, according to the record, had proven his bravery fighting the Vietminh. He was also known for his mastery of political infighting. In January 1964 Khanh had moved against the fellow generals with whom he had worked to overthrow Diem and put himself in the catbird seat.

The prime minister thanked the ambassador for bringing me, said my services were badly needed, and promised me an office near his own. Somehow I had the impression that both the ambassador and the prime minister were play-acting. Lodge was obviously anxious to return to the embassy and the incoming telephone messages about his political future. The prime minister's shrewd eyes kept darting toward the anteroom, where some of his aides were waiting to talk with him.

The prime minister then suggested I meet his press officer, a man with whom I would soon be working. When this individual entered the room, the bright sunlight from the window made it momentarily difficult to see his face.

"Ah, Sim-son!" the new arrival exclaimed. It was Monsieur L, the Vietnamese colleague I had known from the days of the Franco-Vietnamese–U.S. psychological warfare effort. He had since served as a director of *Vietnam Presse*, the government news agency, and held various positions in the Ministry of Information—despite the changes in government. My grudging admiration for anyone with such a gift for political survival was tempered by the recollection that he had also been in close liaison with French Intelligence Services. Now he was obviously holding a key position in the prime minister's entourage. I mentioned this paradox to the ambassador on the way back to the embassy, but his mind seemed to be elsewhere.

On my first day at work I cooled my heels for more than an hour before being shown a small office down the hall from the prime minister. My first priority was to get to know Khanh and begin to understand his character, priorities, and working methods. A request to see him was tactfully countered by one of his military aides. I called the office of Monsieur L but he was out. After a long search I found some paper and began to jot down the outline of a program that would get the prime minister out of Saigon and into the field and villages for direct contacts with ARVN units and the population. Ambassador Lodge had mentioned this project as a priority need, but without more input from Khanh or his close aides I was working in a vacuum. I was also suffering from the lack of a typewriter, a telephone directory, and other office needs. I made out a shopping list, called for a car, and headed for the JUSPAO office in central Saigon.

I was in an ambiguous position in regard to JUSPAO. As an adviser to the prime minister, my principal office would be at the palace, but I was carried on the JUSPAO personnel roster. My assignment had been classified, primarily to fuzz increased U.S. participation in GVN operations and spare Vietnamese sensibilities, but I couldn't operate in the goldfish bowl of Saigon as a clandestine "press adviser." It would have been a contradiction in terms, particularly since some of the old media hands were already aware of my role, thanks to the normal leakage from U.S. and Vietnamese government sources.

JUSPAO was housed in a tall, blocklike colonial building looking out on the broad, busy Avenue Le Loi. Barry Zorthian's office on the third floor, with its adjoining, secure conference tank, was the nerve center of the U.S. information and psywar effort in Vietnam. Here Zorthian held his special briefings and "deep background" disclosures for selected newsmen. He also worked the telephone and communications net to keep on top of developments and maintain his authority, even if it meant chewing out unresponsive generals or disagreeing with an ambassador. The same floor contained the JUSPAO press section, a busy office dedicated to briefing visiting journalists and transporting them where they wanted to go to observe the war. The press section also produced the "Five O'Clock Follies," a daily press briefing conducted by civilian officials and military officers, held in an auditorium on the ground floor.

JUSPAO field operations in support of the Vietnamese Revolutionary Development and Pacification programs were headquartered near the press office. The "field reps" were the spearhead of the psywar campaign in the field. From the steamy Delta towns south of Saigon to the villages of the Central Highlands, these JUSPAO officers worked with regional representatives of the Vietnamese Information Service to build popular acceptance of the GVN, attack Vietcong morale, and encourage enemy desertions. It was an unusual assignment for a USIA officer, particularly as many called to Vietnam had left posts in Europe, where they may have been serving as cultural attachés or information specialists. Within days of leaving Rome or Paris they had found themselves in a Vietnamese rice paddy accompanying a black-clad, armed propaganda section of Vietnamese psywarriors or arguing with the local province chief about the merits of the *chieu hoi* defector program. The JUSPAO field reps, like their counterparts in other government agencies, operated at considerable risk, far from the privileges and pleasures of Saigon.

Other JUSPAO offices housed film, radio, publication, and TV sections manned by American officers supported by local employees. The shrunken cultural section was bravely carrying on in this wartime atmosphere, maintaining contact with Vietnamese students, and running a cultural center and an exchange program.

To maintain a semblance of normality and keep me in the fold, Zorthian had insisted I maintain a second office at JUSPAO. He had given me carte blanche to operate as I saw fit, with the proviso that I keep him informed on a daily basis. I also had immediate access to his lair if I judged it necessary. Space in JUSPAO was hard to come by, but I managed to squeeze a desk into Paul Garvey's cubbyhole. I'd no sooner begun to gather the material needed for my other office when my first visitor appeared.

Joe Fried of the New York *Daily News* slipped into the narrow room and introduced himself. Short, thin, intense, and highly skeptical of all information from official sources, Fried had a justified reputation as a reporter who sinks his teeth terrierlike into a story and doesn't let go until he's shaken the truth out of it. He was known for using JUSPAO and its small coffee shop as his operating base. While other correspondents ranged the countryside in search of copy, Fried panned for rumors, events, and trends; read between the lines of communiqués; picked the brains of JUSPAO personnel; and came up with nuggets of information that he burnished during the daily briefings. His interrogations, designed to box in nervous briefing officers, were worthy of a prosecuting attorney from The Bronx. During our first encounter, he told me he'd heard about my assignment and would like to maintain contact in order to present the Vietnamese side of things. When I instigated evasive action by telling him he should go to the press section for his information, he smiled knowingly and promised to drop by again.

Once my office at the palace was in working order, I set out to find Lou Conein. Requests for directions to Conein's office produced puzzled silences and blank faces among the prime minister's staff. I was about to give up when one of Khanh's aides and bodyguards intervened.

"You want to see Lou?" He asked in English. "Follow me." Conein's bare office was housed in a nearby building. He obviously didn't spend much time there and I was lucky to find him in. The elusive colonel was in civilian clothes, and as closed-mouthed as ever about his activities. He knew about my arrival. After some reminiscences of the old days in North Vietnam, he asked if I needed any help. I told him of my doubts about the prime minister's enthusiasm at being saddled with an American press adviser and asked that he feel Khanh out on the subject. If I was going to be kept in limbo, I explained, the assignment would be of no use to anyone. I hesitated a moment before mentioning a second request. My previous experience in Saigon and current worry about the security of my soon-to-arrive family had left me feeling naked, without a weapon of some kind to fall back on in an emergency. Conein, who had had a Special Forces team guarding his wife and children during the anti-Diem coup, promised a quick solution to my problem. A few days later we met in a small bar near the embassy and he passed me a wrapped package containing a snub-nosed .38 caliber Colt with a supply of ammunition. I would never be facing the threat or risks Conein lived with, but in the context of time, place, and situation it was a perfectly normal transaction.

The American Mission increased the pressure on Khanh to spend more time in the field in contact with his "rice-roots" constituency and the district chiefs and unit commanders responsible for the pacification program. Ambassador Lodge, with nostalgic memories of his own days on the campaign trail, emphasized the importance of visiting outlying villages and hamlets where the war would be won or lost. Other Americans added their urging and I joined the chorus with my memo to the prime minister. It had always been hard to tear Vietnamese officials away from the capital, but it was also hard to expect the Army or the population to pledge loyalty to a leader they neither knew nor respected. To most Vietnamese, Saigon was the seat of the mandarinate, the source of their troubles: taxes, agricultural levies, press-gang "recruitment" for the military, and blind repression. The Vietminh—and now the Vietcong—had taken full advantage of this attitude in their use of a Machiavellian blend of propaganda, civic action, and ruthless but carefully targeted terrorism.

At the beginning of his mandate Diem had made a reluctant attempt to play the populist, but he had never been convinced of the importance of "the people" in Vietnamese politics. In his world a regime had governed by making decisions and enforcing them. The population had then obeyed. He had also known that every hour he and his immediate circle spent away from Saigon could create an exploitable political vacuum for his enemies. Prime Minister Khanh, while adapting the clichés of Revolutionary Development, had much the same outlook. His role in successive coups and the thinly veiled hostility of certain military colleagues made him wary of leaving Saigon unless the situation was comparatively stable.

My first official sortie with Khanh in Phouc Tuy Province came close to disaster. I had not been privy to the planning for the trip and had only two hours warning before lift-off. Khanh's staff was behind the initiative and, I suspect, responsible for freezing me out of the preliminaries. To complicate matters, a team from French national television was to accompany us. As a qualified pilot, the prime minister flew his own chopper while the television team accompanied us in another. At our first stop the two security choppers went in first, settling like awkward mosquitoes on the sand near a coastal village. It was a "hot" zone and the villagers were scheduled for evacuation. The prime minister's visit was designed to show concern for his people and allow him to explain in person the need for their relocation. A sullen, bedraggled group of peasants was flushed from the huts as we landed. They listened uncomprehendingly as an aide shouted over the din of the rotors. He identified Khanh and attempted to raise a cheer. No luck. The French TV team jogged up to join us. When the villagers heard French being spoken, an old man with open sores on his scalp came forward. Hands joined together, he bowed and spoke in rapid French.

"It isn't just!" he protested to the French journalists. "They are making us move. We don't want to move. Tell them. It is not just!" Sniffing a good story, the French reporter flicked his notebook open and ordered his camera and soundmen to get the old man on film. "The Americans don't understand," the old man wailed. "Tell the Americans we don't want to leave!" The camera continued to whir as one of Khanh's security men hustled the old man out of range.

With the chopper rotors still turning slowly, the prime minister addressed the villagers. It was a wasted effort. They kept their eyes on the ground. As far as they were concerned he could have been a man from Mars. A sudden explosive *crump* jarred the earth. It was followed by another. Incoming mortar rounds were bracketing the far end of the village, and gray smoke hung in the still air. The villagers were gone within seconds. We scrambled unceremoniously back to the choppers, piled in, and lifted off, swinging low over the sea, heading back to Saigon.

Other, more successful field trips were to follow. They were usually aimed at the provinces close to Saigon. The provincial authorities hung out flags, gathered local dignitaries, and mustered schoolchildren to greet the prime minister; but there was little real, direct contact with the people. Blankets, medicine, and special funds were distributed and medals were presented to militiamen or ARVN personnel. But the astute peasants knew from experience that the stocky man with the beard, his well-armed entourage, and his foreign advisers would soon depart for the capital in a cloud of rotor dust. The villagers would remain in place, caught in the middle between government forces and the Vietcong and alternately wooed or punished by both.

In reality, what we were trying to do was graft our idea of "hit the hustings" democracy onto a resistant, centuries-old tree of Vietnamese history and culture. A "people's war" worked well in the Asian tradition of revolt and resistance. Adapting some of the same tactics to an established, authoritarian government was to prove unworkable.

CHAPTER 16

A Climate
of Coups

By the summer of 1964 Saigon was undergoing a surface Americanization. The U.S. government had taken over several of the city's hotels and large buildings as billets to house some of the 16,000 military personnel then in Vietnam. A small commissary had been established across the street from the multistory Brinks Bachelor Officer's Quarters (BOQ) near the Continental Hotel, and American military advisers and technicians in Hawaiian sport shirts roamed the busy Rue Tu Do. Some of the BOQs boasted roof-garden bars, barbecue facilities, and air-conditioned restaurants where American military and civilian officers could relax over cheap drinks during "happy hour" and listen to slinky Filipino vocalists belt out the latest hit tunes. These insular pockets of Americana isolated U.S. headquarters personnel in the capital from the Vietnamese and enclosed them in a sanitized cocoon far from the realities of the war. As the United States had not yet committed combat troops to Vietnam, only those serving in the field as advisers, Special Forces teams, and chopper crews had experienced the brutal, steadily escalating violence in the countryside.

American enlisted men on leave found plenty to keep them occupied at the small bars proliferating in the city's center and along the road to Tan Son Nhut Airport. La Normandie and Chez Yvette had given way to the San Francisco and the Blues Bar. Bar girls had replaced the more discreet professionals operating in bordellos. Younger, louder, and more aggressive, the B-girls perched on the stools of the Tu Do watering holes like chattering magpies, waiting to descend on GI customers. Their naïve idea of Western glamour often produced

173

grotesque, strangely touching combinations of dress and makeup. Armed with a few phrases in English, they competed for the attention of fresh-faced, home-sick GIs, hoping to hook a regular customer who might return. Many of the girls were helping to support their destitute refugee families or providing for their fatherless children with the money left after their pomaded "protectors" had skimmed the day's take.

The influence of Hollywood Westerns on a new generation of Americans was apparent in Saigon and the main Delta towns. Some GIs had taken on the air of swaggering gunfighters from a John Wayne epic. Kennedy had spoken of a New Frontier and they had found it. Under the threat of attack from an omni-present guerrilla enemy, the advisers and even the GIs in service units wore sidearms. They were also inventing a new vocabulary with links to the old West. The Vietcong were "hostiles" and the ARVN were "friendlies." After their arrival in March of 1965, the Marines would organize their Vietnamese irregulars as "Kit Carson Scouts," and the 1st Air Cavalry Division would later bring the full panoply of its Indian-fighting tradition to Vietnam.

I was now established in the prime minister's office and accepted by most of his staff. I had proven helpful to Khanh as an additional, more informal link to the embassy and JUSPAO. The prime minister was heeding my recommenda-tions to grant interviews to specific journalists, but he preferred to use Monsieur L as a buffer between us on more weighty suggestions while he played his politi-cal power games. I was also supplying the embassy with information on develop-ments and trends at the palace. This function was to take on more significance as we approached the period of coups, demicoups, and coupettes that would bring the war effort to a standstill, disrupt the shaky cohesion of the ARVN, and infuriate an uncomprehending Lyndon B. Johnson.

The prime minister introduced me to Col. Pham Ngoc Thao during a trip to the Mekong Delta and announced that Thao would soon come to Saigon to replace Monsieur L. General Khanh did *not* tell me he wanted Thao in close proximity because he didn't trust him and wanted to keep an eye on his activi-ties. Thao was a thin, walleyed Southerner and devout Catholic who had fought the French while commanding a Vietminh regiment in the Delta. At one point he'd supervised the Vietminh intelligence apparatus in South Viet-nam. With the end of the Indochina War he'd rallied to the Diem government and run a "successful" pacification program in Ben Tre Province. During this period his apparent candor and reasoned approach to counterguerrilla opera-tions had endeared him to a number of foreign correspondents.

A born plotter, Thao had been involved in the coup to topple Diem. Al-though he maintained close contact with certain Vietnamese combat com-manders, the majority of high-ranking ARVN officers distrusted him. Well they might. The man I was to work with for the next few months would spend most of his time planning future coups, using his press officer position as a cover. Not until 1981, during a trip to Vietnam to gather material for his book *Vietnam: A History,* did Stanley Karnow discover the truth about Thao. Tor-tured and killed by President Nguyen Van Thieu's special police in 1965, Thao had been reburied in Ho Chi Minh City's "Patriots' Cemetery" in recognition of his work as a key Communist agent.

I took time off during this period to greet my family at Tan Son Nhut. I picked them up in a small, newly purchased gray Mercedes with a sliding roof—without mentioning Garvey's description of the latter amenity as a "grenade trap." We settled into a villa in the same colonial compound on Rue Tu Xuong that housed George Hellyer's old residence, now occupied by Mel Manfull, the chief of the embassy's political section. I had hired a Vietnamese cook trained on French merchant vessels, a Chinese *amah*, and washerwomen. Within days of my wife's arrival she contacted Dr. Dé, who agreed to deliver our fourth child. The doctor assured us there would be no replacement obstetrician this time. As a former minister of health in the Diem government, Dé was under house arrest and could not leave his clinic. There was now an American School in Saigon, but we decided to put Shawn and Lisa into Les Oiseaux, a French institution run by nuns several blocks from our villa. We preferred to have our children blend into the Saigon scene rather than ride in a U.S. military bus guarded by an MP wielding a pump shotgun.

I returned to the palace to find my office occupied by a chain-smoking Vietnamese major. He explained that my effects had been moved across the street to an annex where I would be more comfortable and in close working proximity to Colonel Thao and his staff. The prime minister later cited the space shortage as the reason for the move. A more likely explanation was that he preferred not to have an American adviser so blatantly present on his doorstep and didn't relish my observing and identifying his palace visitors.

Working with Colonel Thao was a unique experience. It was as if he were performing a high-wire act without a safety net, an act written and directed by the Marx Brothers. We had adjoining offices, but he was seldom in his own. He was forever off on mysterious missions in a jeep driven by his bodyguard, a dour gunman with heavy-lidded eyes. When he returned, he'd invite me to his office, close the doors with the dramatic gestures of a stage conspirator, and relate tales of unrest and intrigue in Saigon. Either the Buddhists were "not happy" with Khanh's regime, the Catholics were "worried," or the ARVN was on the brink of "revolt." Once delivered of his foreboding predictions, Thao would relax in his chair and smile beatifically, his good eye scanning the untouched paperwork on his desk while the other fixed somewhere on the ceiling. I was duty bound to relay Thao's comments to the embassy and he undoubtedly knew it. But the glut of his doom-and-gloom pronouncements produced a wall of skepticism. The mere mention of Thao as a source soon brought groans from the embassy's upper echelons. But, despite his eccentricities, Thao was still considered a member of Khanh's inner circle and his comments could not be totally ignored. The problem lay in separating the truth from the fiction.

Thao lived in a small villa not far from the prime minister's palace. A large, sweet-smelling kumquat tree shaded the interior court, and the day I was invited to lunch a table had been set under its spreading branches. Thao's wife, a charming, attractive woman, had introduced me to the children. I recall having been impressed by their wide-eyed beauty, manners, and seeming vulnerability. They had been painting with watercolors when we arrived, and their deft oriental brushwork showed great promise. It was a pleasant, idyllic interlude. I had the impression that Thao had wanted to show me the other side of his character: that of a someone who would be content as a family man in time of peace. The only jarring note was the hovering presence of his bodyguard, whom Thao referred to as "my very old friend."

Shortly after moving to my new office, I was put on the restricted distribution list of a periodic government press roundup. I expected it to be a summary of international news stories or a condensation of editorials from the Vietnamese press translated into French. My first look at the mimeographed sheets provided an unexpected shock. I was reading the raw copy of foreign correspondents filed the day before via the international cable facilities of the Saigon post office. This meant that high-ranking Vietnamese officials were reading news stories before they were printed abroad and classifying Saigon-based journalists as "friendly" or "unfriendly" depending on the slant of their articles. In addition, the press roundup often contained the correspondent's personal notes to an editor: brief comments outlining plans for future coverage, touching on subject matter considered sensitive by the GVN, or pointing to sources the government might wish to shut off.

I found myself in a difficult position. As a former journalism student brought up on the ideals of Peter Zenger and freedom of the press, I saw the roundup as a violation of confidence. As the press adviser to a beleaguered wartime prime minister, I had to recognize the advantages of a "first-look" privilege. A quick investigation revealed that the practice, begun by the French, had been perfected and expanded by the Diem government. I mentioned the roundup to Thao, describing it as a public relations time bomb that could explode at any minute, souring GVN relations with the foreign press. He was obviously not interested. Barry Zorthian and I discussed the problem at length and agreed that I should do what I could to discourage the daily outtakes. In the end I succeeded only in reducing the distribution list. Discreet soundings among some Saigon-based journalists left me with the impression I'd been needlessly spinning my wheels. Most of them realized that their copy would be scrutinized by GVN officials the minute it was passed across the counter at the post and telegraph office. Their prime concern was that it reach its destination without delay or censorship. I did learn one truth from the press roundup hassle. Many American journalists, thanks to the demands of their job and well-cultivated sources, knew more of what was really going on in Vietnam than their government counterparts.

The summer of 1964 found Nguyen Khanh under pressure from a Buddhist coalition demanding a larger role in government. Catholic officers mistrusted him, and his intriguing had alienated some key Vietnamese generals. What little authority the Vietnamese government had in the provinces was deteriorating. The "oil-slick" technique of pacification so dear to the American Mission was in trouble. These operations called for the ARVN to secure a provincial sector and move out from its center. Regional and Popular paramilitary forces would then maintain security while government officials carried out enlightened pacification programs. This meticulously planned program was plagued by a lack of backup and coordination and the fluidity of Vietcong tactics.

It was also apparent that national unity remained a major problem in South Vietnam. Not only did the Buddhists, Catholics, and certain elements of the ARVN pose potential threats to Khanh, but the Cao Dai and the Hoa Hao had made a comeback following Diem's removal. The Binh Xuyen had never recovered from their military defeat, and the survivors had either fled to France or joined the Vietcong. The Cao Dai and the Hoa Hao had managed to maintain a certain power and influence in their regional fiefs, rebuilding their private armies on a relatively smaller scale. Their support and assistance were now needed against the Vietcong. With strong encouragement from the embassy, the Khanh government decided to sponsor a "National Unity Day." A ceremony was planned to bring the leaders of the sparring factions together on the same reviewing stand in central Saigon. The prime minister would then give a speech urging that old rivalries be forgotten in the interest of national survival.

I was asked to contribute to the first draft. Armed with some salient points provided by the embassy's political section, I isolated myself in Zorthian's office and tried to put some stirring, conciliatory words into Khanh's mouth. Members of the prime minister's inner circle were then to produce the final version. The text was also designed to avoid ruffling the feathers of the various political and religious groups. I was told the prime minister was pleased with the result, and preparations went ahead for the public rally. Security was particularly tight on the big day. Lou Conein haunted the grandstand area, his trained eye peeled for unwanted interlopers and possible assassins, while Khanh's security men checked for explosives.

The usual "hire a crowd" civilians and claques for the various participants had been augmented by the purely curious. The sunbaked square facing on Le Loi Boulevard was almost filled. Buddhist, Cao Dai, Catholic, Hoa Hao representatives; labor leaders; decorated war veterans; and a sampling of Vietnamese politicians took their places as the prime minister arrived in his escorted limousine. I was standing beside a Vietnamese-speaking officer from our embassy's political section when Khanh approached the microphone. He smiled toward the cameras from various international television networks and began to speak.

The political officer, who had been reading from his Vietnamese text, reached for my English text and began to compare the two papers. He then put both texts together, folded them, and began noting down the prime minister's words.

"It's not the same speech," he announced flatly.

In an ill-advised attempt to save his faltering government and distract both friends and enemies from the real problems at hand, Khanh had decided to change "National Unity Day" to "March to the North Day." In a situation where the ARVN was having problems holding its own against Vietcong units throughout the country and at the very doors of Saigon, he was advocating an invasion of North Vietnam!

Our much-touted national-unity project dissolved in an atmosphere of confusion and recrimination. The participants, who had been reluctant to lend their support to Khanh from the start, felt duped. No one at the American Mission was happy with Khanh's surprise innovation. It was obvious that all of us had been kept in the dark as to the prime minister's intentions. This episode confirmed our fears that Khanh's chronic unpredictability put him in the loose-cannon category. Hanoi radio and the Vietcong's propaganda outlets lost no time in underlining the prime minister's unrealistic proposal as the bombastic ravings of a desperate man.

In the following weeks I spent some time in the field wearing my other hat as adviser to the political warfare section of the ARVN. It was my first real glimpse of the war since my return. Barring the change in uniforms and equipment, it was the same old conflict. I listed the mistreatment of villagers, torture of suspects, and blind "interdiction" fire by artillery as prime faults in the ARVN's pacification program. Even more devastating was the inordinate tendency of Vietnamese commanders to call in air strikes or artillery on "suspect" hamlets before ordering their units to advance. The shift of the population's allegiance to the VC cause after such murderous attacks was often inevitable.

One evening, after returning to Tan Son Nhut from the Delta, I was about to call for a car from the prime minister's office when a well-polished but venerable Hotchkiss sedan pulled to a stop beside me. It took me several seconds to recognize the general in the rear seat. It was Pham Van Dong, the tough, combatwise Nung captain I had first met at the battle of Nasan in 1952. Laughing and shaking hands, he offered me a ride into Saigon. Dong was now commander of the Saigon-Cholon Military Region. He had put on weight since I last saw him, but he still resembled a Sioux chieftain. Climbing into the Hotchkiss, I noted the loaded .38 on the seat beside him. He saw my interest, smiled, and told me he had many enemies in Saigon and not all of them were Communists.

Weeks later my wife and I gave a small dinner in General Dong's honor. It was catered by the Jade Palace Restaurant of Cholon, and a circular table was set on the grass of our walled compound. There was much to eat, many incidents to recall, and too many toasts to be drunk to old friends. Halfway through the meal there was the sudden rumble of artillery from the direction of Co Cong. The firing grew in volume till it reached the proportions of a minor barrage. Frowning, the general put down his bowl of baked river fish and black mushrooms and asked if he could use the telephone.

For the next fifteen minutes our villa echoed to Dong's shouting as he took personal charge of blunting a VC feint on an ARVN position. That done, he returned to the table and helped himself to a good three fingers of scotch. A second interruption occurred as the dessert was served. A din arose from the kitchen. The general ordered the two Nung bodyguards who had been hunkered down near his Hotchkiss to investigate. They reappeared carrying our cook. He had inexplicably collapsed and was totally unconscious. The general sent him off to a hospital under the care of his chauffeur. A few days later the cook returned, smiling, to hand me a doctor's report diagnosing his problem as tertiary syphilis.

Ambassador Taylor and his deputy, U. Alexis Johnson, a top U.S. diplomat who also held the rank of ambassador, were operating in tandem at the embassy, trying to bring a semblance of order to the Vietnamese-American war effort. They were assisted by William Sullivan, a cool, witty Far East specialist who had worked as an aide to W. Averell Harriman, the assistant secretary of state, and to Secretary Dean Rusk. The top-floor offices of the embassy were busy nerve centers of the growing American effort in Vietnam. Typewriters clacked, telephones rang, and highly classified telegrams from Washington slugged "flash" and "immediate" were rushed in from the code room. Direct calls from the Oval Office were not uncommon when President Johnson's frustration level caused him to reach for his favorite working tool.

Ambassador Taylor's "mission council," the senior officers of all U.S. agencies and commands active in Vietnam, were attempting the herculean task of bolstering the South Vietnamese war effort without effective hands-on authority, monitoring VC activities and North Vietnamese infiltration, and formulating contingency plans for future U.S. initiatives. The White House, the State Department, the Pentagon, the Joint Chiefs of Staff, CIA headquarters, and CINCPAC in Hawaii were filling the role of kibitzers, pushing their favorite projects and plans with bureaucratic determination and insistence. But the computer-enhanced studies, flip charts, and statistics in Washington had little to do with reality. The Tonkin Gulf incident in early August, involving an alleged North Vietnamese patrol boat attack on an intelligence-gathering U.S. destroyer and the retaliatory U.S. sea and air bombardment of North Vietnamese targets, had distracted Washington from the growing internal crisis in Saigon.

Buoyed by the U.S. reaction in the Tonkin Gulf and interpreting it, in part, as a justification of his "March to the North" initiative, Khanh produced a new constitution, named himself president, and dumped Gen. Duong Van "Big" Minh, the popular central figure in the revolt against Diem. Khanh also instituted a number of draconian measures, including censorship, under a wide-reaching state of emergency. Considering the volatile political atmosphere in Saigon during late August of 1964, Khanh's actions had the effect of someone throwing a firebrand into a powder keg.

Students, Buddhists, and Catholics demonstrated against the government and then turned on each other. Alerted by the ominous, angry chanting of a crowd, I slipped out of our villa one morning to watch a mass of students armed with clubs and knives sweep along Cong Le Boulevard on their way to the center of the city. Small groups of Saigon policemen, nicknamed "white mice" for their lack of temerity, were swept aside by the militant mobs. I found the palace under siege. Armored cars blocked the main approaches. I had to argue with sentries manning a barrier of concertina wire to get to the office. The prime minister's press staff, in the tradition of detached, French-trained bureaucrats, were calmly peering out the windows and fretting over whether they would be allowed to leave the office early due to "events." Colonel Thao was nowhere to be found.

Once again blood ran in the streets of Saigon. Rival mobs clashed on the avenues and nervous ARVN troops threatened to open fire on the demonstrators. In a series of secret negotiations, Khanh tried to come to terms with the Buddhists, placate the students, and reassure the Catholics. At one point, protected by a thin ring of military police, he clambered atop a vehicle to face a chanting mob outside the palace. Microphone in hand, he tried to win the crowd over, but it was in no mood to listen. Visually shaken, he climbed down to be manhandled to safety by his bodyguards.

At the height of this crisis the loud voice of the security guard at the gate of our compound awoke me well after midnight. Colt in hand I went to the door to find a smiling Colonel Thao. He was wearing a holstered .45 on his thin hip and was profuse in his apologies for disturbing me. I asked what had brought him to my door. Thao calmly explained his mission. General Khanh wished to see Ambassadors Taylor and Johnson as soon as possible at his villa near General Staff Headquarters. Couldn't it wait till morning? No, it was of the utmost urgency that the two highest-ranking Americans in Saigon see the president immediately.

I dressed hurriedly and joined Thao in his jeep. He drove us through the deserted streets while his bodyguard rode shotgun in the backseat, a submachine gun on his lap. Thao got us through the Vietnamese sentries at the outer approaches to the ambassadorial residence, but the U.S. Marines guarding the entry were more meticulous. They were not prepared for an impromptu, post-midnight visit from such an odd couple. After several minutes of explanation and the showing of identity cards, the sergeant in charge went off to seek the duty security officer. Luckily, he knew me by sight.

Once inside, I explained the urgency of our mission and the security officer agreed to wake the sleeping ambassadors. Ambassador Johnson came down the stairs first, adjusting his bathrobe. Maxwell Taylor, silver hair askew, was not far behind. He rubbed his eyes, shook hands with Thao, and gave me a "this-better-be-important" look. They sat side by side on a divan and Taylor signaled for me to explain the purpose of our visit. I repeated what Thao had told me while the colonel beamed and nodded in agreement. When I'd finished, Ambassador Taylor informed Thao he'd be glad to see General Khanh at any time and suggested he could come to the residence right away if he felt it necessary. Colonel Thao, still smiling, shook his head slowly. The ambassador did not understand. Khanh wanted the ambassadors to come to him. It was a matter of "great importance."

Thus it was that a small convoy of one jeep and the ambassadorial sedan sped through the high-risk, empty streets of Saigon to a mysterious rendezvous with the Vietnamese chief of state. To say that I was nervous over Thao's initiative would be a gross understatement. Our security and firepower were minimal. We constituted a choice ambush target for the VC or any number of antigovernment factions then active in Saigon. Reflecting on that early-morning drive, particularly since learning of Thao's role as a Communist agent, remains an unsettling experience. I still have visions of what could have been the worst-case scenario: a sudden burst of firing, two dead ambassadors, Thao nowhere to be found, and myself—miraculously spared—trying to explain why I'd led the former chairman of the Joint Chiefs of Staff and one of America's top diplomats into a setup ambush.

We arrived at Khanh's villa without hindrance or trouble. While Thao and I cooled our heels in a reception room, Khanh and the ambassadors conferred behind closed doors for over three hours. The upshot of the long nocturnal meeting was that Khanh was determined to step down, relinquish his claim to the presidency, scrap his hastily conceived constitution, and allow the "military revolutionary council" of ARVN generals to form a new government. Generals Duong Van Minh and Tran Thien Khiem, whom I had known as a young, bespectacled captain with a *groupe mobile* in North Vietnam, joined Khanh in a shaky coalition to provide some semblance of government. Now "*trés fatigué*" from the tensions and strains of the crisis, Khanh left Saigon for a rest in the mountain resort town of Dalat.

The situation in Saigon remained fluid and threatening while Khanh recharged his batteries and plotted in Dalat. He had named Nguyen Xuan Oanh, a Harvard-trained economist, as prime minister, but few in the capital took the appointment seriously. Oanh (today an economic adviser to the Hanoi government) was destined to be pushed aside when Khanh felt it was time to move back into the palace. Khanh tried to mend his bridges with the Buddhists and appear conciliatory to the students and the Catholics, but his absence from the seat of power had emphasized his weaknesses and encouraged the dissidents. While Khanh attempted to "pacify" the marauding factions of Saigon, certain ARVN units were moving to take things into their own hands.

One bright morning in mid-September I drove to the palace to find tanks pulled up near the gate. Considering the situation, I took no particular notice, thinking their presence was a reassuring demonstration of Army loyalty or a simple precaution to prevent further rioting. Only after I'd parked and begun to walk to my office did I notice the tank's guns were leveled at the government buildings. I found a heavily armed squad of ARVN Rangers in my office. Everything on my desk had been swept onto the floor, the desk lamp was broken, and they'd used the corner of the room as a latrine.

A frowning Ranger lieutenant with tattooed forearms, wearing a camouflage uniform and dark glasses, was sitting in my chair, his boots braced on the desk. There was an awkward moment of silence as we eyed each other. My only thought was to leave as soon as possible, but I could sense that a precipitate retreat would have been unwise. The South Vietnamese Rangers had a well-earned reputation as tough and ruthless "cowboys." I was in no hurry to push my luck. Without thinking I fell back on a spontaneous French expression.

"*Eh bien, merde!*" I said quietly, surveying the mess. I couldn't have chosen a better phrase. A smile wiped away the lieutenant's frown, the boots came off the desk, and he stood up.

"You speak French?" he asked, puzzled. "But you are not French?"

For the next fifteen minutes we clarified our respective positions, the Marx Brothers once again in charge of the script. The lieutenant knew he was involved in a coup, but he didn't know who his adversaries were. He thought they might be VC collaborators in the government. He was piqued that those in the palace had not surrendered. But he and his men were ready to go in after them once the tanks started firing. He did know that Gen. Duong Van Duc, the ARVN commander in the Delta, was in charge of the operation. I sketched a brief outline of my role as an adviser. For some reason the lieutenant found this vastly amusing. He repeated it to his men and they all had a good laugh. When I explained that the palace was being defended solely by ARVN colleagues from other units, his frown returned.

The lieutenant allowed me to use the telephone and I called Zorthian, explaining my predicament. He listened with interest and some amusement. With the calm of someone who'd experienced tight situations himself, he suggested I leave the vicinity of the palace as soon as possible. He told me that Air Vice Marshal Nguyen Cao Ky, the commander of the Vietnamese Air Force (VNAF), was threatening to bomb the coup forces into oblivion. As I put down the phone a tanned American captain appeared at the door. He, too, was an adviser, attached to the ARVN Rangers. I suggested we talk outside. He was as much in the dark regarding the true situation as his Vietnamese counterparts. The Rangers had been ordered to Saigon to preserve law and order, he told me, perhaps to block a VC uprising. He turned red in the face when I told him he was participating in an antigovernment coup. I warned him of Ky's intentions while edging toward my Mercedes. I also suggested that it might be wise to leave his ARVN colleagues to sort out their own problems. When I turned on the ignition, he was still pondering his predicament, doubtless torn between loyalty to his Vietnamese comrades-in-arms and the thought of dying under Ky's bombs in a coup d'état. By the time I'd rolled out of the driveway and past the tanks, I was relieved to see the captain striding purposefully away from the palace complex.

Ky's threats had the desired effect. The officers and men of the ARVN had mopped up too many battlefields in the wake of heavy air strikes. They had a deep respect for the deadly results of bombs and napalm. The two coup leaders, Gen. Lam Van Phat and Gen. Duc, surrendered and the chastened coup forces returned to their sectors. From this point on, Air Vice Marshal Ky, a flamboyant, mustachioed character with a taste for purple jump suits and pearl-handled revolvers, would act as a deciding factor in future coups.

Colonel Thao had been conspicuous by his absence during the abortive coup, and the prime minister's press office had been marking time. Most of the civilian staff had not reported to work. Their excuses ranged from "liver attacks" to simple fatigue. The military officers in mufti whom I worked with appeared daily for a short period to sniff the wind of change, trying to decipher whether Khanh would remain in power or be replaced. As far as I was concerned it was just as well. The birth of our fourth child was imminent and I was waiting for the phone to ring. When the time came, my wife drove herself to the clinic and I met her there. Dr. Dé was summoned from his daily roller-skating sessions in the clinic's courtyard to deliver our youngest daughter, Maggie. It was October 18, 1964.

On November 1 the Vietcong mounted a classic, successful guerrilla attack on Bien Hoa Air Base, twelve miles north of Saigon, destroying six U.S. B-57 bombers, damaging twenty other aircraft, and killing five Americans. It was a clear message to Saigon that the real threat to South Vietnam lay beyond the feuding cabals of the capital. It was also a signal to the United States that the Vietcong and their North Vietnamese allies had no qualms about challenging a superpower.

CHAPTER 17

Who Is That Man?

Saigon could not shake its bad case of coup fever. At one point I found myself rushing to Colonel Thao's house in a cyclo-pousse, the driver straining at the pedals and ringing his bell to clear the way. A member of the prime minister's staff had passed the word that certain officers were planning to eliminate the colonel. I'd rushed from the office to find my car hopelessly blocked in the drive and run into the street to flag down a cyclo. When we'd skidded to a stop I bounded to the villa and banged on the door. I was soon staring at the business end of a riot gun. The colonel's faithful bodyguard told me that Thao and his family had already fled to an unknown "safe house." Not long afterward Khanh removed Thao from the scene by sending him off to Washington, D.C., as press attaché to the Vietnamese embassy, where General Khiem, a former comrade whom Khanh also mistrusted, had been sent as ambassador.

Days later an American newsman came to me with a letter he had agreed to deliver in Saigon for a Vietnamese general exiled in Paris. It was addressed to a member of the General Staff. Worried about the letter's possible contents, the newsman had asked his Vietnamese assistant to read it. The assistant had immediately suggested it be shown to an American official. I rushed the letter to the embassy for translation. Within minutes our worst suspicions were confirmed. The text was a straightforward pledge of moral and material support for a planned coup. It was the type of message that could easily have changed the local balance of power and torn the shaky government apart. I eventually returned the letter to its innocent bearer with a strong recommendation that it be delivered only after the coup clouds had cleared.

The constant political change produced a swinging-door policy in Vietnamese government offices. Time after time Barry Zorthian and I climbed the steep stairs of the Ministry of Information to call on a newly appointed minister and urge a continuation of previous psywar programs that had barely gotten off the ground. The various succeeding ministers listened politely, promised full cooperation, and saw us on our way. One such visit found us face-to-face with the resilient Monsieur L. He had bounced back from political limbo to occupy the minister's desk for a short period of time. During each getting-to-know-you meeting, I observed the appearance of the "eye-glaze" syndrome. Zorthian sat forward in his chair, poking his stubby index finger at documents—or the minister—in an attempt to emphasize the urgency of the situation. One after the other the ministers withdrew behind fixed smiles into their protective shells.

The sound of tank engines and the sudden appearance of unfamiliar troops at strategic points in Saigon had now become commonplace. It was always hard to tell whether they were pro-coup or anti-coup forces. ARVN units had taken to wearing colored armbands to identify themselves and prevent the exchange of fire between friendly elements. But lack of coordination led to confusion, and the varied colors were often misread. The presence of Ky's bomb-heavy aircraft flying low over the city, their landing lights blinking on and off, had become a sure sign that another coup was brewing or under way.

Nguyen Khanh was still playing his political games. He had resigned as prime minister but retained real power as commander in chief of the Armed Forces. A figurehead regime of doddering civilians had been moved into the palace. Phan Khac Suu, a politician in his eighties who had once served Emperor Bao Dai, had been named chief of state. Tran Van Huong, the aged former mayor of Saigon, had become prime minister. They were both unlikely leaders for a nation in crisis. Suu, wearing his mandarin gown and traditional round hat, had to be hand-guided to official functions. The portly Huong, gray hair in a brush cut, appeared to be operating in his own dreamworld.

My function at the palace was fast becoming redundant. Normally I would have concentrated on working with Gen. Huynh Van Cao, the chief of the ARVN political warfare section, but he too was caught up in the coup waltz. As it was, I went through the motions of offering my services to the new prime minister. Huong received me graciously, we sipped tea, and I did most of the talking. After fifteen minutes I thanked him for his time, reminded him my office was across the street, and took my leave. As I walked to the door he turned to one of his aides and whispered, "Who is that man?"

The anarchy continued. Buddhist mobs defied the police and the ARVN while Suu and Huong sat isolated in their offices. Finally, in desperation, Huong declared martial law. Within days Khanh and a group of young generals, including Thieu and Ky, had moved on their military rivals, imprisoning General Minh and his supporters and establishing an Armed Forces Council.

This was the last straw for Ambassador Taylor. Prior to Khanh's move, President Johnson had been insistent in his demands that Taylor bring some order out of the mess in Saigon. Now, although Taylor had already warned the "Young Turk" generals of the American government's lack of patience with their antics, he was faced with another coup. The ambassador's frustration boiled to the surface. On December 21 he summoned the generals to his embassy office and gave them the type of dressing-down normally reserved for recalcitrant U.S. Regular Army subordinates. I had been in the hallway when the generals left the embassy. They'd swept by, white-faced with fury and so upset they'd failed to return the salutes of the Marine guards.

The contained tension that had been building between the ARVN generals and the embassy exploded. Ambassador Taylor had done the unthinkable. The generals had lost face under Taylor's tirade, and Khanh wasted no time in striking back. Unknown to me, he gave a press interview stating that American "colonialism" could be as dangerous as Communism. He also began to push for Ambassador Taylor's recall. The ambassador then suggested that Khanh would best serve Vietnam by resigning and leaving the country. A meeting of the Armed Forces Council was called on December 23 to discuss Taylor's insulting demeanor, and plans were made to unseat him as the U.S. ambassador. A secret "immediate" telegram to Washington dated December 25, 1964, contains one of my reports underlining the seriousness of Khanh's intentions:

CHIEF OF ARVN PSYWAR INFORMED US PRESS ADVISER THIS AFTERNOON THAT ARMED FORCES COUNCIL MEETING YESTERDAY INVOLVED THREE MAIN EFFORTS: KHANH'S CHARACTERIZATION OF AMBASSADOR'S POSITION DURING MEETING WITH YOUNG TURKS AND WITH KHANH AS INADMISSIBLE AND INSULT TO ARMY AND NATION; (2) EXPLANATION OF PLAN TO PRESENT PETITION TO HUONG DEMANDING HE REQUEST AMBASSADOR TAYLOR'S RECALL; (3) OUTLINE OF EMERGENCY PLAN IN EVENT HUONG REFUSES SIGN PETITION, IN WHICH PROVINCIAL CHIEFS WOULD SEND IN PETITIONS SIGNED BY THEIR OFFICERS DEMANDING THE GVN ACT ON AMBASSADOR'S RECALL. REGARDING LATTER POINT PETITIONS WOULD BE COORDINATED WITH PRESS CONFERENCE BY KHANH AND YOUNG TURKS IN WHICH AMBASSADOR WOULD BE ATTACKED AND "CERTAIN RECORDINGS" MADE PUBLIC. SOURCE COMMENTED THAT KHANH IS IN HIGHLY NERVOUS STATE.

The previous day—Christmas Eve—we had been forcefully reminded of the *real* enemy's operational presence in Saigon. Barry Zorthian was giving a background briefing to a group of newsmen at JUSPAO when a heavy explosion smashed the picture window facing on Le Loi Boulevard, showering the correspondents with pulverized security glass. Luckily no one was injured. François Sully of *Newsweek*, an old Indochina hand, had been first out the door, notebook in hand. The rest of us had followed. Black smoke billowed into the sky behind the Hotel Continental. Running across the street, we passed frightened Vietnamese civilians fleeing in the opposite direction.

A charge had been detonated in the Brinks BOQ. Ambulances were careening to the scene, and some young sidewalk venders had been cut by flying glass. The entrance to the BOQ'S basement parking area was blackened with smoke. Firefighters were unreeling their hoses to fight the yellow flames, and American officers in blood-spattered sport shirts and slacks were being helped into the ambulances. The sharp, cloying odor of high explosive hung in the air. It had been too early to know the extent of the casualties, but a final tally would show 2 Americans killed and 52 wounded. Vietnamese wounded totaled 13.

I helped some Vietnamese firefighters with their hose in an attempt to be of use, but nervous MPs with M-16s braced on their hips were warning everyone off, fearing a follow-up explosion. I left the newsmen to their work and crunched over the broken glass to a small bar run by a Corsican I'd known since the early 1950s. I found him standing on the sidewalk assessing the cost of his broken windows.

"*Alors?*" He confronted me, hands extended, palms up. "What is happening, Sim-son?" he demanded. "At least, when the French were here we had security!"

The Brinks attack was later proved to be a well-planned action carried out by Vietcong agents in ARVN uniforms. But, given the conspiratorial climate of the time, rumors were soon circulating pointing to General Khanh as the instigator.

While Saigon was stewing in its self-destructive juices, the Communists were proceeding with a massive project that would have a decisive influence on the outcome of the war. Hundreds of miles to the north, the Ho Chi Minh Trail was being developed and perfected as an infiltration and supply route for the North Vietnamese and the Vietcong. As early as 1959, after the North Vietnamese politburo had decided to back the Vietcong effort, the network of footpaths, trails, and small roads running south through Laos and Cambodia was being improved and linked. Using the techniques perfected during the struggle for Dien Bien Phu, the North Vietnamese were establishing special waystations where porters, working in relays, could rest and be fed. Labor brigades constructed camouflaged vehicle parks, bridges, and storage dumps for ammunition, food, and medical supplies.

At first the spiderweb network of jungle trails was used by agents, small units, and snakelike columns of porters humping backpacks or pushing fully loaded bicycles. This had changed by 1964. While some of the ARVN's best units and most of its General Staff were involved in Saigon's coups and countercoups, North Vietnamese main-force units were joining newly trained Southern guerrillas on the trek south. Over 10,000 hardened North Vietnamese regulars were estimated to have used the trail by the end of the year.

Despite a heavy toll from sickness, exhaustion, increasing U.S. air strikes, and harassment on the ground by daring long-range patrols carried out by American and Vietnamese Special Forces, the infiltration would continue and grow. Soviet-supplied Molotova trucks, and Dodges captured from the French, would augment the backpacks and bicycles, increasing the volume of matériel and facilitating the movement of artillery and rocket launchers. By 1966 the estimated movement of North Vietnamese Regulars would reach 90,000, and by 1970 the weekly count of transported supplies would be estimated at 10,000 tons.

Once again we were stepping into the two principal traps set for the French: underestimation of the enemy's capability and overreliance on the effectiveness of air power. Officials in Washington with little or no knowledge of Vietnam were misreading the signals. The reaction of the Pentagon was understandable and inevitable. What do you do with an enemy supply route? You interdict it by bombing and strafing. But the very name "Ho Chi Minh Trail" was misleading. It might have helped if someone had added an "s" to the word trail.

Layered, thick jungle provided a permanent, impenetrable cover for the trail and road network. Thick clouds and filthy weather over the jungled mountains often supplied a secondary defense, and camouflaged antiaircraft positions threatened low-flying fighter-bombers. One of the enemy's greatest advantages lay in his trail discipline and passive-defense procedures. Tire tracks and footprints were routinely obliterated by sweeping with leafy branches. An elementary aircraft-warning system relayed short notice of an impending attack, imposing a freeze on all movement. Regulars, porters, and construction teams huddled, head down, in shrub-covered ditches and ravines, munching their riceball rations while our hi-tech jets, loaded for bear, screamed over the jungle canopy.

The day after the Brinks bombing my wife and I, like other American families in Saigon, were trying to erect the façade of a normal Christmas. A sparse tamarind tree in the corner of our living room sagged under the weight of colored lights, ornaments, and recycled tinsel. The children's stockings were hung from the stairway, a skinny, long-legged turkey was sputtering in the oven, and the ceiling fans stirred the heavy air. We exchanged presents with the servants, and our cook, whose infection had proven much less serious and treatable, produced a serviceable *bûche de Noël*. But it was difficult to generate spontaneous Christmas cheer in the oppressive heat with the thump of distant artillery counterpointing the carols and the phone threatening to ring with news of yet another coup.

Just prior to the holidays I'd been informed that General Khanh had ordered Colonel Thao back to Saigon. In fact, I'd been looking forward to seeing him again. My queries on Thao's return date had gone unanswered. It was only after Christmas that I learned Thao had returned to Saigon and—aware of Khanh's plan to seize him on arrival—had managed to slip into clandestinity.

The next coup came in late January 1965. Khanh deposed Huong in the wake of violent anti-American Buddhist demonstrations in Hué and Saigon. Rumors of Khanh's desire to seek an accommodation with the Vietcong had begun to be taken seriously by the embassy, and Thieu and Ky, Khanh's former allies, were considering his removal. On February 7 the Vietcong mounted a surprise attack on the airstrip at Pleiku in the Central Highlands that killed eight Americans, wounded over a hundred others, and destroyed eight U.S. aircraft.

President Johnson had resisted previous advice to retaliate following the attack at Bien Hoa and the Brinks bombing. Now he had been pushed too far. McGeorge Bundy, Johnson's national security adviser, who happened to be visiting Vietnam at the time, called the White House, urging prompt retaliation. He and Ambassador Taylor followed up the call with a strong cable supporting such action. Johnson then gave the order for Operation Flaming Dart, a series of reprisal air strikes against North Vietnamese military targets.

While the USS *Ranger*'s pilots were returning from their first raid on a North Vietnamese base at Dong Hoi, the president's decision was having an immediate effect in Saigon.

To "clear the decks for action," the White House ordered the evacuation of all American dependents from Vietnam. The calls came late, the telephones jangling in the hot stillness of the night. I sleepily argued the twenty-four hour notice with an insistent administrative officer. When he failed to capitulate, I called Zorthian to cite doubtful reasons that would make the Simpson family an exception. Zorthian listened patiently, made it clear that Lyndon Johnson was taking a personal interest in the speed of the evacuation process, and granted me an extra twenty-four hours.

It all happened very fast: the calls, the stunned responses, the vain arguments, the waking of sleeping wives, coffee and confusion in the early-morning hours, packing and dressing the drowsy children. In the rush of the moment there was little time to realize the implications of the coming separations, the slipped moorings. It was almost all over in forty-eight hours, concluding with a farewell glass of tepid champagne at Tan Son Nhut, much forced gaiety, and hurried goodbyes. As the leased commercial jets lifted off, the husbands and fathers sighed with relief, realizing for the first time how worried they'd been about the safety of their families. Returning to the city, they joked like men off on a hunting trip. But, once back at the silent villas, they looked at the empty closets, the lone place setting on the table, and knew that everything would be different.

The weekly escalation continued. The VC became bolder, attacking a U.S. military billet in Qui Nhon. The White House then decided to prepare for Operation Rolling Thunder, a progressive bombing of preselected military targets in North Vietnam. In Saigon the workday lengthened and the tension became palpable. The temporary bachelors teamed up to share living quarters. It was both practical and more secure. Civilian officials who had never fired a handgun took to keeping one by their beds and slipping it into their briefcases on the way to work.

Harold Kaplan, who had arrived to serve as Zorthian's deputy, moved in with me to share the villa on Rue Tu Xuong. A former member of the Office of War Information (OWI), Kaplan's USIA assignments had been limited to Europe prior to his posting to Vietnam. A thoughtful, quiet intellectual, Kaplan was stunned by the grim farce of Saigon's political circus. He considered me a hopeless cynic—until he himself had to deal with his opposite numbers in the GVN. One evening not long after his arrival he returned to the villa beaming to announce an agreement he had just reached on a psywar project with Gen. Huynh Van Cao. When I opined that the project would never see the light of day, Kaplan reproached me for my negative attitude. Within the hour Cao's office called to inform Kaplan that the general had changed his mind and the project had been shelved. Despite our differing backgrounds we enjoyed each other's company. Kaplan's Saigon "education" was to serve him well when he was assigned to the Paris Peace Talks on Vietnam in 1968.

The womanless, quiet villas were increasingly difficult to face after a twelve-hour day in the pressure-cooker atmosphere of crisis. The new bachelors began to discover Saigon by night. The "hostesses" of the city, like sharks in an azure sea, sensed vulnerability and closed in on their prey. The experienced, educated professionals, former mistresses of Vietnamese Army officers or government officials, and the younger bar girls, shifted their targeting. A mature American civilian official alone at a reception or in a bar was a more lucrative mark than a GI on R&R. Houseboys and cooks, saddened by the loneliness of their "masters" and ever ready to increase their own income, passed the word, and a sudden spate of job seekers appeared at the door. Uncommonly attractive "sisters" and "nieces"—obviously uncomfortable in tight servant's jackets—were introduced as accomplished laundresses, outstanding housecleaners, and dependable substitute cooks. Never before had American diplomatic residences in Saigon had such appealing servants.

As always, there were those who succumbed and those who held out. Normally, discretion was the key, but some "plungers" insisted on flaunting their new female companions. They appeared at official receptions accompanied by sultry Vietnamese courtesans in expensive ao dais under the envious but critical gaze of their senior officers. Others drew attention to their "arrangement" by frequenting the better restaurants with doe-eyed prostitutes. Worried American officials pondered the security implications of the new permissiveness, concerned that unguarded pillow talk would now have a direct line to VC agents seeded throughout the city. This may have been true to some extent, but the VC infiltration of Saigon was so widespread, so well established over the years, it was more likely the gems of their intelligence collection were mined by long-time "sleepers" and "plants" in government offices, the ARVN, and the American Mission.

The temporary bachelors who did not succumb worked longer hours, read thicker books, wrote more frequent letters to their wives, poured stronger drinks, swam more often at the Cercle Sportif, and crossed off the days on the calendar. Some actually thrived on this priestlike existence, amused by the antics of those who had fallen and strengthened and surprised by their own virtue.

By mid-February General Khanh was once again pulling the strings in Saigon. Nguyen Xuan Oanh, whom Khanh had once again moved into the frontman position as acting prime minister, was unceremoniously removed and replaced by Dr. Phan Huy Quat, a physician from the North. I'd known Dr. Quat briefly in Hanoi, where he had served as a ranking government official under the French administration. He was a thin, courageous politician who had endured constant threats from the Vietminh and various opponents throughout his career. Meeting him again at General Staff Headquarters shortly after his appointment, I experienced a fleeting moment of encouragement. He mentioned the importance of national unity and spoke of the need for broadening the government's base. Here, finally, was a civilian who might have the strength and integrity to stand up to the military. Quat's appointment certainly did not signal McNamara's "light at the end of the tunnel," but his presence as prime minister did represent a slight flickering of hope.

Five days after Quat's installation a new coup hit Saigon with the force of a body blow. Tank treads were once again chewing up the sun-softened macadam, and ARVN troops, like ambulant mushrooms under their heavy helmets, were moving on key government installations. Colonel Thao emerged from the shadows as a co-conspirator with the unrepentant Gen. Lam Van Phat. During the first confused hours I'd found it hard to believe that Thao had embarked on such a rash move, but an American journalist confirmed Thao's role. Seeing the colonel leading a group of tanks toward Radio Vietnam, he'd banged on the turret to get Thao's attention and asked "what the hell" he was doing.

"Go away!" Thao had replied in English. "I am making a coup!" His English pronunciation of the French word came out as "coop."

Thao's attempt to capture Khanh failed, and Air Vice Marshal Ky reemerged in his role of avenging angel. Ky's air force helped Khanh escape to safety, and Ky threatened Thao and Phat's forces with a bombing attack. Thao and Phat eventually agreed to call off the coup, but only if Khanh agreed to leave the country. This brief synopsis appears simple and uncomplicated, but each action, threat, proposal, and initiative took place on the edge of a political-military precipice. Excerpts from the embassy's cable traffic, now unclassified, accurately reflect the tension and uncertainty of the moment:

SECRET/FLASH/LIMDIS
FEB 19, 5PM
    ... GENERAL KY AT BIEN HOA HAS JUST TALKED TO GENERAL PHAT WHO CONTROLS TAN SON NHUT. ACCORDING TO VIETNAMESE WHO OVERHEARD PHAT END OF CONVERSATION, PHAT EXPLAINED THAT COUP WAS TO OUST KHANH AND WAS NOT ANTIGOVERNMENT. KY APPARENTLY GAVE PHAT SOME ENCOURAGEMENT AND INDICATION OF SUPPORT. I HAVE JUST TALKED BY TELEPHONE TO QUAT WHO IS IN CONFERENCE AT HIS RESIDENCE. NO ONE HAS BOTHERED HIM AND HE INTENDS TO CONTINUE BUSINESS AS USUAL.... TROOP INVOLVEMENT IS STILL FAR FROM CLEAR BUT APPEARS SLIGHT. MOST VISIBLE UNIT IS THE 5TH AR-

MORED GROUP WHICH IS VERY MUCH IN EVIDENCE. TROOPS AT
TAN SON NHUT ARE RANGERS OF AN UNIDENTIFIED UNIT. . . .
TAYLOR

SECRET/FLASH/LIMIDS
FEB 19, 8PM
SITUATION IS BECOMING MORE CONFUSED BY THE HOUR. KHANH
HAS ORDERED THREE AIRBORNE BATTALIONS PRESENTLY IN VUNG
TAU AREA TO MOVE ON SAIGON AND RESTORE ORDER. HE EX-
PECTS SEVENTH DIVISION TO SUPPORT THE OPERATION. WE ARE
NOT SURE WHETHER HE CAN COUNT UPON THESE TROOPS TO
OBEY HIS ORDERS. AS A MATTER OF FACT NOBODY IS SURE OF THE
LINE UP OF THE SIDES. PHAT SEEMS TO HAVE SOME OF THE
RANGERS ALTHOUGH KHANH IS CLAIMING THEM BY TELEPHONE.
ADMIRAL CANG HAS WITHDRAWN TO A SHIP OFF NA BE IN THE
SAIGON RIVER AND CLAIMS HE IS NEUTRAL. IN THE MEANTIME,
KY IS THREATENING TO BOMB TAN SON NHUT IF PHAT DOES NOT
REMOVE HIS FORCES FROM THE FIELD. HE FIRST SET 1830 FOR
BOMBS ON TARGET BUT HAS NOW CHANGED TIME TO 1900. (THIS
FIRST HOUR IS NOW PAST.) AT 1845 GENERAL WESTMORELAND
TALKED TO KY BY TELEPHONE AND IN THE STRONGEST TERMS
URGED HIM TO PUT ASIDE SUCH NONSENSE. . . . TAYLOR

Nonsense or not, Ky's threats produced results. General Phat and Colonel
Thao agreed to surrender with the condition that Khanh be deposed and leave
the country. The next day the Armed Forces Council removed Khanh from
power, appointed him ambassador-at-large, and made arrangements for him to
fly to Hong Kong. Ambassador Taylor provided a trenchant summation of the
crisis in a "no distribution" telegram to President Johnson:

SECRET/PRIORITY/FOR THE PRESIDENT/NODIS
FEB 23, 8PM
THIS HAS BEEN THE MOST TOPSY-TURVY WEEK SINCE I CAME TO
THIS POST: A NEW GOVERNMENT INSTALLED, A COUP ATTEMPT
AGAINST THE COMMANDER IN CHIEF, THE COUP SUPPRESSED, THE
COMMANDER IN CHIEF DEPOSED BY THOSE WHO HAD PUT DOWN
THE COUP. . . . PHAT'S UNSUCCESSFUL EFFORT DID HAVE THE EF-
FECT OF BREAKING KHANH'S SPELL OVER HIS COLLEAGUES IN THE
ARMED FORCES COUNCIL AND OF BRINGING THEM TO A DECISION
TO UNSEAT HIM. THIS ACTION APPEARS TO HAVE BEEN SUCCESS-
FUL AND KHANH'S APPOINTMENT AS AMBASSADOR-AT-LARGE
HAS JUST BEEN ANNOUNCED. I UNDERSTAND HE WILL DEPART SAI-
GON FOR HONG KONG ON 25 FEBRUARY: BUT ONE CANNOT EX-
CLUDE POSSIBILITY OF HIS MAKING ANOTHER LAST MINUTE MA-
NEUVER TO SAVE HIMSELF. WITH KHANH, THE TROUBLEMAKER,

REMOVED FROM THE SCENE, WE HOPE THAT QUAT GOVERNMENT CAN GET UNDER WAY WITH OUR JOINT PROGRAMS.

The same telegram reflected the effect of such coups on the war effort:

THE EXCITEMENT OVER THE COUP TENDED TO DIVERT ATTEN-
TION SOMEWHAT FROM THE VIETCONG AMMUNITION SHIP SUNK
OFF THE COAST OF PHU YEN PROVINCE. THE CARGO OF THIS SHIP
FURNISHES BY FAR THE MOST DRAMATIC EVIDENCE OF HANOI IN-
VOLVEMENT YET UNCOVERED IN THE WAR. . . . PACIFICATION
CONDITIONS REMAIN UNSATISFACTORY IN MANY PROVINCES,
PARTICULARLY IN BINH DINH AND PHU YEN. THE DETERIORATING
SECURITY SITUATION IN THIS LATTER AREA HAS REQUIRED A CUT-
BACK IN OUR ECONOMIC PROGRAMS, SINCE USOM (AID) REPRE-
SENTATIVES ARE GENERALLY UNABLE TO LEAVE THE PRINCIPAL
TOWNS. WE CAN HARDLY EXPECT TO REVERSE THIS SITUATION IN
CENTRAL VIETNAM UNTIL THE QUAT GOVERNMENT IS ABLE TO
INCREASE ITS OPERATIONAL MILITARY AND PARAMILITARY
STRENGTH.

I had been busy gathering what information I could during the coup and passing it on to the embassy. Now, with the heat off, I returned to my office. The annex building was semideserted, as if the prime minister's press office staff were still expecting a series of political aftershocks. Quat's inner circle had not yet spread its authority across the street. Our domain was a landscape of empty desks, unanswered telephones, and dusty floors covered with unread official documents. While I tried to make some sense out of the telephone messages I'd found speared on my desk pen, the unperturbable Colonel Duc, wearing red suspenders and a striped shirt, sat with his feet up, telling scatological jokes and musing that I would return in an afterlife manifestation as a Buddhist elder named "Tich Tam Simpson."

One of the messages I'd found was from a former aide to Ba-Cut, the piratical Hoa Hao leader executed by the Diem regime. It was marked urgent and listed a telephone number to call. I was puzzled and intrigued enough to follow up the contact. Two nights later I was invited to dine at l'Amiral Restaurant with Ba-Cut's widow. I arrived early, in time to trade stories of the Indochina War with the French proprietor, a former para who was learning to overcook steaks for his American clients.

I wasn't sure what to expect, but I had recalled seeing a photo of Ba-Cut's child bride back in 1954, a fuzzy snap of a sullen teen-ager with large dark eyes. The 1965 reality was breathtaking. She arrived in a chauffeur-driven black se-dan accompanied by the former aide. The black silk of her *ao dai* seemed to have been melted over her shapely body. She was elegantly coiffed, and her makeup was subtle but effective. In short, she was a casting director's dream. With a little imagination the candle-lit interior of l'Amiral could have been the set of a 1940s Hollywood version of the Far East or a panel from *Terry and the Pirates*.

But Saigon of the 1960s was no place for romantic fantasy. By the time the sizzling *steak au poivre* had reached the table I knew why I had been invited. It was a scratchy replay of the same message I'd listened to at Binh Xuyen head-quarters ten years earlier. After the flattery—I was one of the few Americans who "really understood" Vietnam—came the pitch. The Hoa Hao could once again become a "viable anticommunist force." All they needed was money, arms, *and* American support. I fell back on the fail-safe jargon of the profes-sional diplomat, promising to relay the message onwards and upwards. The meal ended, Ba-Cut's widow smoothed her clinging *ao dai* and offered me a ride home. I hesitated briefly, but an embassy car was waiting for me and I declined her offer. Once back at the empty villa on Rue Tu Xuong I cursed myself for thinking and acting like a bloodless bureaucrat.

CHAPTER 18

The Media War

The small black-clad figures were running along a dusty dike near the thatch roofs of a distant village. Heat rose from the rice paddies in shimmering waves, distorting the green and yellow foliage of a treeline to our front. The battalion's point scouts were barely visible as they moved laboriously through the muck ahead of us. The sight of the running figures had galvanized the somnolent battalion commander into action. The major had climbed up on a dike, binoculars in hand, and was shouting in Vietnamese to his staff. The husky American adviser beside me, using his own binoculars, muttered, "Oh shit!" He was a West Point captain with more than a rudimentary knowledge of Vietnamese. He pushed his binoculars into my hand. Once I'd focused them, I could see the faraway group fading from sight. Some of them wore conical peasant hats but I couldn't tell if they were men or women.

"They look like villagers to me," the adviser murmured, frowning into the distance.

The battalion commander was already working his field radio, asking for artillery. He paused to call to the adviser. "We need air!"

"VC, VC!" he shouted in English.

As if on cue, three cruising ground-support aircraft appeared overhead. They looked like dark, pregnant hornets in the blue wash of the cloudless sky. The major became even more agitated, pointing to the aircraft and performing a little dance. "Call them!" he yelled. "VC escape!" The adviser, who had the last word on air strikes, shook his head slowly. I stood beside him, watching the aircraft fly out of sight. "They're not fighting the same war," the captain murmured. Then he methodically noted the battalion commander's request and his refusal on a small clipboard. The Vietnamese major shrugged his shoul-

197

ders in a petulant gesture and turned back to his radio as the first howitzer round wooshed overhead and slammed into the now deserted landscape.

After Thao's coup I had opted to spend some time in the field. I wasn't seeking glory, but I had felt a need to get out of the political morass of Saigon. I had joined an ARVN battalion in the Delta for a few days. Daily sweeps in search of the VC had proven fruitless. We'd received some sniper fire and some men had been wounded by booby traps, but the enemy had evaporated into the countryside, reserving the right to give battle at a time and place of his own choosing. It had been ten years since my operational days with the French and it showed. The long lunches and receptions of diplomatic life, the endless hours behind a desk, and the added years had slowed me down considerably. Squelching through the evil-smelling mud of the Mekong Delta, fording leech-filled streams, and enduring the scorching sun were proving increasingly difficult. My self-confidence had received another blow when the battalion commander began referring to me as "*père*."

Another trip took me to the coastal town of Qui Nhon. My objective had been to link up with an ARVN airborne battalion holding the strategic mountain pass at An Khe. I was still technically an adviser to the ARVN's political warfare section and I wanted to see for myself a crack Vietnamese unit performing a difficult task. I'd also promised to observe what I could of JUSPAO's press operation in the field, to report how correspondents were being treated and the extent of military cooperation on JUSPAO projects.

I had left Saigon with all the necessary clearances, including one from the Airborne command. As always, things in the field proved to be different. A suspicious American Special Forces officer in Qui Nhon had promised to do what he could to get me into An Khe. It soon became obvious that someone in the chain of command had decided otherwise. I did learn that An Khe was under pressure from the VC and that the ARVN Airborne had taken casualties. I was told the commander at An Khe was too busy to receive visitors. It had been frustrating enough in the past to have my movements blocked by the French. I now found it particularly irritating to be stonewalled by my own people. But I was in no position to argue. They were fighting a war and, although I could have argued the point, my mission was not absolutely essential. There was little sense in remaining at Qui Nhon, so I went in search of a flight for Saigon.

The Air America C-47 bound for the capital had been warming up at the Qui Nhon strip when I arrived. I didn't have time to question the pilot before throwing my gear aboard and finding a seat among the crated ammunition and cases of canned beer. Once in the air, I could see we were flying north along the coast rather than south to Saigon. Shouting above the din of the engines, I asked the crew chief our destination. He explained we had a supply stop at Tam Ky, in Quang Tin Province, before heading for Saigon.

I had done enough dicey flying in Indochina to consider myself inured to surprises, but the Air America pilot at the controls was the ultimate skyborne cowboy. I was unaware that Tam Ky was a "hot" zone and that bringing the

C-47 down while avoiding possible ground fire called for aerobatics normally reserved for fighter aircraft. We made three passes over the Tam Ky strip, each more hair-raising than the last. At one point, during a steep bank, the ground seemed to be above us. During another swoop the CIA-hired Nung mercenaries guarding the strip scattered beneath us like hawk-threatened chickens.

Once we'd thumped onto the ground and rolled to a stop, a weapons carrier reversed up to the cargo door to unload the supplies. A reception committee of young officers from the Tam Ky CIA field office greeted us. The pilot jumped to the ground and led us all to the rear of the aircraft. He removed his baseball cap and scratched his balding head.

"Look at that!" he exclaimed in a strong Southern accent. "I knew I felt somethin'." A hole the size of a small fist had been punched in the fuselage near the tail section. The projectile had exited the other side of the plane, narrowly missing the rudder cables. "God damn!" the pilot swore, running his fingers over the jagged hole. "What kinda people you got 'round here?"

The pilot had another stop to make and we were asked to wait at Tam Ky for his return. The C-47 revved its engines, bounced along the strip, and rose abruptly in a stall-defying climb. The CIA officers invited me to share their lunch, someone handed me an M-16, and we were soon speeding toward Tam Ky in a jeep. The region had always been a VC stronghold and it was still "bandit territory." The telltale signs were there. Empty villages, no children on the roads, no dogs among the huts, and an all-pervading silence. The CIA officers were installed in a sandbagged colonial villa surrounded by barbed wire and protected by impassive Nung sentries armed with Swedish K submachine guns. The American operatives were involved in the same "war in the shadows" their French counterparts had experienced earlier, supervising black-clad Provincial Reconnaissance Teams that tracked and eliminated local VC officials and gathered intelligence on VC strength, plans, and movements.

We lunched on hamburgers and thawed French fries, drank bourbon chased by innumerable cans of Budweiser, and rolled back to the strip feeling no pain. Our errant pilot returned at dusk and we took off into the last streaks of a scarlet sunset. A tropical thunderstorm was waiting for us south of Quang Ngai. The C-47 bucked, pitched, and swiveled through black clouds as white lightning flashed the length of the fuselage. One of the officers from Tam Ky ripped open a case of beer and popped some cans. The sudden lurches sent beer sloshing onto the metal floor. By the time we reached Saigon the interior of the C-47 smelled like a brewery. I returned to Rue Tu Xoung at midnight and crawled into a bed that continued to pitch and yaw. Before falling asleep I resolved that my days in the field had come to an end.

I now had only three months left to serve in Vietnam and found myself eager to leave. The frustrations of my assignment, the constant flashbacks of that "other war," and the cruel realities of "our war" had produced a certain fatigue. One incident had affected me more than I realized. Returning from a visit to an ARVN unit northeast of Saigon, the chopper I was riding put down near a burning village to pick up some wounded ARVN troopers and civilians. The badly wounded were laid out on the metal flooring and the others were squeezed onto the seats. A sober Vietnamese boy of seven or eight sat next to me and I shifted my weight to give him more room. The pilot had some trouble getting off the ground, but he finally made it. We rose over the emerald-green paddies and set a course for Phan Thiet. It was a beautiful, sparkling day and the temperature cooled as we gained more altitude.

The boy didn't appear to be hurt. I wasn't sure why he was on the chopper, but I presumed a parent or relative was among the wounded. To take his mind off the growing slick of shimmering blood on the floor, I attempted to make contact. Like a parent trying to bring a pouting child out of a funk I winked and made faces. The boy stared at me with opaque, expressionless eyes. Remembering a piece of candy saved from a ration can, I dug in my pocket and offered it to him. He turned away. Only then did I notice the daylight showing through his left bicep. The hole was undressed, clean, and surprisingly round, as if made by a large drill. There was no bleeding, but a bit of white bone was showing. Feeling like a callous clown, I shouted to the door gunner, asking if he had a blanket for the boy, who had now begun to shiver. The gunner looked at me as if I were crazy and shook his head. When we landed at Phan Thiet I handed the boy down to an ARVN medic and watched as he was carried to an open weapons carrier serving as an ambulance. The vision of that child's dark, morphine-dulled eyes haunted me for weeks.

In addition to a surfeit of war I also missed my family and was anxious to join them in Marseille, where they were waiting in a rented apartment. Zorthian had made some noises about my staying on, but we both knew that my usefulness in Saigon had ended. The Quat government was staggering along, making a doomed stab at effectiveness, but the Armed Forces Council was still calling the shots. Air Vice Marshal Ky had assumed the catbird seat. He and his clique of VNAF officers, sweeping into council meetings like a pistol-packing Mafia, dominated military and political decision-making. Although no one had reclaimed my office at the palace annex, I had been marked as a former adviser to General Khanh. Neither Quat's entourage nor the Young Turk generals felt comfortable with an American hanger-on from the Khanh period. My work now consisted of retaining liaison with the GVN and the ARVN, assisting Zorthian on special JUSPAO projects, and preparing Harold Kaplan to take over some of my duties after I'd left Vietnam.

On March 8, 1965, a landing force of U.S. Marines had arrived at Danang, to constitute the first American combat units in Vietnam. They had come ashore in full combat gear as if they were landing on a hostile beach. Instead of the chattering of AK-47s wielded by VC in black pajamas, they were greeted by an official GVN welcoming committee including lithesome Vietnamese girls bearing flower garlands. The surprised, flower-festooned leathernecks smiled sheepishly for the cameras of the international press and pondered their first lesson in the vagaries of the Vietnam War. Although their announced task was to protect U.S. air installations, thus freeing ARVN units for combat, the Marines would soon extend their operations to include pacification projects resulting in bloody clashes with local VC units. They would be followed by an American Airborne Brigade, the spearhead of the Army's combat forces in Vietnam.

On March 29, while Zorthian and I were conferring at the prime minister's office with Quat's new information staff, a heavy blast reverberated through the city. An urgent telephone call informed us the embassy had been bombed. Zorthian rushed to the scene and I followed. The VC had exploded a powerful car bomb beside the embassy building, splattering the wall with the remains of a Saigon policeman and killing and mutilating customers on the terrace of a nearby café. An American secretary and a Vietnamese consular employee had been killed and a number of American and Vietnamese staff were badly wounded. Ambassador Taylor had not been in his office at the time of the explosion, but the top of his desk had been pierced with jagged shards of glass from a shattered window. The VC had once again shown their ability to strike in the heart of the city despite the precautions and counterterrorist measures of the security forces.

With little more to do in the prime minister's office, I began to spend more time at JUSPAO. Barry Zorthian, as chief of JUSPAO and Mission spokesman, had earned the respect and confidence of Ambassador Taylor and General Westmoreland. He had, in fact, become the controlling czar of all information and psywar programs involving the U.S. effort in Vietnam. It was a once-in-a-lifetime opportunity for USIA. Because of JUSPAO's clout in Saigon, the agency was enjoying a preeminence it had seldom experienced in government circles. Recruitment for Vietnam had top priority, and USIA officers from Washington and distant posts were arriving in Saigon still shaken by the speed of their immediate transfers.

A policy of "maximum disclosure" was in force at JUSPAO, based on the supposition that American and foreign newsmen should see the war as it really was. It was hoped this policy would obviate charges of official obstructionism and allow correspondents to draw their own conclusions from firsthand exposure to the facts. A busy JUSPAO office arranged flights to various military regions and helicopter lifts to operations for resident and visiting journalists. A daily list of travel possibilities was posted so newsmen could plan their field trips, often with the option of returning to Saigon the same day to file their copy.

Maximum disclosure may have been a praiseworthy effort in the American tradition of open journalism, but the Vietnam War was hardly the time or place for such a trial run. If the U.S.-Vietnamese war effort had been progressing successfully, maximum disclosure might have worked. But that was not the case. The government-provided mobility of the press corps coupled with the newsmen's ability to get to the heart of a story often produced a worst-case scenario for American officials. Correspondents fresh from an action in the Mekong Delta or the Central Highlands would walk into the daily "Five O'-Clock Follies" briefing at JUSPAO to hear a MACV briefer giving the official version of the clash they had just witnessed. A confused firefight in which the journalists may have seen ARVN troops perform badly and take heavy casualties had, in the official version, undergone a miraculous transformation into a minor victory. It wasn't a question of someone telling an outright lie. It was simply that an accumulation of half-truths, the withholding of information for security reasons, wishful official thinking, and the knowledge that the superior officers at MACV, the Pentagon, *and* the occupant of the White House were avid for success and progress, combined to produce a flawed picture. Briefers often underlined the fact that the VC had left the field to the ARVN, as if this signified some sort of battlefield success. Anyone with a basic understanding of guerrilla warfare and Vietcong tactics would have been profoundly surprised if the VC had done otherwise.

Deskbound briefing officers, with only hurriedly copied notes to go by, would find themselves in the impossible position of arguing with newsmen who had actually been on the spot. It was an ordeal not to be wished on anyone. At one briefing a major with little previous exposure to the press walked directly into the mouth of the beast. He had been describing routine U.S. air activities in South Vietnam. In passing he mentioned "armed reconnaissance" flights before proceeding to the boring litany of small ground actions, body counts, and captured weapons. But the phrase "armed reconnaissance" had rung an alarm bell for the journalists. Within seconds the hapless briefer was under a drumfire of questioning. Within minutes the pieces of a major story were fitting together. "Armed reconnaissance" meant that for the first time U.S. fighter-bombers had been given carte blanche to shoot up targets of opportunity in South Vietnam. While half the newsmen rushed out to file the story, the other half stormed Zorthian's office for more background details. The American Mission had neither expected nor planned to release the story at that particular time. But somewhere, along the military chain of command, the phrase had been dropped unwittingly into the briefing material.

A definite change had also taken place in the makeup of the Saigon press corps. The old Asian hands who had learned their trade during World War II, in Korea, and during the French Indochina War were now infrequent visitors. They had been replaced by a new generation of correspondents, some of whom had never heard a shot fired in anger before arriving in Saigon. The visual media had come to the fore. Network television teams were constantly on the move, seeking sensational footage that would make the evening news slots at home. They were joined by young freelance photographers willing to risk their lives to make a name for themselves. This new breed, often profoundly shocked by what they had seen in the field, became outspoken critics of the war and natural antagonists of the military hierarchy.

JUSPAO was the daily meeting place of the media and those officials assigned to feed them the news. A potpourri of seasoned correspondents, young tyros, prima donna TV anchormen, famous pundits, harried military briefing officers, USIA public affairs experts, confused Vietnamese liaison officers, and MACV specialists—sent to the Five O'Clock Follies to explain their part of the war— shared space and rumors in the corridors and offices. Maximum disclosure did have its limits. But those officials walking the verbal tightrope between what the press needed to know and what they wished it would never find out some-times slipped into the abyss of unintentional exposure. The rooftop officer's club bar on the JUSPAO building was an added hazard for the military informa-tion officers. Some of them were too new to the business to realize that a jour-nalist's day never ended. The closedown of a briefing session and an adjourn-ment for drinks at sundown may have signaled the end of a working day for the uniformed briefers. As far as the newsmen were concerned, it simply meant the pursuit of a story by other means. Many novice public information officers, relaxing over one too many happy hour martinis, quickly learned that anything they might say could rapidly appear in print with or without attribution.

General Westmoreland's ramrod-stiff, painfully cooperative appearances at JUSPAO briefings often had the effect of waving a red flag at a bull. His Eagle Scout demeanor, his firm-jawed handsomeness, his by-the-book replies, and the suspicion that he had no real understanding of Vietnam could bring out the worst in his interrogators. The general appeared at one session shortly after a VC attack that had cost the United States both casualties and aircraft. He made his presentation in an attempt to minimize the gravity of the action and reassure the U.S. public that all necessary security measures were being taken to block a repeat attack. Joe Fried, of the New York *Daily News*, slumped in his usual front-row seat, took no notes during Westmoreland's presentation, but he was first off the mark when the general agreed to take questions.

"General," Fried asked, "are you finished?"

"Yes, Joe."

"Good," Fried said, producing a list of hard-edged questions. "Now let's get serious."

This war within a war between officialdom and the media extended far be-yond JUSPAO into the field where the first U.S. combat units were soon to be tested in battle. The material from a well-prepared JUSPAO briefing would be jettisoned in favor of meatier fare if a war correspondent or a network camera team stumbled onto combat-weary grunts willing to talk or found evidence of the ARVN's mistreatment of villagers. Few U.S. field commanders welcomed the media visits facilitated by JUSPAO. Their superiors in Saigon revealed their frustration with the U.S. press by demanding why the American correspon-dents didn't "get on the team" in support of the war effort. Much of this adver-sary relationship stemmed from the fact that the military measured success in terms of body counts, arms captured, and VC "withdrawals." The majority of the media recognized the war as guerrilla in nature; a contest in which those who controlled the countryside and villages and maintained a durable political infrastructure were, in fact, winning. The reference point of the Algerian con-flict was readily available as an example of how a modern Western nation had won militarily but lost the more important political struggle.

Media relations were particularly difficult for the military, as no two newsmen or newswomen were alike. One day the American officers might be visited by a thoughtful professional, working on a think piece, who asked all the right questions and revealed a deep knowledge of his subject. The next day they might see an unshaven, pot-smoking freelancer approaching their CP with the prime objective of finding unusual material and stomach-churning photos to feed a tabloid's requirements for violence and sensation. To the consternation of their temporary hosts, these roles could be reversed. The respected veteran newsman might be the one to uncover a scorching story, while the journalistic "hippie" might accept the official line without a murmur. There was no litmus test available to categorize the media.

The unhomogenized mix of journalists in Vietnam produced numerous incidents and clashes. A story by Arnaud de Borchgrave, an editor of *Newsweek* and one of the old Indochina hands who had been among the first newsmen into Dien Bien Phu, had infuriated the Saigon-based American newsmen. De Borchgrave had written a colorful, action-packed personal account of a firefight between a unit of U.S. Marines and the Vietcong. So far so good. What had galled his colleagues was de Borchgrave's printed admission that he had personally thrown grenades along with the Marines to smash a VC assault. This was a no-no in the unwritten code of the war correspondent. Not only did they feel de Borchgrave had succumbed to self-glorification in his own copy, but worse, he had exposed them all to summary justice at the hands of the VC as combatants who used their profession as a cover. A group of American newsmen delivered a protest to JUSPAO but *l'affaire de Borchgrave* did not go much further. The irrepressible de Borchgrave remained as aloof and impervious to criticism then as he was later as editor of the Washington *Times*.

The outwardly tolerant attitude toward the media meant that news-hungry journalists had a more or less free run in the JUSPAO building. Normally they frequented the small coffee shop and the briefing area, but they might also stray down the halls in search of flight confirmations or looking for friends among the JUSPAO staff. Certain JUSPAO projects in the psywar field were understandably classified, and most officers were well aware of the security procedures to be observed.

Unfortunately, a publications officer had taken to posting samples of his printed output on the walls of his office. Normally these wall hangings consisted of *chieu hoi* surrender leaflets, cartoon presentations of basic hygiene tips for village use, and patriotic posters featuring determined ARVN troopers under a Vietnamese flag. In this particular instance a sharp-eyed newsman spotted a most unusual sample of the printer's art pinned to the office door: a sinister, single eye peering out from a small square of paper. Some adroit questioning clarified the mystery. The all-seeing-eye symbol, printed in large numbers, was for the use of Armed Propaganda Teams and Provincial Reconnaissance Units. They were to be placed on the corpses of eliminated Vietcong cadres as a demonstration of the GVN's omnipresence and a warning to VC collaborators. Once again there was a rush to Zorthian's office for background information followed by a spate of "killer squad" stories in the U.S. press. The chastened publications officer became much more selective thereafter in exhibiting his section's handiwork, and an effort was made to limit media access to certain sections of the JUSPAO building.

This was just as well because the JUSPAO field operations office was also running armed propaganda teams under the supervision of its director, Ev Bumgardner, a Vietnamese-speaking veteran of the Diem period. These black-clad counterguerrillas were led by Frank Scotton, a young risk-taker with a good understanding of revolutionary warfare. Scotton, who also spoke Vietnamese, had modeled these units on the VC's successful agitprop sections. They were not the naïve, untrained psywarriors that had been decimated by the Vietminh years before. His men were tough veterans drawn from the ARVN and certain militia units. Some of them were VC deserters whose life span would be counted in minutes in the event of capture. Ambushes and the neutralization of VC cadres were as much a part of their task as the dissemination of propaganda. In many ways Bumgardner and Scotton's initiative was much more effective than all the leaflet drops, loudspeaker broadcasts, and posters generated by JUSPAO. Fortunately those newsmen who blundered into Scotton's office while he was slinging his Swedish K prior to another trip to the boondocks realized the seriousness of his business and little word of the teams leaked out.

The Saigon-based press corps often came to JUSPAO with complaints about the GVN's Press and Information Center. I was asked to do what I could to remedy the situation. The center was vaguely modeled on JUSPAO, but its limited facilities weren't meeting the media's requirements. In addition, most American newsmen were covering the U.S. war effort. With the exception of headline-making defeats or scandals, they remained blithely uninterested in day-to-day ARVN activities.

The real problem could be traced to Kipling's old adage about "the twain" never meeting. We were trying to force-feed the Vietnamese our brand of press relations and it just did not work. To many educated Vietnamese, "the press" was a commodity that politicians and officials bought and sold. Journalists, in their eyes, were very low on the social scale, considered as failed poets struggling to fill their rice bowls. The young officers I worked with at the center were pleased to be far from the combat duty. But their dull briefings before a minuscule, yawning audience reflected extreme caution, a desire not to offend their superiors, and the naïve belief that transparent propaganda presented as truth would be accepted by the Western press. Those Vietnamese press officers I brought to the Five O'Clock Follies to see how American briefings were handled went away wide-eyed with shock at the vehemence of the questioning and in no hurry to encourage the same performance at their own center.

Through all of this media circus Barry Zorthian sat at the top of the seething JUSPAO pyramid "leveling" with trusted journalists, soothing ambassadors and generals, dispensing "deep background" information like a well-earned reward, and blocking indiscreet queries with an enigmatic smile and a shrug.

I was now preparing to leave Vietnam for the second time. I'd moved my office furniture out of the palace annex; and the Vietnamese press staff, those civil servants and military officers who had survived the coups and successions, organized an impromptu going-away party. We drank *vin mousseux,* nibbled on nuts, and made vain promises of continued contact. Colonel Duc speculated that I would find it hard to live without a weekly coup and proposed a toast wishing me a happy reunion with my family. After the fall of Saigon, Duc was to spend many years in a Communist reeducation camp until he convinced his jailers he was not quite right in the head and qualified for release. Once outside, and perfectly sane, he promptly fled to Paris.

Two weeks before my departure I received word of my assignment as information officer to the embassy in Paris. I had also learned that my second novel was being published by Harper & Row. It was all good news, but it didn't seem to register. I had the feeling that I wouldn't be part of the outside world until my flight had left Tan Son Nhut. The last days in Saigon fused in a rush of activities. I sold our small Mercedes to a pompous diplomat at the French embassy and was amused to see him being driven down Rue Tu Do in his new acquisition by a uniformed chauffeur. My Vietnamese friends insisted on a round of stag dinners in Cholon marked by enough down-the-hatch toasts to poleax an ox. A flurry of curious, whisper-filled comings and goings among the servants culminated in their ceremonious presentation of a dragon-handled brass incense urn as a departure gift. Little matter that my first name was engraved as "Howad," the gesture was unexpected and touching.

I bequeathed my handgun to Kaplan with a certain feeling of liberation and spent my last day in Saigon on a sentimental tour of some old haunts. I sipped a drink in the rooftop bar of the Majestic Hotel, watching the sampans glide over the muddy surface of the Saigon River. I stopped for a Kronenbourg in a Corsican bar on Nguyen Hué and said goodbye to the *patron* who had been one of the regulars at Chez Yvonne in the early 1950s. Finally, I sat alone on the terrace of the Continental Hotel over a gin fizz as the sun set, the heat faded, and the ghosts of an endless war paraded in my memory.

Zorthian and some friends from JUSPAO saw me off at Tan Son Nhut. We left a forest of empty "33" beer bottles on the Formica table when my flight was called. Within hours I was luxuriating in the calm of Raffles Hotel in Singapore, and the next day I took off for France. My wife and four daughters met me at Cannes Airport. It was cool and crisp on the Riviera. Saigon seemed far away. A few days later, while we prepared to depart Marseille for home leave, I picked up the daily *Le Provençal* to read that there had been a bloodless coup in Saigon. On June 11, 1965, the Armed Forces Council had removed Dr. Quat as prime minister, replaced him with General Ky, and named Gen. Nguyen Van Thieu chief of state.

CHAPTER 19

"It Is Not Good"

The Vietnam War followed me to France. Lee Brady, my first boss in Saigon, was now in charge of the USIA operation at the Paris embassy. As information officer, I was soon involved in the daily explanation and justification of U.S. policy in Indochina. Fresh from the scene, I became an in-house expert. My first briefing was directed at the Country Team. The bleak picture I painted didn't jibe with the hopeful optimism being generated in Washington. The reaction was far from positive. Strangely enough, the military attachés expressed appreciation for my candor, but some of the civilian officials obviously thought I was much too pessimistic.

Nevertheless, I was soon briefing skeptical French newsmen and speaking before French organizations or groups on our role in Vietnam. It was a thankless task. The de Gaulle government was against U.S. policy in Vietnam and wasted no opportunity to attack us officially and in the media. The French Left was targeting the embassy with weekly, often violent, protest demonstrations, and the Right, still blaming us for their loss of Indochina and to a lesser extent Algeria, was gloating on the sidelines at our discomfiture.

It was difficult to push the official line from Washington when I was aware of what was really going on in Saigon, but I concentrated on what I knew to be true: the heroism of *some* ARVN units, the courage of *some* GVN officials, and the veiled but real brutality of the Communists in pursuing their goals. It had come as a shock to find that the prevailing picture in France of events in Vietnam was being painted in stark black and white. The Vietcong were portrayed as starry-eyed peasant soldiers going forth barefoot and ill-equipped to fight for freedom against a puppet army of cruel mercenaries supplied and directed by the Pentagon. Little mention was made of the presence of well-equipped North Vietnamese Regulars in the South or the fact that the Ho Chi

Minh Trail system had ensured that the VC were now provided with AK-47 assault rifles, Degtyarev light machine guns, and rocket-propelled antitank grenades. Anyone familiar with Vietnam would have known that the war could only be reflected in shades of gray. This was not the case in the France of 1966.

Nor were these constant reminders of Vietnam limited to the office. I caught a glimpse of General Cogny while riding the Paris Métro, his tall, once-erect frame bent with age and the legal battle he had fought to justify his role in the battle of Dien Bien Phu. I encountered Colonel Fourcade, who had retired as a general. We had lunch together in a small bistro near the embassy and he came to a cocktail party at our apartment on the Rue Vaugirard. He too seemed smaller, as if shedding his uniform for civilian clothes had torn away a carapace and lessened him physically. A mysterious, well-dressed Frenchman appeared in my office to inform me Gen. Nguyen Van Hinh wished to see me, but the emissary declined to explain for what reason. I refused the invitation: I didn't like his manner, and I didn't want to get involved in any Saigon-oriented intrigue. I met with Ho Thong Minh, a former defense minister under Ngo Dinh Diem, for periodic lunches in a Vietnamese restaurant off the Rue Faubourg Saint-Honoré. The sincere and indefatigable Minh, active among the large colony of Vietnamese exiles in Paris, was a constant source of fact and rumor on Vietnamese political developments in Paris and Saigon. I dutifully reported his comments to the embassy political officer charged with Vietnamese affairs until, swamped with Minh's offerings, he begged me to be more selective. I also renewed contact with a number of French journalists I had known in Saigon, including Pierre Schoendoerffer. He had turned to writing fiction and film directing. His *317th Section*, a film of a small French unit retreating from Laos, had won a number of prizes including one at Cannes.

But Vietnam was not my prime preoccupation. De Gaulle was withdrawing France from NATO in 1966 and losing no opportunity to express his dissatisfaction with "Anglo-Saxon" foreign policies. Following his lead, most French officials were being as difficult as possible in dealing with their American counterparts, and we were tempted to respond in kind. Ambassador Charles E. "Chip" Bohlen, a calm and wise Foreign Service professional who ran the embassy with a benign but firm hand, managed to temper our responses to such goading.

We countered anti-American attacks in the media, produced a monthly French-language magazine for national distribution, encouraged European unity through French organizations, and kept Washington informed of the trends in French public opinion. I returned to the International Film Festival at Cannes as a U.S. delegate and traveled to Strasbourg, Lyon, Bordeaux, Perpignan, and Marseille on official business. For wartime service in France and time spent with the French Expeditionary Force in Indochina I was decorated—with Bohlen's permission—as an *officier* in the Military Order of French Combat Engineers. The ceremony, including the traditional kiss on each cheek, took place at the French Army's Engineer headquarters at Angers. Some of the initiative for this decoration undoubtedly stemmed from the fact that the order's hierarchy was staunchly anti–de Gaulle. Pinning a medal on an American official at that time was the equivalent of thumbing your nose at the de Gaulle government.

During this period Pierre Schoendoerffer came to me with an ambitious project. He wanted to return to Vietnam to film the U.S. war for French television. His aim was to attach himself and his crew to an American combat unit and film exactly what happened over a period of several weeks. I knew I could trust Schoendoerffer to be objective, but some of my colleagues in both Paris and Washington were not so sure. French national TV at that time was noted for its broken promises and hatchet jobs on the U.S. effort in Vietnam. JUSPAO, several times burned, was not eager to greet another French camera crew. With Brady's backing, I piled on the assurances, sent a personal telegram to Zorthian, and the Schoendoerffer project was approved. The final result was *The Anderson Platoon*, a gripping documentary of combat, comradeship, and loss among the men of a 1st Air Cavalry platoon led by a black West Pointer. The subsequent international distribution of the prize-winning film—even to Yugoslavia—attested to its quality.

After two years in Paris I received a letter from the agency assigning me as the USIA student for the one-year senior course at the School of Naval Warfare of the Naval War College at Newport, Rhode Island. Like the other war colleges, a few civilian officials from State, USIA, and CIA were seeded into the class each year. Halfway through the course, in late January 1968, the Tet offensive erupted in Vietnam. It was a somber time at the War College. Not only was the unexpected Communist effort a jolting surprise, but most of my fellow students had close friends involved in the fighting. Stunned Army and Marine Corps colonels followed the news between lectures on transistor radios. Despite their combat experience in "Nam," it was as if a new, hidden aspect of the war had been revealed. They all knew "Charlie" as a dangerous foe, but few considered him capable of mounting such a well-coordinated major offensive.

My own Indochina experiences had prepared me for such a disaster. I could imagine how the sterile bubble of illusion surrounding the upper strata of the U.S. Mission, and MACV had managed to reject or sanitize realistic intelligence reports and warnings from the field. I was to find later that this supposition was partly unfair, as some warnings had been heeded and acted upon. In fact, Lt. Gen. Fred Weyand, commander of the III Corps area surrounding Saigon, had been warning of a worrying buildup of enemy units within striking distance of the capital prior to the Tet attacks. The fact remains that the scope and force of the enemy action had caught us flatfooted. As the days passed, it became clear that if the North Vietnamese and the Vietcong had taken heavy casualties and not won a major victory in a military sense or instigated the popular revolt they were seeking, they had won a psychological victory in the United States. Those who had supported the war with misgivings now dropped out completely, the staunch supporters began to waver, and the antiwar movement received a shot in the arm.

Word began to filter through about friends involved in the fighting. General

Dong and his Nungs had set an ambush not far from his Cholon villa and wiped out an overconfident section of North Vietnamese sappers as they headed for downtown Saigon. Barry Zorthian had been in the thick of it from the start, rousing newsmen with early-morning calls and briefing them on the fighting for the American embassy and the attacks in Saigon with what he could glean from sketchy telephone conversations with MACV, the ARVN, and from monitoring the embassy security radio net. I could picture it all clearly, and felt some of the same frustration I'd experienced when Dien Bien Phu fell. The "fire horse" syndrome had me wishing I was there. At the same time I realized how lucky I was to be in Newport.

Upon graduation, thanks to a thesis I had written on "The Psychological Aspects of Guerrilla Warfare," I was asked to remain at the Naval War College as a faculty adviser and consultant to the president. Once again I was deeply involved with Vietnam, teaching a course on the subject of my paper and another on "The French Experience in Indochina." In 1969 we were at the height of our involvement in the war. My "students" were senior officers of all services who had either served in Vietnam or would soon be headed in that direction. It was an eerie experience when describing a particular Vietminh ambush of the French war to be interrupted by a Marine colonel who, after confirming the exact location of the action, shook his head in disbelief and murmured, "Son of a bitch, they did the same thing to us in approximately the same location!"

My next assignment took me to Washington as deputy director of the Public Affairs Office of the State Department's East Asian and Pacific Bureau. Here, once again, Vietnam was the order of the day as we prepared daily briefing papers for the State Department spokesman. But I had joined the Foreign Service to serve overseas, and this Washington assignment, with its stratified bureaucracy and deskwork held little appeal. I quickly passed the word that I'd be willing to consider the first foreign post available. Four months later, much to the consternation of my family, who had just settled into the pattern of Washington living, I accepted the assignment as counselor of public affairs at the American embassy in Canberra, Australia.

Any thought that the distant "down under" continent would be an isolated, quiet post soon faded. To begin with, the Australian Department of External Affairs on entering my name and position on the official diplomatic list had dropped the l in "Public." I thus became the first "counselor for pubic affairs" in the history of our Canberra embassy, much to the amusement of the diplomatic community and the local press.

Within days of my arrival I was contacted by the Vietnamese ambassador, whom I had known as a government official in Saigon, for help in convincing Australians of the validity of his government's cause. A few months later I found myself repeating my War College lectures at the Australian Joint Services College. Meanwhile the embassy was under heavy fire from Australian antiwar organizations and some of the media. Australians had been involved in support of the South Vietnamese since 1962, when they first sent a team of thirty military advisers to Vietnam. The advisers had been followed in 1965 with combat troops. By the time I arrived in Canberra, the Australian commitment of fighting men to Vietnam was close to 8,000. The Australian presence had fitted perfectly into President Lyndon Johnson's "More Flags" campaign to present the war as a Free World response to Communist aggression. The Aussies weren't alone. Thanks to continued diplomatic arm-twisting from Washington and certain economic advantages, South Korea, New Zealand, Thailand, the Philippines, the Republic of China (Taiwan), and Spain had sent contingents to Vietnam.

Despite Australia's pride in its fighting traditions, as exemplified by the military trappings of the annual ANZAC Day, participation in the Vietnam War was even less popular among the public than it had become in the United States. Antiwar spokesmen were comparing Australia's past sacrifices in "Britain's wars" to its "subservient" role in supporting U.S. policy designs in Southeast Asia.

Our cause was not helped by an inopportune official visit from Vice President Spiro T. Agnew. Designed to demonstrate continued U.S. support of Australia and gratitude for its role in Vietnam, Agnew's arrival had almost the opposite effect. His abrasive and domineering staff managed to alienate the normally easygoing Australian officials we worked with. This simmering diplomatic crisis reached epic proportions when the Agnew staffers informed the Australians there would only be room for the accompanying White House press when the vice president laid a wreath at the Australian War Memorial. Already smarting from what they considered second-class treatment, the Australians exploded. Twenty-four hours of vituperative negotiations, with the embassy acting as middleman, ultimately resulted in the Australian press being allowed into their *own* War Memorial. By this time all we could do was count the hours till the departure of the vice presidential aircraft in order to begin assessing the diplomatic damage.

One crisp sunny morning in Canberra I found a priority telegram waiting on my desk. I read it twice with growing disbelief. The agency was sending me to Saigon to participate in an "orientation" tour. These tours for the senior officers at USIA posts were designed to provide an up-to-date exposure to the U.S. effort in Vietnam so that America's overseas spokesmen could better explain American policy in their host countries. I decided that someone in Washington had made a mistake. Surely I wasn't in need of any Vietnam orientation, and my place in the program would be better used if allotted to an officer who had never been there before.

I called the agency to make this point but was overruled. Australia was an ally in Vietnam, antiwar feeling was spreading down under, and I *would* take part. The program was ambitious and expensive. I was to join the small group of participating officers in Washington for preliminary briefings before flying out to Vietnam. We were a mixed bag, including career Foreign Service information officers from European and Central American posts and politically appointed officials from the agency's Washington headquarters.

The briefings at the State Department and the Pentagon were the usual amalgam of positive pablum and impressive figures. At the White House we were received by Col. Alexander Haig, then a staff member of Henry Kissinger's National Security Council, who briefed us as if we were members of a visiting Rotary Club rather than members of the same official team. When Colonel Haig completed his presentation and agreed to take questions, I asked him for his estimate of the current use of drugs among U.S. military personnel in Vietnam. It was a valid query considering the prevalence of such stories in the American media and the effect narcotics could have on a GI's fighting ability. It was also the type of question I'd soon be facing in Australia. Haig's steely, blue-eyed glare was of such intensity that to this day I can't remember his reply. It was clear I had touched a raw nerve. The future secretary of state obviously did not consider such subjects as narcotics use and the "fragging" of unpopular officers and noncoms by tripping GIs as proper subjects for a White House briefing.

My fourth return to Vietnam was like walking onto a familiar stage to find the cast and the play completely changed. Our small band of visitors was met at Tan Son Nhut and bundled into an air-conditioned JUSPAO van for the drive into Saigon. In a sense the air conditioning was a symptom of the American presence in Vietnam. No one could argue its necessity, but it automatically provided a barrier of isolation: no street noises, a minimum of smells, and escape from the reality of Saigon's overpowering heat.

We were housed in the Hotel Caravelle—the Continental was considered obsolete by most Americans—and presented with our schedule. It called for perpetual motion from the time of our arrival. Our tour would take us to Nha Trang, Da Nang, and Hué, My Tho, Rach Gia, Chau Doc, and Hien Hung. We were to visit isolated fire bases near the Cambodian border, Revolutionary Development projects in the Mekong Delta, and a division headquarters in the Central Highlands. My schedule had been adjusted so I could spend a few days with the Australians in Phouc Tuy Province, southeast of Saigon.

We didn't fully realize it, but we had arrived in Saigon at an inopportune moment. Nixon's Vietnamization program, designed to shift combat responsibility to the ARVN, had just undergone a major reversal. Operation Lamson 719, an ARVN thrust into neutral Laos designed to cut the Ho Chi Minh Trail, had begun on February 8, 1971, and ended with a heavy loss of ARVN lives and a disastrous retreat back across the border. The American military and civilian officials who briefed us, smarting from the reverse and trying to pick up the pieces, were under tremendous pressure from Washington to explain and justify what had happened. Little wonder they seemed less than enthusiastic when we trooped into their offices to ask probing questions on the progress of the war.

Ambassador Ellsworth Bunker reflected this attitude. The seventy-seven-year-old diplomat made it clear we were taking up valuable time, deflected our questions, and returned again and again to the same theme. We were *winning the war* and that should be the message we carried back with us. The curmudgeonly Bunker lectured us as if we were troublesome newsmen. When I left his office, I wondered if we were the targets of a psychological warfare campaign by our own people.

Our meeting with Bill Colby, the CIA official in charge of the controversial Phoenix program, was an exception. Colby, a veteran of the wartime OSS in Europe, greeted us in a relaxed manner and answered each question in as much detail as he could. The Phoenix program called for the infiltration of the Vietcong infrastructure by Vietnamese government agents and the capture or "neutralization" of enemy cadres. Colby's reports, soon to be made public, were to confirm that more than 50,000 active VC cadre and agents had been captured, killed, or had defected thanks to the Phoenix operations. There was little doubt that such a clandestine program of political denunciation and elimination spawned abuses. Critics focused on Phoenix as an official version of "murder incorporated," and the CIA's Provincial Reconnaissance units were labeled hit teams. Nevertheless, the Phoenix program had hurt the Vietcong badly. Stanley Karnow was to confirm this during a number of interviews with former Vietcong officials in 1981. The bespectacled, soft-spoken Colby, who would soon become CIA's director, resembled nothing more than a tired college professor as we listened to him speak calmly of hazardous operations in the war for the hamlets and villages.

It was soon time for our tour of the bush, and we flew off in an Air America plane to see things at first hand. It was a week of takeoffs and landings in pulsating choppers, hurried meals, quick jolts of bourbon, and interminable briefings. Even the most isolated base in the boondocks boasted a briefing board and a pointer-wielding officer ready to "put us in the picture." One U.S. fire base surrounded by wooded hills in the shadow of a shattered French pillbox and ringed by defensive wire could have been a strongpoint from that other war. Questioning the commander, I learned that the fire base was buttoned up at night and ready to repulse any attack. This didn't dovetail with Ambassador Bunker's briefing. If we were *winning the war*, why did the VC still control the countryside and the villages at night?

At Pleiku in the Central Highlands we were greeted by local officials and escorted to a Montagnard village, where we were offered *choum*, a potent rice wine drunk from earthenware jars through hollow reeds. Young girls in tribal costume came forward to bend brass bracelets around our wrists following the drinking ceremony. It was all colorful stuff, worthy of a tourist agency, but the Montagnards were just bit players in a charade. The Vietnamese still referred to them as *moi*, or savages, and the Montagnards detested the Vietnamese, be they Vietcong or ARVN. When I explained this to my traveling companions, they accused me of cynicism—and they were right.

U.S. and Vietnamese psywar officers in the Mekong Delta gave us an upbeat briefing and took us out to see their efforts. We were following a well-worn track in a comparatively secure area used regularly for orientation tours. We barreled along narrow canals in ARVN assault boats driven by powerful outboards. Villagers waved to us from the banks, and the hamlets we visited were hung with GVN propaganda banners bearing the government's message. At one point, after we had stopped in a village to drink coconut milk and roared out onto the canal again, I glanced astern to see that our roiling wake had capsized three dugout canoes manned by women on their way to market with manioc. Considering what those small cargos meant in terms of labor, sustenance, and income to the villagers, I decided that our psywarriors must be operating in a vacuum of perception. The ARVN helmsman only laughed when I called his attention to what he had done.

My solo visit to the Australians in Phuoc Tuy Province provided a welcome break from our official traveling circus. The Aussies, aware that I was stationed in their capital, greeted me like an old friend. A can of iced Foster's lager was never too far away, and the Australian officers were particularly candid in expressing their views on the war. They were outspokenly critical of large-scale U.S. operations that they saw as counterproductive and unnecessarily destructive.

Using small-unit tactics developed during the anticommunist war in Malaya, the Australians were doing a credible job of separating the VC from the population, thus depriving the enemy of local support. They believed in continual patrolling, day and night, to keep the VC off balance. But they had their problems too. Located in a nasty zone surrounded by enemy forces, the Australians found the struggle to pacify Phuoc Tuy Province like trying to shovel sand with a rake. When political pressure at home forced them to leave Vietnam later the same year, the VC quickly filled the vacuum.

I rejoined our group in time for a visit to an isolated U.S. installation deep in "bandit territory." One of our briefers was the unit's intelligence officer. The captain's tour was coming to a close, and he would soon be heading home. His entrance into the cramped room was marked by the unmistakable odor of bourbon. His briefing was detailed, if hesitant, and at one point he dropped a rolled map on the floor and kicked it aside. There was some meaningful throat-clearing among his superior officers, who were anxious for the briefing to end. Then the captain decided to digress. He pushed aside his notes and told us a story.

Six months previously his men and their Vietnamese counterparts had captured the wife and children of the local VC commander. Each month, the captain had sent a message to the VC leader informing him that his wife and children were in good health and well cared for. The messages had also contained exhortations to give himself up and explanations of the *chieu hoi* surrender program. The repeated messages had gone unanswered until recently. The last one had finally drawn a reply. Our unsteady briefer drew a wrinkled piece of paper from his pocket, smoothed it, and read the translation.

"I will never surrender," the VC commander had replied. "We will be here long after you Americans have gone."

"That," the captain told us, "should give you an idea of the problems we face."

It was then time for refreshments before we boarded our chopper. The captain was noticeably absent when the drinks were poured. A senior officer joked about short-timers being entitled to a shot or two during working hours, but no further reference was made to the captain's digression. It had, however, made an impression on all of us. For a few brief moments the veil of official optimism had been drawn back and we had had an unsettling look at the future.

Back in Saigon we were invited to dinner at the villa on the Rue Tu Xuong I'd occupied with my family in 1964. It had been renovated and enlarged and was now home to a senior JUSPAO official. Halfway through the meal I heard laughter from the house across the street and excused myself to see if the French neighbors we had known were still there. I arrived as the dinner guests were leaving, but the host, who had attended our dinner party for General Dong seven years earlier, insisted I stay for a cognac and a cigar. He told me he was leaving Vietnam. The taxes being levied by the Vietcong on the oil barges his company was sending up the Mekong to Phnom Penh had become too steep. He managed a laugh when I asked him if he'd requested protection from the Vietnamese government. "I've been paying them, too!" he replied.

A few days before our departure from Vietnam I found a message waiting for me at JUSPAO. Gen. Pham Van Dong, now minister for veterans affairs, had heard of my presence in Saigon and wanted me to dine with him at his villa in Cholon. On the appointed night a JUSPAO sedan delivered me to Dong's doorstep. The villa's entrance was well fortified by two low, slitted embrasures housing automatic weapons. An unsmiling Nung sentry escorted me to the door, where I was greeted by a jovial Dong. Both of us had aged since our last encounter. We joked about his gray hair and my increased girth as he led me to the dining room.

A long hardwood table was set for two, one place at each end, each marked by a full bottle of Johnnie Walker Red Label. We took our seats and a barefoot, black-clad servant poured a generous measure of whiskey into our glasses. One of Dong's poker-faced bodyguards positioned himself near the door, his arms folded. We toasted each other and drank while I looked unobtrusively for a receptacle of ice or a water jug. I knew I wasn't going to survive a full meal on straight whiskey, but I decided to bide my time. We reminisced about the early 1950s and he told me of the whereabouts or fate of Vietnamese officers I'd met at Nasan and Ninh Binh. I could hear children's voices from the kitchen, and I realized that in all the time I'd known Dong I'd never been introduced to his family.

The meal was delicious. There was steaming crab and asparagus soup, a whole fish stewed in a piquant black sauce, tiny roast quail with hard-boiled quail eggs, plentiful rice, and a dessert of tropical fruit. Unable to down another four fingers of whiskey, I had finally asked for beer when the quail appeared on the table. At my request the general described his part in the Tet action. His intelligence network in Cholon had been fully alerted when the first attacks came, and he knew he would be a likely target of Vietcong assassination teams. The fortified villa was fully manned and provisioned to withstand a siege.

Nung agents monitored the movements of advancing enemy units, keeping in radio contact with the general. When it became obvious that a North Vietnamese sapper contingent was moving toward the villa, Dong had led a group of his men into the street to set an ambush. He told the story in a matter-of-fact, self-effacing way. When the sappers came into sight, he had been shocked by their lack of caution. He said it was as if they were out for an evening stroll. He said they were very young and that one of them was whistling. His battle-tested Nungs opened fire when the North Vietnamese entered the killing zone and it was all over in minutes.

We later adjourned to a sitting room for coffee and brandy, and General Dong went on to speak of continued North Vietnamese infiltration and constant political infighting in Saigon. Then it was time to go. Dong walked me to the door and instructed his driver to take me back to Saigon. It was a clear, starry night; there was the scent of charcoal fires in the air and the distant buzz of cyclomotors from Cholon's main street. We stood together for a moment looking up at the stars, two old comrades from widely divergent backgrounds pulled together by the drama of Indochina. Then we shook hands.

"Simpson," General Dong said gravely, "it is not good."

Four years after my farewell to General Dong, North Vietnamese T-54 tanks rammed their way through the gates of the presidential palace in Saigon, and sixteen Communist divisions began mopping up the last remnants of the demoralized ARVN. During these and the following years further assignments took me to Algeria as USIA chief, to Marseille as consul general, to the University of South Carolina as a diplomat-in-residence, and to Paris as deputy counselor for public affairs. On my retirement from government service in 1979, I became a full-time novelist and freelance writer.

CHAPTER 20

Closing the Circle

The Air Vietnam pilots brought the Tupolev jet down onto the glistening, wet runway of Hanoi's airport like a feather. The flight from Bangkok on March 8, 1991, was packed with Vietnamese returning from a purchasing spree in the Thai capital. The aisle was blocked by packages and carrier bags. A man across from me, sporting a porkpie hat of shiny black leather, was clutching the keyboard of a Japanese-made electric organ. Some of the passengers were half hidden behind bouquets of brightly colored, sweet-smelling tropical flowers.

Returning to Hanoi after thirty-seven years' absence, I wondered what I would find and how I would react now that the long-planned trip had become reality. A journalist's visa had been stamped in my passport by the Vietnamese embassy in London. An exchange of fax and Telex messages with the International Service Center of the Vietnamese Ministry of Information had ensured a tentative working schedule, including an interview with Gen. Vo Nguyen Giap.

I was also looking forward to joining Pierre Schoendoerffer on the set of his film, *Dien Bien Phu*. Pierre, now a prize-winning director, novelist, and member of the *Académie-française*, had finally received the funding and support needed to shoot his script on the battle of Dien Bien Phu. He had also written me into the film—using my real name—as one of the principal characters.

We taxied to the terminal, the passengers springing up to unload the overhead racks despite the stewardess's pleas to remain seated. A sifting *crachin* rain was blowing across the tarmac, the northern mountains floated above a wash of mist, and tiny, far-off figures labored in the fields under conical hats.

My guide, and minder, from the Ministry of Information greeted me in English and hurried me through the customs and police checks. He was a young man with an outwardly pleasant manner, but there was something about him that spelled "security." It was nothing I hadn't expected. After all, a former American official who had spent his time in Vietnam working against "the Revolution" and was now returning as a journalist was bound to incite some official curiosity. The news that my wife and daughter Lisa would soon join me in Hanoi was greeted with a definite lack of enthusiasm.

We drove into Hanoi in a new French sedan while my guide reviewed the program. I was listening to him with half an ear. There was too much going on outside. It was as if I'd taken a long step back to October 1954. Cars, overloaded trucks and buses, massed bicycles and motorbikes vied for space on the potholed road at various speeds, horns honking steadily. Women selling sugarcane sat dangerously close to the roadway, and water buffalo driven by children sloshed through the black mud of the paddies. The weaponless turret of a French tank, cemented into a sunken pillbox, reminded me how many times I'd traveled the same road.

Another impression was that of prevailing poverty. Tonkin's years of war and economic isolation appeared to have left its people treading water, barely surviving in a changing world. I was pondering this depressing thought when it became obvious that everyone in view appeared to be particularly busy. Road repairs were under way with the most primitive of equipment, women were working in the tobacco fields, a roadside sawmill was producing rough boards, and numerous small, two-story dwellings were being constructed of cinderblock, wood, and cement. Small children in neat school uniforms were returning from their classes, and vendors had arrayed their wheeled carts filled with eggs, onions, lettuce, eggplant, peppers, and cabbage to form an impromptu market at the edge of a village. These displays of vitality and enterprise seemed to blur the images of poverty. The poverty was undeniably there, but somehow it didn't seem irreversible.

Entering Hanoi's broad, tree-lined boulevards, we drove past the old, mustard-colored buildings of the French colonial government. Weather-streaked and badly in need of paint, they had maintained a certain majesty. The wet streets were filled with bicycles, cyclos, and motorbikes. The new cars belonged to government offices, foreign missions, or international aid organizations. Most private vehicles were relics of another time, old Citroëns and Peugeots, kept functioning by recycled spare parts and mechanical ingenuity. We pulled up at the Rose Hotel, a fairly new establishment catering to hard-drinking Aeroflot crews and traveling businessmen. It offered clean, air-conditioned rooms, a bar, and a restaurant staffed by attractive, giggling waitresses badly in need of basic training.

That evening, after convincing my guide that I was tired from the voyage, I walked out to get the feel of the city. The *Petit Lac* helped orient me, and I was soon on familiar ground. It was rush hour and the streets were filled from curb to curb. Crossing them was a hazard until I learned not to run. The drivers and cyclists showed an uncanny ability to gauge your progress and miss you by inches—if you didn't change your pace. The sidewalks were crowded with food stalls, cigarette vendors, small cafés, bicycle repairmen, and busy barbers. Laughing children pointed me out to their parents, and small groups of uniformed police eyed me with a surprising lack of professional interest. I paused to watch a barber plying his trade under a makeshift canvas awning.

"Where you from?" he asked in English. I told him and he passed the word to his smiling cronies that I was a My, or American.

"Bush good!" he volunteered, with a thumbs-up gesture.

Later, I rounded a corner to see a walled prison building that looked vaguely familiar in the fading light. I had seen it before, probably in a photo. A lounging cyclo-driver solved the mystery.

"Hanoi Hilton!" he shouted, "Hanoi Hilton!" pointing and nodding to the infamous prison that had housed downed American airmen during the war.

The next day Maj. Gen. Tran Cong Man, a slight, gray-haired man of sixty-five, received me over tea in the offices of the Vietnam Journalists Association. Although still on the active list, he was now a columnist for army publications, writing for both "soldiers and generals." He had begun his military career fighting the Japanese in May 1945 and recalls the help received from Maj. Archimedes Patti and other OSS advisers at that time. Later he fought both the French and Americans as a regimental commander of Engineers. Speaking with slow, deliberate authority and considerable humor, he told me the Chinese were more actively involved in the Indochina War than admitted, stating that he had "many Chinese soldiers in my unit" while fighting the French. But he was quick to underline that although there was much cooperation, the Vietnamese made their own tactical decisions. Man explained that "we didn't follow Mao's tactics," and avoided costly attacks on strongpoints to concentrate on the weakest enemy positions.

The Americans, the general said, relied too heavily on advanced weaponry and air power. He also believes they underestimated the capability and dedication of the VC. Although he still believes artillery the "key to victory," he praised the role of his Doi Dac Cong (Special Force units) in "carrying the fight" to the enemy. "We slipped in to cut their belts," he said, referring to the October 1964 attack on the American air base at Bien Hoa. He told me "several months" of preparation were needed to launch only one night attack on a U.S. position, and they succeeded only thanks to "help from the people." General Man said he had continually drummed into his men the need to stay as close to the Americans as possible "to avoid B-52 strikes."

My escort and two Army officers arrived early one morning to drive me to the headquarters of the Hanoi "Capital Division," a unit responsible for the defense of the Hanoi region and the reception and training of recruits. Both officers, one taciturn, the other talkative, had fought in "the American war" and more recently against the Khmer Rouge in Cambodia. They explained that

their trainees were beginning two years of obligatory active service before joining the reserves.

Maj. Pham Quang Hoi was waiting to receive us at the division's concrete
headquarters building. The thirty-eight-year-old officer, a chain-smoking veteran of Cambodia, appeared uneasy and wary. I had the impression that my
visit had been forced on him. We sat sipping tea while I posed a number of
questions about the division's tasks, equipment, armament, and training. Hoi,
who had graduated from the military academy at Dalat, said his men were
"ready to defend the national territory" and that their tasks were divided between defense and reconstruction. My queries on equipment and armament
were answered with an oblique statement that such matters "depended on the
economy." He ended our brief interview with a wish that a normalization of
relations between our countries would soon take place and suggested we accompany him to watch a training session.

The company was drawn up on a drab rural plain under a lowering sky. The
men's uniforms were disparate in varying shades of dark khaki, beige, and
green. The soldiers wore red-starred, canvas-covered pith helmets, and the officers short-visored, round cloth caps. There were no weapons in sight. I was
told it was to be a martial-arts session. The major nodded to the monitor and
the training began. It was all deadly serious. The force of the kicks and blows
was impressive. Feet thudded into ribs, stiff-handed chops whacked into shoulders, and bamboo staves thumped against kidneys hard enough to raise dust
from uniform jackets. One trooper went down for the count and had to be
assisted to his feet.

The demonstration closed with a few minutes of close-order drill: dressing
the ranks, hand salutes, and calls to attention. Watching these comparatively
awkward and unkempt soldiers, it occurred to me that a Western observer with
limited experience in Asia could easily go away with a misleading impression.
I recalled a dispatch written at the time of the Tet offensive describing the
struggle for Saigon. "The tenacity of the enemy continues to surprise top military spokesmen," Gene Roberts of *The New York Times* had written. "It also
baffles the American and South Vietnamese ground troops." The story ended
with an on-the-spot quote from an American infantryman. "Every day we
think we got him this time, and he keeps coming back." These men, with their
impassive, high-cheekboned faces and calloused peasant hands, were the type
that would keep coming back.

An early-morning telephone call confirmed that the role of my character in
Schoendoerffer's film had gone—not to Mel Gibson or Tom Cruise—but Donald Pleasence. This was a bit of a disappointment. Admittedly, Pleasence is an
outstanding actor, but I was twenty-nine at the time of Dien Bien Phu and
Pleasence is a well-preserved seventy. This blow to my ego image was cushioned
by a luncheon invitation from Schoendoerffer. I joined him and his wife, Pat,
at the complex of lakeside government villas housing the film company. We
renewed our long acquaintance over a drink and I learned of the trials and
tribulations of filmmaking.

Schoendoerffer was dealing with a complex project not much different from a military operation. He was many miles from his base, Paris; his logistical tail was tenuous; communications were difficult; the procurement of uniforms and equipment posed a major problem; and his actors, assistant directors, cameramen, set designers, script assistants, and grips were talented but temperamental. The fact that he was working in an underdeveloped Communist country shooting a film with inevitable political-military overtones, dealing with a French defeat and a Vietminh victory, only added to his daily preoccupations.

A stickler for authenticity, Schoendoerffer explained the difficulty of obtaining the proper matériel: Uniforms and such items as belts, boots, and weapons had changed considerably since the 1950s. In addition, as the film re-creates the airdrop on Dien Bien Phu, he had to locate three C-47 Dakotas in the United States and have them flown to Vietnam. Jeeps, trucks, and period cars had been shipped from France. The shortage of Europeans as *figurants* was remedied by the willingness of some Soviet diplomats based in Hanoi to moonlight as extras for $10 a day. Schoendoerffer had used all his diplomatic talents to obtain government permission to fly the French tricolor over the National Theater and the old Citadel—now a war museum—for the purposes of his film. The Vietnamese official who granted the permission made it clear that such an arrangement was "for the *last* time." The Vietnamese were providing facilities, troops for the battle scenes, and technicians. One of the Vietnamese working with Schoendoerffer had been a combat cameraman with Giap's forces during the battle.

We ate in the large dining hall of the complex with the film's company, technicians, actors, and the colonel in command of a company of serving French parachutists from the same airborne units that fought at Dien Bien Phu. The colonel and his men, seconded by the Army, were there to lend veracity to the battle scenes with their true *têtes des paras*. The cooks and bakers, flown from Paris to keep the crew well fed, had filled the long serving tables with plates of *hors d'oeuvres variés, saucisson sec, jambon cru,* and *salade.* Main courses of *steak pommes-frites* and *poisson grillé* were followed by *fromage* and *café.* Red and white wine in unmarked bottles was on all the tables. The sound of French being spoken, the odors of the food and wine, the clink of cutlery and glasses, the overhead fans, and the palm-dotted landscape produced another flashback. Suddenly, for a few seconds, I was back in a French Army mess, or *popote*, of the 1950s. Schoendoerffer introduced me to the cast and crew as "the real Howard Simpson." They seemed surprised. "You mean," an assistant asked, "the character really exists?"

The same consternation was apparent when I visited the sound stage and met Donald Pleasence. The actor, who appeared somewhat discomfited by my presence, asked Schoendoerffer, "You used his name?" The set was a reconstruction of the interior of the Café Normandie, the Hanoi rendezvous for parachutists and Legionnaires during the Indochina War. The designers had done a good job. The bar was a perfect replica, and the walls were hung with photos of General de Lattre de Tassigny, Edith Piaf, and the regimental insignia of various French units. Once the shooting started, I was amused to see that Schoendoerffer had heeded one of my script suggestions regarding the Simpson character. I had been a heavy cigar smoker in the 1950s. Now a propman hovered near Pleasence, popping a lighted stogie into his mouth before each take. I only hoped the actor enjoyed the pleasures of the rolled leaf. But filmmaking, with its long pauses, consultations, and repetition, is not a spectator sport and I had other commitments.

Throughout my meetings in Hanoi the same theme was repeated: The war is over, let us put it behind us, let us work together as friends. At the same time the Vietnamese insist on exposing their visitors to memories of the war. Viewed objectively, such a fixation is understandable. Their "finest hours" were the victories over the French, the Americans, and their Vietnamese "puppet" allies. I found it difficult to reconcile putting the war "behind us" and the almost obligatory visit to Hanoi's War Museum. It is one thing to be proud of the wartime achievements and sacrifices of your people. It is another to expect your former foe to relish the sight of his nation's downed aircraft, captured armor, and displays of "war crimes."

I trailed a group of young schoolchildren through the exhibits: the worm-eaten poles used to rip the bottoms out of an invading Chinese fleet on the Bach Dang River in A.D. 43; shackles and leg irons used by the French colonial authorities; the T-54 tank that seized ARVN headquarters at Ban-ma-thuot in March 1975; and fragments of a wing and fuselage from a downed B-52. A large diorama of Dien Bien Phu keyed to a slide show occupies one building, and the war crimes section is primarily an exhibition of yellowed photographs depicting French or U.S. personnel standing over the bodies of Vietnamese dead.

The schoolchildren listened to their guide, whispered to each other, giggled, pushed, and gaped at the strange foreigner in their wake. It was hard to say what impression the museum was having on their young minds. Later, in Hanoi and Ho Chi Minh City, I discovered that a number of Vietnamese, particularly those working to expand the lucrative tourism business, were questioning the inclusion of such museums as compulsory stops on the tourist itinerary.

A tall, immaculately uniformed noncom of the guard of honor escorted me up the broad stairway to Ho Chi Minh's tomb. The huge, blocklike edifice of stone and marble dominates a broad park in central Hanoi. A blast of frigid air greets the visitor as you step into the air-conditioned interior. Another flight of stairs takes you to a silent, dimly lit room and the airtight, glass-enclosed bier guarded by four ceremonial sentries. The embalmed corpse of the Vietnamese leader appeared unreal, like a waxen effigy. I stood in silence contemplating the corpse of the old revolutionary, the man of many aliases, the revered Uncle Ho, the enemy. It was a strange sensation to see the individual we'd so often targeted as a symbol of evil now revered as an icon in his own land. My reverie was broken by a sharp tap on the shoulder. A frowning sentry gestured abruptly toward the exit as if I'd overstayed my welcome.

I had heard that the many Soviet advisers and technicians working in Vietnam had never been popular with the Vietnamese, but I'd taken such reports with a grain of salt. Even with the Cold War ended, I suspected Western visitors were spreading such rumors with a certain relish. A few days in Vietnam changed my mind. A huge Soviet technician in my hotel had to be restrained by his comrades from assaulting a slight but determined Vietnamese desk clerk who had denied him permission to take a street prostitute to his room. At the Hanoi Airport a stout Soviet female official refused to return to the Air Vietnam desk to clarify a question on her tickets. She had obstinately remained in her seat, forcing the embarrassed young hostesses to make several trips back and forth till the matter was settled. In Saigon a disgruntled, Vietnamese-speaking Soviet, wishing to push ahead of my wife at a reception desk, was told to wait his turn by the Vietnamese woman on duty. Throughout the wait he mumbled in Vietnamese about *Hoa-Ky*, the Southern usage for "American."

These brief encounters with the Soviets indicated the Vietnamese have been enduring a new form of colonialism. They had no specific name for their Sovophobia, but it took little to bring it to the surface. Cyclo-drivers complained that the Soviets never used their services, restaurant employees blanched at their shouted complaints, and government officials hinted that their Russian contacts could be overbearing. Events in the Soviet Union, economic retrenchment, and the cutting of Soviet aid to Vietnam by two-thirds, have put the USSR in the position of a withdrawing power. The Vietnamese are clearly turning to the noncommunist world for economic assistance. Individual Russians, sensing the change, are reacting with frustration and bitterness. A young Vietnamese mother who runs a two-table, sidewalk beer stand in Hanoi put her national preferences in business terms. "The Russians," she told me, "drink too much and refuse to pay. The Americans drink a lot and pay too much!"

As the time approached to leave Hanoi, it was officially recommended that the same guide accompany me to Ho Chi Minh City. I, of course, would have to pay for his return air travel, board, and lodging. My budget didn't provide for such an expense and I declined. A second attempt was made to convince me. After all, I was "not young" and traveling alone "anything could happen." I had already been reminded of the Vietnamese male's preoccupation with age. More than one official, seeking a hopefully flattering response, had asked me to guess his age, and even the cyclo-drivers were calling me *"Ba-Ba,"* a Vietnamese phrase for someone over the hill, and showing surprise that I was still operational at sixty-five. My second refusal to finance a traveling "minder" was more emphatic than the first, and I sensed a certain coolness in the atmosphere. My interview with General Giap appeared to hang in the balance.

Prior to my arrival I had also asked to visit the grave of Col. Pham Ngoc Thao in the Patriots' Cemetery near Ho Chi Minh City. Understandably, this had created a problem. Why would a former U.S. official want to visit the grave of a Communist agent? I had not been absolutely sure myself when I'd made the request. Now I knew there were two reasons. I wanted to prove to myself that Thao had been honored as a "hero of the Revolution" and—despite what had happened—the Thao I had known had also been a friend. Pressing for a favorable reply, I was told it would be impossible. His remains had "been moved." Forty-eight hours later I was told I'd have to leave for Ho Chi Minh City the next morning if I wanted to see General Giap.

Tan Son Nhut Airport sweltered in a shimmering midday heat as we taxied past the long rows of U.S.-built concrete aircraft shelters. I thought I recognized the buildings that had housed the Air America installation in the distance. Another English-speaking guide was waiting for me in the terminal building. He explained that he was filling in for a friend who was busy with other visitors. It seemed I had arrived on the last day of a "Forum for International Investment" that had brought over 400 foreign businessmen to the city.

We drove into Saigon (most Vietnamese find HCMC too much of a mouthful and still use "Saigon") in a dilapidated Dodge sedan doubling as a cab. It was like being on home ground. We passed what had been the entrance to MACV and the old ARVN General Staff headquarters, sped through the crowded suburbs, and clattered onto the tree-shaded boulevards. Posters in English near the Cathedral Square and the former presidential palace announced the investment forum. Air-conditioned Mercedes and BMWs with tinted windows purred past, and the Japanese motorbikes buzzing in and out of the traffic were shiny and new. What had been Rue Catinat in the 1950s and then Tu Do Street was now Dong Khoi (Uprising) Street. A resplendent, renovated Hotel Continental looked out onto the square. The hotel's colonial façade had been retained, and purple bougainvillea clung to the balconies. Gival's snack bar across the street was crowded with customers, and the National Theater, freshly painted a canary yellow, was surrounded by sidewalk cafés. The "hostess" bars of old Tu Do Street had been replaced by shops, art galleries, and restaurants.

There were no rooms available at the Hotel Majestic, and the luxurious, Australian-run "Floating Hotel" on the Saigon River was too rich for my blood. I settled into the Huong Sen Hotel, on Dong Khoi Street, a new establishment complete with air conditioning and a roof-garden bar, massage parlor, and sauna. The following days were filled with impressions, frenetic movement, interviews, and echoes of the past.

My Saigon escort appeared late on Sunday night to find me nursing a beer at a roof-garden table. He had an air of authority and a toughness about him that went with a long-healed facial scar. He'd brought an interpreter along and we began to review my schedule. I asked about the Giap interview. After a hurried consultation in Vietnamese the interpreter turned to me with a nervous smile.

"It is impossible," he said. "General Giap cannot see you."

Even former diplomats have a boilover point. Cursing, I thumped the table.

The escort's eyes hardened as I went on to enumerate the preparations for the interview. It had all been agreed by the Ministry in Hanoi! I'd rushed to Saigon on their instructions!

The escort's grim stare slowly dissipated. He said something to the interpreter. Then a shadow of a smile crossed his face.

"It is all a joke," the interpreter told me. "He makes a joke. You will see the general."

Relieved but still angry I told the interpreter that from now on I'd call his boss "the joker." This produced some laughter. But my query on the visit to Colonel Thao's grave cut the hilarity. Such a visit was truly impossible, I was told; Colonel Thao's remains had been sent to the North. I later learned from a non-Vietnamese source that the man I'd labeled the joker was a senior officer of the security police.

Returning to Saigon stirred a deep well of nostalgia and brought back memories. I found myself drawn to our old residence on Tu Xuong Street, the Hotel Continental, and the apartment building where I'd watched the Vietminh make their noisy departure from Saigon in 1955 and my wife had announced her first pregnancy. I had paused to look up at the balcony of Dixie Reese's old apartment, passed Ed Lansdale's former villa in a cyclo, and sipped beer at sunset at a small café on the banks of the Saigon River while the overloaded ferries fought the current and the latest Madonna disk belted out of a flag-bedecked floating restaurant.

For old time's sake I'd taken the elevator to the rooftop restaurant of what had been the JUSPAO building and is now the luxurious Rex Hotel, catering to Japanese businessmen. A plaque of sculpted concrete on the wall of the former Brinks BOQ commemorates the Christmas Eve VC bombing of 1964. "Cheap Charlie's" restaurant across the street is now the CA-LI-PHO-NIA HAM-BU-GO, with a chicken logo. A long cyclo ride to Cholon past the *Arroyo Chinois* helped me retrace the killing grounds of the Binh Xuyen revolt. The front gate of the former American Embassy building—now the government office for petroleum development—was closed. A one-legged VC veteran was begging nearby. Many cyclo-drivers are ARVN veterans, both officers and men. Most are "graduates" of Communist reeducation camps and are now restricted to manual labor. Some former Marines who park their cyclos near the old Naval Headquarters still "square" their fatigue caps in the leatherneck manner.

"Miss Saigon" is alive and well but much more discreet. Years of doctrinaire "purity" have swept the streets clear of blatant hustlers. Well-dressed professionals can be found idly leafing through magazines in the lobbies of some hotels. Discotheques have their share of "hostesses" in fluffy pastel gowns. The back route to Cholon boasts a sector of open-fronted cafés, manned by shapely "waitresses" and reverberating to rock, where curtained doors lead to rear rooms. My cyclo-driver, a former ARVN sergeant, peddled *Ba-Ba* Simpson speedily past such temptation with the warning, "No good!"

One of my first appointments was with Dr. Nguyen Xuan Oanh, the distinguished former prime minister who had been bounced in and out of office during the coups of the 1960s. He received me in his office at IMC (Investment & Management Consulting Corporation of Ho Chi Minh City). Now managing director of IMC, Oanh is also a deputy in the National Assembly, a bank official, and an economic adviser to the government. He was enthusiastic about Vietnam's economic future and has made several trips to the United States to lobby in Washington and speak at Harvard for a lifting of the U.S. trade embargo. Outspokenly stating that "socialism is not conducive to economic development," Oahn reviewed Vietnam's potential in agriculture, minerals, offshore oil, and tourism, predicting an "explosion" of economic activity once the embargo has been lifted. He then showed me a checkerboard map of offshore oil allotments already granted to foreign companies and informed me that five U.S. companies had been invited to send teams to explore possible American participation. When I asked him what message he might have for American businessmen, he thought for a minute, smiled, and said, "Hurry up and come back!"

I had almost given up my attempts to visit Colonel Thao's grave when one of the Information Ministry's staffers discreetly asked if I still wanted to see the Patriots' Cemetery. He was a former VC officer and had been one of Thao's friends. Taking me aside, he promised to arrange an unofficial visit.

The next day we drove out of Saigon in his battered personal vehicle, speeding through the dense mass of heavy trucks and bicycles while he sounded his horn by touching an exposed wire to the steering column. On the way he told me that members of Thao's family had approved my visit and relayed their apologies for not being present. The sunbaked cemetery was on the edge of a small rubber plantation. Tombstones of varying size spread out from a central obelisk. The hot air was filled with the sound of cicadas. On some tombs, photos of the dead were encased in plastic insets. Most of them depicted young people, some in uniform and others in civilian clothes, some smiling, others serious. The more mature dead were Vietcong officials, members of the National Liberation Front. A new section of the cemetery, marked by some freshly dug graves, had been allotted to those killed fighting the Khmer Rouge in Cambodia.

It took us some time to locate Colonel Thao's grave. It was marked by a modest headstone bearing a star and the dates of his birth and death. I stood for a moment in silence, contemplating the small strip of cracked earth that the colonel had claimed as his own.

My escort produced some joss sticks, lit them, and handed them to me, indicating I should place them in the sand-filled urn at the foot of the grave. This done, we returned to the cemetery office where the supervisor, another Vietcong veteran, served us green tea. As we spoke—of the Vietnam War and the action in the Gulf—it suddenly dawned on me that Colonel Thao had been buried as a Buddhist. I asked about this, explaining that I had known Thao as a devout Catholic. My guide only shrugged his shoulders and smiled. Once again Thao had left a mystery in his wake.

The meeting with General Giap was confirmed at the last minute. My guide picked me up at the hotel and I squeezed into the backseat of a small sedan between an interpreter and a sound technician. We drove through the gates of the old presidential palace under a punishing midmorning sun. The broad stairway and lobby of "Reunification Hall" were crowded with Vietnamese officials welcoming a German delegation. We were led through the crush and up another flight of stairs to a long, air-conditioned reception room decorated with lacquer paintings of Vietnamese historical scenes and large blue and white vases. Classic Vietnamese weapons, spears and pikes from another age, were displayed behind a central divan.

After a short wait Gen. Vo Nguyen Giap, vice president of the council of ministers, victor of Dien Bien Phu, and commander of Communist forces in the Vietnam War appeared with an entourage of government officials. The seventy-nine-year-old general wore casual civilian clothes, an open-necked shirt, and comfortable shoes. His gray hair was brush-cut. He smiled as we were introduced and shook hands.

"Do you speak French?" he asked. When I told him I did, he warned me that he might not answer all my questions and suggested I sit beside him. He handled the interview like a public affairs professional. Some questions were ignored—in the style of de Gaulle—while he introduced his own subject matter. He moved easily from flights of dialectic to reminiscences, from seriousness to humor. We discussed history, strategy, tactics, politics, and personalities as the tape recorder ground on and his staff sat in rapt silence. The following excerpts give the flavor of the interview:

On Historical Personalities That Influenced His Career
"For example, Kutuzov [the Russian general who forced Napoleon's retreat from Moscow]. I studied him and there are things about Kutuzov that are useful, but other methods that better fit the situation. It is often said that I studied Napoleon as a professor of history—but we don't make war in the same way, we make war in the Vietnamese manner. . . . We had to defeat superior forces with very little. President Ho Chi Minh said it was the fight of the grasshopper and the elephant. . . . Those who had the most influence on my strategy were the strategists of Vietnamese history. For example, the Trung sisters, Tran Hung Dao, Nguyen Hue. We created our own military art."

On Soviet Reaction to His Victories
"A Soviet marshal once asked me how I defeated the Americans. He asked me how many infantry divisions, tank divisions, artillery divisions I had. How much aviation. [Laughter] If we had fought like that we would have been beaten in less than two hours, but we fought differently and we won."

On Dien Bien Phu and Nasan
"The most difficult battle *and* the most difficult decision was at Dien Bien Phu. . . . They [the French] thought it was impossible, a thousand times impossible, to solve our logistics problem. But we succeeded in resolving first of all the strategic and tactical problems, then we addressed the logistics problem . . . . If we had continued to fight night and day as we had at the beginning, they would have wiped us out. But no, we attacked little by little, trench by trench—The day I gave the order to our troops to pull back and to start work on the trenches was the most difficult.

"Just before Dien Bien Phu there was Nasan. . . . I gave the order to attack Nasan. We didn't attack the whole camp. We attacked hill by hill. The method of combat was sound, but the troops were not yet well trained. We did succeed in wiping out—I recall, two battalions. It wasn't a defeat—but we suffered losses."

On General de Lattre de Tassigny

"As to the French and American generals, one must say that as men, I have esteem for their learning and knowledge. I see that they are soldiers who obey their governments. I understand that. I can say that de Lattre, who was later named a marshal, was a general of value. That's why he defeated the Germans. But he was *badly used*. . . . de Lattre said it was necessary to hold Indochina, otherwise the French Empire would disintegrate, which was true. And then he lost the battle. He didn't understand that it was a war of an entire people, against a people's army, an army that fights for its people, supported by the people. He made war against the people. He didn't understand all that. It wasn't his fault."

On General Westmoreland

"Now, Westmoreland. He was a soldier, like the Americans who studied in military school. He had a military culture but he didn't understand the sense of the war we were fighting in Vietnam. For example, after the Tet offensive— he asked for reinforcements. . . . If they had come it wouldn't have changed the situation. Naturally, it would have been more difficult for us, but it wouldn't have decided anything."

On People's War

Some think that a people's war means guerrilla. That's not true. A people's war is certainly carried out by all the people with different forms of organization, from small actions to that of a whole army. That is why that division, a bit mechanical, is not correct. This is the first time I've said that. What does guerrilla war mean? In other words a war fought by guerrillas. Are there rules? Certainly. That's why combatants who fight well as guerrillas adapt to changes when encadred into regular units. . . . "

On Discipline

"I can say that the army I commanded was extremely well disciplined. For example, when I was at Dien Bien Phu our dispositive was in place and ready to open fire, but I gave the order to pull back. The decision was made because the situation had changed. I decided to change our method of combat and retire immediately. So we withdrew. They [my troops] weren't happy—not happy at all. [Laughter]"

On the French and the American Soldier

"The French soldier knew the terrain, particularly those who participated in the colonial campaigns. The commanders also. But—they didn't understand that times had changed. The times *had* changed. When they came, they thought they had the same authority as at the time of the governor general. But no, it was an entire people in revolt. . . .

"The American soldier, he was better armed. When he was in the field there were helicopters that brought provisions, even water. He knew the terrain less well, the Vietnamese people even less. As to the American commanders, they knew less than the soldiers they were commanding. They conformed to the manual, but the American soldier was on the ground. He may not have known the terrain that well, but at least he was there. He saw; he saw the enemy. . . . I don't have the intention of speaking badly of the American commanders. They were doing their job."

On U.S.-Vietnamese Relations

"The job of our army is to guard our independence and peace. . . . The war was imposed on a people that love peace. Tell that to the Americans. That is why, when the American veterans, including generals, come to Hanoi, I've received them and they're surprised by my attitude . . . Man to man, there is no lack of friendship. I tell them: You arrived with the Thompson, [submachine gun], we received you in another manner. Now you arrive as representatives of the American people, we have respect and friendship for you. . . .

"There will be a normalization of relations, that is certain. When? The intelligence of a government is measured in time. Maybe it will be another thirty years! We are optimists. The Vietnamese people draw optimism from their history. . . . "

It was soon time to leave. One last balmy sunset as the golden clouds darkened over the Saigon River, a dinner of spicy pepper crab, some hurried packing, and a night of restless sleep to the thrumming of an overaged air conditioner. Then, escorted by "the joker," we were on our way to Tan Son Nhut.

A piece of blue and white pottery my wife had purchased in the shop of the state museum in Hué almost delayed our departure. Fortunately she'd declared the bowl on our customs forms. Despite this, a surly customs officer impounded the piece until we could obtain the required additional papers. This small, innocuous incident triggered a certain anxiety. I suddenly realized that despite the friendliness I'd encountered and the journalistic tasks I'd been allowed to accomplish, I was still carrying some heavy baggage from the past. No one had threatened me, no one had blocked my way to the aircraft, but I breathed a genuine sigh of relief when the Tupolev lifted off and headed for Bangkok.

Epilogue

What I saw and heard during my return trip convinced me that Vietnam, despite its current problems, is destined to play an important and growing role in Southeast Asia. Optimistic foreign observers point to the liberalization of trade, reduction of inflation, encouragement of private enterprise, opening to foreign investment, and the potential of untapped natural resources as solid foundations for future development. The pessimists identify the tenacity of aged, doctrinaire Communist Party officials, continued poverty and unemployment, lack of modern infrastructure, and the penury of the state as justification for an outlook of doom and gloom.

The truth lies somewhere between these extremes. While some economic experts see Saigon as the "future Hong Kong of Southeast Asia," and certain political observers predict an eventual and dangerous North-South divide, Vietnam is on the road to inevitable change. With the collapse of Communist hegemony in Eastern Europe and the defection of its Soviet ally, this strategically placed nation of more than sixty-six million people is turning toward other Asian nations and the West in search of trading partners and assistance.

The U.S. trade embargo of Vietnam, which continues as this book goes to press, has become redundant and vindictive. It is punishing the people of Vietnam, not the wartime leaders, many of whom are now dead or out of office. It also provides the surviving hard-liners with an excuse to keep Vietnam isolated in a political vacuum. The embargo is preventing American businessmen and trading companies from entering the active international competition for contracts and joint ventures covering everything from offshore oil production to fisheries development, and from mineral ores to tourism.

Vietnam's position in southeast Asia, its extensive coastline; its frontiers with China, Cambodia, and Laos; its long, bellicose history; and its slightly dimin-

231

ished but real military strength make it a nation of political and military significance. We have invested too much in blood and fortune to ignore what is happening in the region. Granted, the wounds of the Vietnam War are barely healed. Despite progress, the MIA question remains to be settled, and points of disagreement exist on Vietnam's continued role in Cambodia. But such issues are best resolved by constant on-the-spot meetings, not occasional "unofficial" conferences. A prompt resumption of diplomatic relations and pragmatic, direct contacts with the Vietnamese would be the best method of ensuring "no more Vietnams" in this important part of the world.

I have no plans to return to Indochina. I consider the circle of my Vietnam experience closed. I only hope a resumption of normal relations will soon allow a new generation of Americans to know that fascinating country and its people free of war and enmity.

Index

About the
Author

HOWARD R. SIMPSON is a former Foreign Service officer, a novelist, and a writer on defense matters. During the Franco-Vietminh War, he was a U.S. Information Agency correspondent; a psychological warfare operative with the French and Vietnamese; and, later, a press adviser to Premier Ngo Dinh Diem. After a brief stint with the San Francisco *Chronicle*, he reentered the Foreign Service and served in Nigeria and France before returning to Saigon in 1964 as adviser to Prime Minister Nguyen Khanh. In 1965 he was assigned to the Paris embassy and in 1967 was sent to the Naval War College, later serving as adviser to its president. In 1969 he became the deputy director of the State Department's East Asia/Pacific Bureau of Public Affairs, after which followed diplomatic service in Canberra, Algiers, Marseille, and again Paris. During this period he was also briefly diplomat-in-residence at the University of South Carolina. Since retirement from the Foreign Service in 1979, he has been a frequent lecturer and a consultant on international terrorism. He has written for *Harper's*, *Commonweal*, the *International Herald-Tribune*, *Newsday*, and other publications. His books include *To a Silent Valley* (1961), *Assignment for a Mercenary* (1965), *The Three-Day Alliance* (1971), *The Jumpmaster* (1986), *A Gathering of Gunmen* (1987), and *A Very Large Consulate* (1988). He now lives in Ireland.